INTELLECTUAL PROPERTY RIGHTS UNDER GLOBALISATION

INTELLECTUAL PROPERTY RIGHTS UNDER GLOBALISATION

TALWAR SABANNA
Karnatak University, KRC P.G. Centre
Belgaum, Karnataka (India)

SERIALS PUBLICATIONS
NEW DELHI

First Published - 2006
Second Published - 2019

ISBN : 81-8387-015-5

Published by

SERIALS PUBLICATIONS
4, B.S.S. Hall, Khyber Pass Market
Civil Lines, Delhi-110054 (India)
Phone : 23245225
Fax : 91-11-23272135
E-mail: serials@satyam.net.in

CONTENTS

INTRODUCTION

Talwar Sabanna

Laura J. Loppacher and William A.Kerr explores some of the facets of the TRIPS in developing countries would like to see changed using the particularly contentious case of bio-technology and the potential affect on incentives for investment in innovative activity for firms in that industry. The authors addresses that the agricultural bio-technology is one sector that will be significantly affected by the international protection of IP. Further, the authors states that many developing countries would like to see changes made to the TRIPS agreement. However, the authors concludes that the developing countries would be better off if they instantaneously had access to all of the current technological development on a global basis.

Anju Jain's paper discusses different types of intellectual property, its legal status, economic aspects and TRIPS. The paper highlights that as per the obligations under the trade related aspects of Intellectual Property Systems(TRIPS), all members of the World Trade Organisation (WTO) are supposed to implement national system of intellectual property rights following an agreed set of minimum standard. However, there is an increasing feeling that harmonization is demanded from those that are not equal, either economically or institutionally. The paper concludes that the TRIPS provisions have to be interpreted in the context of promotion of competition, and not its restriction.

C.M. Rajpraveen's paper critically examines the effects of the TRIPS agreement on certain important sectors namely pharmaceuticals, bio-technology, and agriculture. The paper states that the intellectual property rights cases in India have been dealt with according to the provisions as mentioned in the Indian patent act 1970. However, in accordance with the provisions as mentioned in the TRIPS, India has an obligation to modify its IPS regime accordingly. The paper concludes that at present valuable traditional knowledge of developing countries is not protected under the TRIPs and many time exploited by the developed nations without any safeguards.

R. Meenakshi have attempted to present an overview of impact of TRIPs on Agriculture. The study shows that the intellectual property protection is the key factor for economic growth and advancement in the high technology sector. They are good for business, benefit the public at large and act as catalysts for technical progress. In agriculture sector, the role of IPRs is becoming even more important because much of the R &D have been concentrated in public sector so far and private sector R&D is recently emerging slowly. However, the author concludes that the knowledge intensity of Indian agriculture has to go up if it has to become competitive globally.

R.Hiremani Naik's paper reviews Intellectual Property Rights and its relationship with Trade. The author points out that the Global's export profile increasingly features knowledge-intensive, sophisticated and distinctive products and services that rely only effective and affordable intellectual property right protection. This makes a valuable instrument for promoting global trade and investment interest. The author concludes that the intellectual property has a role in transfer of technologies, as investment in new industries often depends on confidence in the protection of the intellectual property rights that emphasizes availability of new technologies.

I. Sundar in his paper furnishes that there is a growing emphasis about implications of intellectual property on life support system particularly in case of agriculture, biological resources and traditional knowledge. The paper takes into account that these days intellectual property rights create a lot of concerns in the form of patenting plants, animals genes and bio-piracy of traditional knowledge and wisdom. The paper concludes with some policy measures to safeguard the interest of indigenous people and developing countries from the negative implications of intellectual property rights.

The paper by **S.Srikrishna and S.Anil Kumar** has discussed the intellectual property rights in the light of protection and enforcement. The paper presents that India showed signs of resistance to quick enforcement of international intellectual property right protection laws as demanded by the developed countries, especially the USA. The paper argues that the absence of international IPR protection for some decades has spawned employment for millions, so an overnight clampdown on IPR violators would foment social unrest.

S.B. Somannavar's study emphasizes Intellectual Property rights and its relationship with technology transfer and economic growth. The study identifies that the development of new areas within IP tests the flexibility of old rules necessitating new ones. Though India, an economically developing country, as far as intellectual capital is concerned, it is treated as a developed country. Because, it is recognized fact that the best intellectual capital is available in India. The author concludes that it is right time to speed the process of liberalisation and privatization of all economic activities except the most important aspects of social sector.

P.L. Sablok and Geetanjali Sharma's paper traces a synoptic account of the approach that India needs to adopt in dealing with the challenges and the opportunities of the WTO system. The paper presents a noteworthy opinion that as per the commitment under the TRIPs agreement, India is all set to move towards a comprehensive IPR regime with product-patent system, and a rigorous copy-right-enforcement framework. The issue of widening the scope of patentable matter, protection, promotion of bio-diversity, protecting the farmers rights etc., would continue to figure prominently at the national and international fora. The paper suggests that India need to invest more in bio-technology research to make it a lead sector of global strength.

H.H. Uliveppa and D.R.Albal's paper raised many issues with regard to India's participation in trade in future, its integration with the world economy and the likely costs and benefits during the regime of WTO. The authors addresses that the Government of India amended the Patents Act 1970 as the Patents (Amendment) Act 1999 on the subject to take advantage of the provisions of the TRIPs Agreement. The new act encourage innovation by rewarding the inventors with the grant of monopoly rights over the commercial exploitations of their inventions for a specified period. However, the authors concludes that discussions on TRIPs and other issues are likely to dominate WTO's agenda in future, and India will have to prepare a national and an international strategy to face challenges.

The paper by **K.A. Rasure** emphasizes the impact of WTO on India's foreign trade. The paper highlights that TRIPs were introduced for protecting the rights of inventors and allowing patent ability only in the final products. Further, the paper states the India's EXIM policy encourages exports through subsidies, incentives, infrastructure development etc. Therefore, the export promotion and import liberalization are twin objectives of EXIM policy. The paper concludes that there is urgent need to invite private or foreign investment on priority basis in power generation, transportation, communication, warehousing etc.

An attempt has been made by **Vishwanatha, Jayasheela, M. Showkat Ali and S. Sudhakar** to look at the Health Insurance in India in the context of Globalisation. The authors states that Insurance provides protection against risk or uncertain events and health insurance protects against the cost of illness and mobiles funds for health services. Further, the authors presents that the health insurance, whether social or private, whether formal or limited, is extremely limited in India. Existing health insurance schemes in India are mandatory schemes, private (voluntary) schemes and employer based insurance. The authors concludes that the health insurance which strengthens the demand side, makes sense only when the supply of health care is reasonable well developed.

J.Cyril Kanmony makes an indepth study on Environmental pollution and human rights with special reference to water pollution in Kanyakurmi District. The study highlights that the right to life is the most fundamental of all human rights and imbalance in environment causes a severe threat to human health and survival. Further, the study presents that outdoor air pollution caused by emission from automobiles, thermal power plants and other industries makes air in almost all the cities highly polluted. From all these, it is clear that human rights violation due to environmental pollution is rampant throughout the India including the study area.

D.N. Patil's paper attempts to analyse the contribution of service sector to GDP in the context of WTO regime. The paper notes that the growth of international trade in services in the last two decades has been much faster than that of the trade in goods. Further, the paper highlights that as far as India is concerned, services sector is not as underdeveloped as in many other developing countries. The paper concludes that the effective negotiations are a must, we can neither procrastinate the day of reckoning nor reverse the imperatives of WTO driven globalisation of the Indian services industry.

Geetanjali Sharma's paper touches the globalisation, intellectual property rights and prospects of Indian agriculture. The paper states that among all intellectual properties, patent is the most important issue these days not only in India, but also world over. Further, the paper presents that the adverse impact on Indian agriculture which was feared by many in the country seems to be unfounded given the inherent competitiveness. The paper concludes that the greater attention needs to be devoted to the provision of inputs such as seeds, fertilizers and un-interrupted power supply to the sector to boost agricultural production.

N.S. Sreenivasulu and C. Basavaraju's paper seeks to examine the bio-technology and patent law. While pointing out the significance of bio-technology, the authors outlines the role to play in improving the capacity of plants producing consumable foods. Further, the authors opines that the patent is an incentive for the inventor to disclose his invention. If an invention is disclosed, then society can use it, and can enjoy the fruits of it. That is how a patent serves for the maximum benefit of maximum members of the society. The paper concludes that the India is getting diverged from its traditional and customary practices to give patent protection to living things produced through bio-technology.

Manish Sharma's paper reflects on the knowledge and nature of indigenous health care practices of Monpa Tribe of Arunachal Pradesh under the new IPR regime. The paper explores that the indigenous knowledge of any society is that which is transferred from generation to generation in a systematic and informal way. With the emergence of the WTO, a lot of discussions are there for Intellectual Property Rights (IPR) raising issues like feasibility of protection of indigenous knowledge system (IKS) with existing intellectual property right system. The paper recommends for further scientific investigation and documentation of indigenous medicine so that we can reap the benefit under the new IPR regime.

This issue presents papers dealing with the Intellectual Property Rights and problems thrown up by the Globalisation and the solutions. Further, it is expected that all the papers included in the Journal will be found to be useful by academicians, teachers, students, economic and law analysts interested in the Intellectual Property Rights and Globalisation.

DEVELOPING COUNTRIES' PROTECTION OF INTELLECTUAL PROPERTY UNDER TRIPS AND INNOVATION INVESTMENT

Laura J. Loppacher & William A. Kerr***

INTRODUCTION

The World Trade Organization (WTO) Agreement on Trade Related Aspects of Intellectual Property (TRIPS) has generated significant controversy since its inclusion in the Uruguay Round of trade agreements which saw the creation of the WTO in 1995. The TRIPS combines provisions from the Paris Convention for the Protection of Industrial Property and the Berne Convention for the Protection of Literary and Artistic Works and adds a significant number of provisions in areas where these Conventions were silent or were felt to be inadequate. After phase-in of TRIPS is complete[1], all countries will be subject to the same standards regarding minimum protection that must be provided but are allowed flexibility in interpreting some of these obligations. Arguments about the standards of protection for intellectual property (IP) have typically been viewed as a North-South divide. Many espouse the position that strong standards are unfair as they force poor developing countries, with little IP of their own, to pay royalties to rich developed countries, where ownership of the majority of IP resides.

Intellectual property rights (IPRs) are granted by governments to attempt to correct a market failure that

* Research Associate, Estey Centre for Law and Economics in International Trade, Saskatoon, Saskatchewan.

** Senior Associate, Estey Centre for Law and Economics in International Trade, Saskatoon, Saskatchewan.

produces less than optimal amounts of investments in innovative activity. Patents are used to protect products and processes. It is often less costly to reverse engineer a product than to undertake the research and development (R&D) to create the innovation. In the absence of any laws preventing companies from engaging in reverse engineering or similar activities and then marketing their copies, all firms would wish to be the "copy-cat" firm and soon there would be no innovations to copy (Boyd et al., 2003)[2]. Innovations are viewed as a very important factor in increasing welfare for societies. IPRs grant the owner the exclusive right to prevent a third party from using, reproducing, selling, exporting or importing the product or process that is protected. In exchange, the owner must disclose all information relevant to duplicating the product or process. This provides the firm with a temporary monopoly in which they can potentially earn monopoly rents[3]. In exchange for exclusive marketing rights, their acquired knowledge is made available to the public. The potential profits available to a firm induce it to undertake expensive and risky R&D (Boyd et al., 2003).

Agricultural biotechnology is one sector that will be significantly affected by the international protection of IP. By undertaking genetic modification of a variety of plants and animal species, scientists are uncovering ways to create nutritionally enriched foods, herbicide, pesticide and disease tolerant crops and increase yields. The potential benefits for developing countries are substantial. Genetically modified cotton in China, for example, has significantly reduced the amount of pesticides used in cotton production, leading to less environmental contamination and a reduced incidence of pesticide poisonings for farmers and labourers while at the same time, increasing yields (Pray et al., 2001). Blindness caused by Vitamin A deficiency may be significantly reduced with the introduction of "Golden Rice" – a genetically altered rice enriched in Vitamin A. The impact will likely be greatest in very poor regions where rice is consumed as the staple food and other sources of Vitamin A are too expensive (Boyd et al., 2003). There are many other potential ways to use agricultural biotechnology to help some of the world's poorest. In order for the maximum benefit to be realized, however, additional funds will need to be invested in areas of research of particular importance to developing countries–for example, in tropical plants. If these funds are to come from private firms, those making investment decisions in research and development activities must be able to foresee a reasonable chance of recouping their investment. Thus, strong IPRs are required.

DEVELOPING COUNTRIES NEGOTIATING AGENDA AT TRIPS AND WIPO

The TRIPS has been a contentious issue with developing countries ever since it was included as part of the Uruguay Round agenda at the insistence of developed countries. Some of their most pressing concerns relate to protecting traditional knowledge, fair and equitable benefit sharing arising from use of genetic resources and human health concerns. Developing countries were successful in getting these issues on the negotiating table at Doha at the WTO Ministerial meeting in 2001. Paragraph 19 of the Doha Ministerial Declaration states:

> *We instruct the Council for TRIPS...to examine, inter alia, the relationship between the TRIPS Agreement and the Convention on Biological Diversity, the protection of traditional knowledge and folklore, and other relevant new developments raised by members pursuant to Article 71.1 (WTO, 2001b).*

A separate declaration was adopted regarding TRIPS and public health. Paragraph 4 states:

> *We agree that the TRIPS Agreement does not and should not prevent members from taking measures to protect public health. Accordingly, while reiterating our commitment to the TRIPS Agreement, we affirm that the Agreement can and should be interpreted and implemented in a manner supportive of WTO members' right to protect public health and, in particular, to promote access to medicines for all (WTO, 2001a).*

Negotiations have been underway on these topics and others at the Council for TRIPS at the WTO and at the World Intellectual Property Organization (WIPO)[4]. At the Thirty-First Session of WIPO, Argentina and Brazil submitted a proposal to establish a development agenda for WIPO. This proposal was subsequently co-sponsored by Bolivia, Cuba, Dominican Republic, Ecuador, Egypt, Iran, Kenya, Peru, Sierra Leone, South Africa, Tanzania, and Venezuela. This was the first time in WIPO's recent history that a proposal calling for development issues to be at the heart of WIPO's activities was put forward. The proposal called development the most important challenge facing the international community and as WIPO was a member of the United Nations system[5], it should be fully guided by the broad development goals that the UN has set for itself. In their proposal, they state,

> *Intellectual property protection cannot be seen as an end in itself, not can the harmonization of intellectual property laws leading to higher protection standards in all countries, irrespective of their levels of development...IP protection is a policy instrument the operation of which may, in actual practice, produce benefits as well as costs, which may vary in accordance with a country's level of development. Action is therefore needed to ensure, in all countries, that the costs do not outweigh the benefits of IP protection (WIPO, 2004a).*

After the close of the workshop, the Geneva Declaration on the Future of the World Intellectual Property Organization was issued by a number of non-governmental organizations. This Declaration went further than the Development Agenda proposal put forward by governments of developing countries, demanding a moratorium on any new WIPO patent treaties in order to create space to address issues that they felt were far more urgent. The Declaration stated the highest priority should be the "long-neglected concerns of the poor, the sick, the visually impaired and others" (Geneva Declaration, 2004). The Declaration also accused WIPO of embracing a culture of creating and expanding monopoly privileges (Geneva Declaration, 2004).

While the majority of countries supported the basic principles behind the formal government proposal, some argued that WIPO already incorporated development into its activities. The strongest and most direct opposition came from the US which stated that the proposal "appeared to be premised on the misconception that strong intellectual property protection might be detrimental to global development goals and that WIPO had disregarded development concerns" (WIPO, 2004b). Further proposals have been tabled arguing that countries at different stages of economic, social and technological development will benefit differently from IP protection and, as such, special and differential treatment should be integrated into all of WIPO's activities and bodies (ICTSD, 2005a). Discussions on this topic are ongoing and are not expected to be settled quickly.

SPECIFIC ISSUES OF CONCERN TO DEVELOPING COUNTRIES

Faced with a spreading AIDS epidemic, one of the most pressing issues for developing countries is the ability to utilize compulsory licensing to manufacture drugs when needed to protect public health when a country has insufficient manufacturing capacity to produce generic versions domestically. This is because the existing rules state any drugs produced under compulsory licence must be "predominantly" for the supply of the domestic market (ICTSD, 2004b). Pharmaceutical companies, particularly in the US, were concerned that if generic manufacturers were allowed to export, these exports may be diverted into markets where a compulsory licence is not warranted or back into the domestic market. An interim waiver from the ban on trade in generic drugs with protected intellectual property was agreed upon on August 30, 2003 but almost two years later, countries had still not come to a consensus regarding how to turn this into a permanent solution (ICTSD, 2005c).

The negotiations on the proper relationship between TRIPS and the Convention on Biological Diversity (CBD) are both very complicated and controversial. The CBD states members shall work to protect traditional knowledge and promote the equitable sharing of benefits arising from such knowledge. The agreement also states that the authority to determine access to genetic resources rests with the national governments and is subject to national legislation and that access to genetic resources shall be subject to prior informed consent of the

Contracting Party providing such resources (Convention on Biological Diversity, 1992). This issue is very important to developing countries which have the greatest wealth in traditional knowledge and genetic resources. One goal of the CBD is to prevent "bio-piracy" where multinational corporations take a plant developed over many generations using traditional methods and make minor changes using modern processes and are able to be granted a patent for it (Isaac and Kerr, 2004). In response, some developing countries have called for the exclusion of life-forms from patentability.

The TRIPS Agreement has significantly different provisions than the CBD. With regards to life forms, TRIPS states that Member may exclude plant and animals, other than micro-organisms and essentially biological processes for the production of plants and animals other than non-biological and microbiological processes. If a country excludes plant varieties from patent protection, however, an effective *sui generis* system of protection must be provided. The tests for patentability are novelty, inventiveness and industrial applicability (WTO, 2005). As traditional knowledge is not novel, it would not be patentable under TRIPS. The rational for these rules is if a monopolistic distortion is to be added to the market, it should promote innovation. As no new product or processes have been created in traditional knowledge, granting a patent, which may be seen as the 'fair' thing to do, would lead to a reduction in total societal welfare (Isaac and Kerr, 2004).

Developing countries have made many proposals regarding the issue of protection of traditional knowledge and equitable sharing of benefits arising from the use of genetic resources. The essential elements of the debate are whether life-forms should be patented at all and whether TRIPS should be amended to make it compatible with the requirement of the CBD. A large number of developing countries believe that life-forms should not be patented and that the TRIPS Agreement should be amended. However, most developed countries believe the opposite (ICTSD, 2003). One of the most recent proposals by developing countries, led by Brazil and

India, is to require patent applicants to disclose the country of origin of genetic resources and/or traditional knowledge used in the invention and evidence of prior informed consent and benefit sharing. The US response was that disclosure requirements were not the best way of preventing "bad" patents or ensuring prior informed consent or benefit sharing. Australia and Japan concurred with the US. The EU, while generally supporting a disclosure requirement for patent applications, opposed the obligation to provide evidence of fair and equitable benefit sharing as they fear patent offices do not have the expertise to determine what is "fair and equitable" (ICTSD, 2005c). It is clear that negotiation positions of developing and developed countries are still very divergent and reconciling these differences could be a significant challenge.

A very substantial issue for developing countries is the cost of implementing an enforcement system for IPRs. Despite the fact that most WTO Members have now adopted legislation implementing the minimum standards required by the WTO, levels of piracy and counterfeiting continue to increase every year (Lamy, 2004). This is a concern not only because of the financial losses to the IPR holders but also because pirated and counterfeit goods can have a serious impact on health and consumer protection. A significant factor in developing countries' failing to enforce IPRs is the lack of capacity to do so. The costs of establishing a fully functioning system from the ground up can be very high, especially for poor countries with limited resources. Technical assistance and capacity building assistance from developed countries will be of paramount importance if developing countries are to provide the degree of protection envisioned in TRIPS commitments (Lamy, 2004).

One aspect of the TRIPS Agreement that has garnered attention recently is the possibility of using TRIPS as an instrument of retaliation. When the Uruguay Round was negotiated, cross-retaliation (i.e. retaliation between the different agreements administered by the WTO) was seen as a way to ensure commitments made in TRIPS are honored. The prevailing expectation was that if a developing country failed to live up to it TRIPS commitments, developed countries could put pressure on the delinquent government to reform through withdrawal of concessions on their goods and service exports (i.e. the imposition of trade barriers on imports of goods from the country not fulfilling its TRIPS commitments). However, as first argued by Ecuador in their dispute with the EU over the EU banana regime, a country can also withdraw concessions made in TRIPS if a country fails to live up to their commitments in the General Agreement on Tariffs and Trade or the General Agreement on Trade in Services (ICTSD, 2000). This is particularly appealing to many members because other retaliation measures put in place against large, rich Members, such as the US and the EU, are unlikely to have sufficient economic impact to induce their compliance with WTO rulings. This possibility has again been brought to the fore in the Brazil-US dispute over cotton subsides[6] (ICSTD, 2005b). While there are complications to ensure this type of retaliation is compliant with WTO rules, if it proves successful there could be a number of developing countries attempting to use this type of retaliation in the WTO.

For those who view strong IP protection in developing countries as inappropriate, a worrisome trend in free trade agreements (FTAs) is the tendency for developing countries to agree to TRIPS-plus commitments in order to secure a deal from developed countries. If a WTO member agrees to TRIPS-plus provisions in regional or bilateral negotiations, the TRIPS Agreement states the member must extend that advantage to all other Members. As the number of FTAs continue to balloon, TRIPS-plus concessions will become more of a rule rather than an exception. Critics worry that the TRIPS-plus requirements will prevent countries from using the flexibilities inherent in TRIPS or adopt industrial policies based on weaker IPR protection (ICTSD, 2004a).

DEVELOPED COUNTRIES AND TRIPS

In developed countries, the interests of IP holders play a much larger role in the formation of public policy than in developing countries. Many governments strive to create an environment that encourages R&D spending and IP policy is one instrument used. As a result of these policies, companies developing products for these markets have a significantly improved chance of recouping their investments. As the public sector spending on R&D has continued to decrease since the mid-1970s, the ability of firms to recover their investments has become ever more important for developing new products and processes of value to society (Boyd et al., 2003).

It is not surprising that high-technology industries have lobbied for the strongest and most comprehensive IP system possible as it is viewed as one of the most important factors for success. In a survey of pharmaceutical, medical device or diagnostic, biopharmaceutical and biotechnology companies, length of market exclusivity, strength of patent enforcement and global IP standards were cited as the most important external factor for accelerating development of health science innovation for 32 per cent of respondents and second most important for 46 per cent of respondents – the highest of all factors given. This survey also found that 87 per cent of respondents said degree of patent enforcement was very important in affecting decisions on the development of health sciences innovation in their company and 77 per cent said length of market exclusivity was very important (Luce, 2004).

Companies involved in the biotechnology sector would like to see strong patent protection for living organisms and are concerned with the proposals of developing countries regarding access to genetic resources. The International Chamber of Commerce (ICC) has stated,

> *the legal uncertainty associated with access to and use of natural genetic resources that has arisen over the past decade has cast a shadow over the patent system and led may of those users to postpone or limit acquisition of new genetic material...The legal uncertainty that is discouraging investment in naturally occurring genetic resources is reducing opportunities for negotiating mutually agreed terms and for the sharing of any resultant benefits...This vicious spiral is contrary to the interests of both the countries and indigenous communities stewarding in-situ genetic resources, and the community of potential users of such resources (ICC, 2005).*

TRIPS AND INVESTMENT

The impact IPRs have on R&D investments has already been well documented in the pharmaceutical industry. Medicines San Frontiers (Doctors Without Borders) published a report outlining the disproportionate amount of R&D spending on diseases of the prosperous. Only about ten per cent of health-related R&D spending is used for research on diseases that account for 90 per cent of the world's health burden (Secretariat of the Global Forum for Health Research, 2004). While certainly not the only factor, this is partially attributable to the fact that private firms, which account for 42 per cent of all global health R&D spending, face a very significant chance of their IP not being protected if they created drugs tailored to diseases prevalent in poor countries. The agricultural biotechnology industry is following a similar path. The first generation of commercialized biotechnology crops are canola, maize, soybean and cotton. The majority of research is directed towards crops grown in temperate climates or a limited number of tropical cash crops such as cotton, rubber, coffee, papaya, and pineapple. Many of the tropical and sub-tropical food crops have received relatively insignificant research investments for the past 50 years. Some of these crops include cassava, the plantain and cooking bananas, sweet potato, taro, sorghum, and millet. Biotechnology has not been applied to tropical or sub-tropical food crops. In addition, little to no work has been done on improving important local varieties of crops such as rice and corn (Fauquet and Taylor, 2003).

When TRIPS was negotiated, developed countries argued forcefully that strong IP protection would benefit not only rich, developed countries because with strong IPRs, private firms, in both developed and developing countries, would begin making more investments in areas of particular concern to developing countries. As shown above, however, in both the pharmaceutical and agricultural biotechnology industries, ten years later this has failed to materialize. Were developed countries simply trying to deceive developing countries? The answer to this is no. Firstly, developing countries have only had to be in compliance with TRIPS for the past five years as they were given until 2000 as a transition period. Least developed countries do not have to comply until January 1, 2006. As such, there has been less time for companies to adjust their long term R&D investment strategies. Despite developing countries having been required to comply with TRIPS for five years, the incentives for private firms to invest in these markets have not improved significantly. Infringement of IPRs is still rampant in many developing countries. This widespread piracy is caused by the lack of resources and political will in many countries to properly enforce their IP legislation. There are localized examples of how strengthened IP standards have lead to increases in R&D investments. For example, Mexico implemented a strong patent regime in 1991 and in the following ten years, R&D investment almost tripled. South Korea experienced similar growth (Ernst & Young, 2002).

Notwithstanding the significant documented evidence of poor IPRs enforcement, there has never been a case taken to the WTO for failure to enforce IPR laws. The US has been undertaking a significant number of initiatives to encourage compliance such as high level meetings, technical assistance and including IP in their FTAs. Progress in China has been a priority but improvements have been small. The Deputy Undersecretary of Commerce for Intellectual Property Stephen Pinkos acknowledged that China's continued poor record of intellectual property right enforcement would likely end up as a WTO case. At the same time, however, he also acknowledged the difficulty arguing this case as there is no precedent to rely on and the standard in WTO rules on enforcement is vague (*Inside US Trade*, June 3, 2005).

Thus far, it appears as if TRIPS has been unsuccessful in inducing widespread additional private sector investments in R&D for products and processes of particular importance to developing countries. The expected return is simply insufficient to compensate for the risk involved in this type of activity. In addition to traditional risks of product development, for example, that after development the product will fail to obtain regulatory approval, the risk of not having marketing exclusivity is much higher in developing countries. Firms must first consider the probability of a foreign government voluntarily enforcing their IP. If this possibility is not sufficiently high, firms must consider the prospect of pursuing civil legal action against the pirate producer(s). This would include an analysis of both the chances of a successful judgement and the costs that would be incurred. Factors such as the efficacy and independence of foreign courts and their potential bias would have to be evaluated. The TRIPS Agreement, in theory, makes it possible for the firm could go to their own national government and petition for action under TRIPS for a foreign government's failure to uphold the firm's IPRs. However, as indicated earlier, there has never been a case on enforcement brought to the WTO and government officials have publicly acknowledged the difficulty that would be faced in obtaining a positive judgement. In addition, if private firms were successful in developing a product with large health benefits for poor countries, developing country governments are within their rights to order compulsory licences which may not be to the satisfaction of the IPR holder. Thus far, TRIPS has not successfully reduced these risks and costs to a level which makes investment in products for developing countries attractive.

CONCLUSION

The TRIPS Agreement has been the subject of considerable debate since its inception in 1995 and it appears that disagreements over it will continue for some time into the future. This is not surprising as optimal provision of intellectual property protection is a delicate balance between the costs incurred to society from granting temporary monopoly rights and the benefits of inducing investments in innovative activities. It is only natural that a variety of opinions would develop regarding what the optimal solution is, especially considering that these costs and benefits are not distributed uniformly across countries and individuals.

Many developing countries would like to see changes made to the TRIPS Agreement. Some of the primary areas of concern are access to medicines, equitable sharing of rewards from genetic resources, protection of traditional knowledge and biodiversity, patenting of life forms, costs of enforcement and appropriate technology transfer. Negotiations are taking place at both the WTO Council for TRIPS and at WIPO. Even issues that have had widespread international support, such as access to medicines for very poor countries, have proved to be difficult negotiations as countries try to ensure strong rules to prevent abuse of exceptions made to TRIPS.

The push for strong international IPRs has come primarily from governments of developed countries that have made *knowledge economy* innovation a central pillar of their industrial strategies (Gaisford et al., 2002). These governments are not, however, only seeking to enhance the interests of their domestic firms. They have recognized the importance of private capital in producing innovations which improve the overall well-being of society and that in a market economy, IPRs are required to induce these investments. There is significant potential for improving the lives of many people in developing countries through improved medicines and agricultural crops. Proposals by developing countries would result in a system where firms could obtain a patent on fewer inventions and that patent would be afforded less protection. As a result, private firms will have even less of an incentive to work to develop products that could help so many poor individuals. Stronger patent protection could actually help create competition in products for developing countries and result in lower drug and input prices for agriculture in the long term. It should be noted that regardless of intellectual property right protection, there are regions that are desperately poor and simply cannot pay for such products even if they are available and at a relatively low price. In these circumstances, research and development cannot be undertaken on a commercially viable basis and will need to be shouldered by the public sector and charitable organizations. Stronger IPRs can still help in this regard by shifting some of the burden off the public sector onto the private sector for products that could be commercially viable. As such, the public sector can concentrate its resources on a more limited number of problem areas and thus have more resources for each problem.

Intellectual property rights are not a perfect means of encouraging innovation. Every government can recognise that they come with costs–allowing a firm temporary monopoly rights. Governments must consider the impact of their actions on the long term well being of their citizens. In the short term, developing countries would be better off if they instantaneously had access to all of the current technological developments on a global basis. Developing countries are, however, in desperate need of technological solutions for some of their most pressing problems that currently have no solution – and few, if any, resources being devoted to finding them. If there is any serious hope that private firms will provide these solutions, at some point developing countries are going to have to prove that they are serious about providing strong intellectual property rights.

NOTES

1. Countries were given different transition periods depending on their development status. Developed countries had one year after the WTO Agreements took effect on January 1, 1995. Developing countries and transition economies (under certain conditions) were given five years, until 2000. Least-developed countries were given eleven years, until 2006. This has now been extended until 2016 for pharmaceutical products.
2. This is not to deny that some spontaneous invention would take place either through the work of inquisitive individuals or by accident. Spontaneous invention, however, represents only a small proportion of innovative activity in modern market economies.
3. It is important to stress that IPRs only provide the opportunity to earn monoploly rents. Of course, many inventions fail in the marketplace and being granted IPRs does not eliminate risk for firms engaging in innovative activity. Critics of IPRs often focus on the monopoly rents associated with inventions that are commercial successes while ignoring the failures and the risks taken by those who do produce a commercial success.
4. The WIPO was established in 1970 to jointly administer the 1883 Paris Convention for the Protection of Industrial Property (i.e.

patents, industrial designs, etc.) and the 1886 Berne Convention for the Protection of Literary and Artistic Works (i.e. copyrights). In 1974, WIPO became a specialized agency of the United Nations. The Paris and Berne Conventions became the basis of the WTO TRIPS Agreement. The WIPO now has a cooperation agreement with the WTO concerning implementation issues and assistance to developing countries. The WIPO now administers a total of 23 treaties and continues to work on new IP issues such as electronic commerce and the internet (WIPO, 2005).

5. WIPO is classified as a specialized agency of the United Nations system of organizations with the mandate to administer intellectual property matters recognized by the member States of the UN.
6. Brazil successfully argued in front of the Dispute Settlement Body of the WTO that the subsidies provided to US cotton farmers were in breach of US commitments. The Panel called for the US to withdraw the prohibited subsidy by July 1, 2005. The US had not complied by this date and the issue of retaliation was referred to arbitration.

REFERENCES

Boyd, S.L., W.A. Kerr and N. Perdikis, (2003), Agricultural Biotechnology Innovations Versus Intellectual Property Rights–Are Developing Countries at the Mercy of Multinationals?, *The Journal of World Intellectual Property*, 6 (2): 211-232.

China Update. *Inside US Trade*. June 3, 2005.

Convention on Biological Diversity (1992), *Convention Text*. Available online at http://www.biodiv.org/doc/legal/cbd-en.pdf.

Ernst & Young, (2002), *Beyond Borders: The Global Biotechnology Report 2002*. Ernst & Young Global Health Sciences. United Kingdom.

Fauquet, C.M. and N. Taylor, (2003), Biotechnology's Greatest Challenge. *Biosafety News*. Issue No. 44. July. Available online at http://www.biosafetynews.com/July03/bi.htm.

Gaisford, J.D., R. Tarvydas, J.E. Hobbs and W.A. Kerr, (2002), Biotechnology Piracy: Rethinking the International Protection of Intellectual Property, *Canadian Journal of Agricultural Economics*, 50 (1): 1-14.

Geneva Declaration on the Future of the World Intellectual Property Organization (2004), Available online at http://www.cptech.org/ip/wipo/genevadeclaration.html.

International Centre for Trade and Sustainable Development (ICTSD) (2000), *Bridges*. Year 4. No. 4. May. Available online at http://www.ictsd.org/monthly/bridges/BRIDGES4-4.pdf.

International Centre for Trade and Sustainable Development (ICTSD) (2003), *Bridges*. Year 7. No. 5. June. Available online at http://www.ictsd.org/monthly/bridges/BRIDGES7-5.pdf.

International Centre for Trade and Sustainable Development (ICTSD) (2004a). *Bridges*. Year 8. No. 7. July-August. Available online at http://www.ictsd.org/monthly/bridges/BRIDGES8-7.pdf.

International Centre for Trade and Sustainable Development (ICTSD) (2004b). *Bridges*. Year 8. No. 10. November. Available online at http://www.ictsd.org/monthly/bridges/BRIDGES8-10.pdf.

International Centre for Trade and Sustainable Development (ICTSD) (2005a). *Bridges*. Year 9. No. 4. April. Available online at http://www.ictsd.org/monthly/bridges/BRIDGES9-4.pdf.

International Centre for Trade and Sustainable Development (ICTSD) (2005b). *Bridges*. Year 9. No. 5. May. available online at http://www.ictsd.org/monthly/bridges/BRIDGES9-5.pdf.

International Centre for Trade and Sustainable Development (ICTSD) (2005c). *Bridges Weekly Trade News Digest*. Volume 9. Number 22. June 22. Available online at http://www.ictsd.org/weekly/05-06-22/story3.htm.

International Chamber of Commerce (ICC) (2005). *Access and Benefit Sharing: Special Disclosure Requirements in Patents Applications*. WTO Discussion paper. Available online at www.wto.org/english/forums_e/ngo_e/posp48_icc_e.doc.

Isaac, G. E. and W. A. Kerr (2004). Bioprospecting or Biopiracy?: Intellectual Property and Traditional Knowledge in Biotechnology Innovation. *The Journal of World Intellectual Property*. 7(1): 35-52.

Lamy, P., (2004), Trade-Related Aspects of Intellectual Property Rights--Ten Years Later. *Journal of World Trade*. 38(6): 923-934.

Luce, C. B., (2004), *Total Value of Innovation: Choosing Metrics that Matter in Health Sciences*. Ernst & Young Global Limited. available online at http://www.ey.com/global/download.nsf/US/WEF_-_Value_of_Innovation/$file/TotalValueofInnovation.pdf.

Pray, C., D. Ma, J. Huang, and F. Qiao, (2001), "Impact of Bt Cotton in China". *World Development*. 29(5): 813-825.

Secretariat of the Global Forum for Health Research (2004), *The 10/90 Report on Health Research 2003-2004*. Ed. Sheila Davey. Available online at http://www.globalforumhealth.org/site/002__What%20we%20do/005__Publications/001__10%2090%20reports.php.

World Intellectual Property Organization (WIPO) (2004a), *Proposal by Argentina and Brazil for the Establishment of a Development Agenda for WIPO*. WO/GA/31/11. Available online at http://www.wipo.int/documents/en/document/govbody/wo_gb_ga/pdf/wo_ga_31_11.pdf.

World Intellectual Property Organization (WIPO) (2004b), *Report of Thirty-First (15th Extraordinary) Session, Geneva, September 27 to October 5, 2004*. WO/GA/31/15. Available online at http://www.wipo.int/documents/en/document/govbody/wo_gb_ga/doc/wo_ga_31_15.doc.

World Intellectual Property Organization (WIPO) (2005), *About WIPO: General Information*. Available online at http://www.wipo.int/about-wipo/en/gib.htm.

World Trade Organization (2001a). *Declaration on the TRIPS agreement and public health*. WT/MIN(01)/DEC/02. Available online at http://www.wto.org/english/thewto_e/minist_e/min01_e/mindecl_trips_e.htm.

World Trade Organization (2001b), *Ministerial Declaration*. WT/MIN(01)/DEC/01. Available online at http://www.wto.org/english/thewto_e/minist_e/min01_e/mindecl_e.htm.

World Trade Organization (2005). *Overview: the TRIPS Agreement*. Available online at http://www.wto.org/english/tratop_e/trips_e/intel2_e.htm.

INTELLECTUAL PROPERTY RIGHTS UNDER GLOBALISATION

*Anju Jain**

INTRODUCTION

Globalization is a term used to describe the changes in societies and the world economy that are the result of dramatically increased trade & cultural exchange. In specifically economic contexts, it refers almost exclusively to the effects of trade, particularly trade liberalization on free trade. Between 1910 & 1950, a political & economic upheavals dramatically reduced the volume & importance's of international trade flows. In the post world war II. Environment, Fostered by International Economic Institution & rebuilding programs. Liberalization & Globalization have dramatically altered perceptions about science & its practice in India. The unbashed drive to patent & protect every conceivable scientific advances, no matter how incremental, has now reached a ridiculous level in the west. American & Multinational Company never known for moderation & thought fullness, when commercial interest are involved have set out to fence vast areas of science under the guise of intellectual property. Issues of generation, protection & exploitation of intellectual property (IP) are assuming increasing importance under globalization. The new IP regime will have wide ranging, technological & political impact. As per the obligations under the trade related aspects of Intellectual Property system (TRIPS), all members of the world trade organization (WTO) are supposed to implement national system of intellectual property rights following an agreed set of minimum standard. However there is an increasing feeling

* Department of Economics, Ganga Singh College, CHAPRA (SARAN) BIHAR.

that harmonization is demanded from those that are not equal, ether economically or institutionally.

INTELLECTUAL PROPERTY

In law particularly common law jurisdiction intellectual property or IP refers to a legal entitlement which sometime attaches to the expressed form of an idea or of other intangible subject matter. The most well known form of intellectual property include copyrights patients, trademarks & trade secrets. Common types of intellectual property rights include conflicting area of law:

(i) Copyrights-which give the holder some exclusive rights to control some reproduction of works of authorship such as books and music, for a certain period of time.

(ii) Patents give the holder an exclusive right to prevent third parties from commercially exploiting an invention for a certain period, typically 20 years from the filing date of a patent application.

(iii) Trademarks are distinctive manes, phrases or marks used to identity products to consumers.

(iv) Trade secrets, where a company keeps information secret, perhaps by enforcing a contract under which those given access to information are not permitted to disclose it others.

LEGAL STATUS

Exclusive rights are generally divided into two categories: those that grant exclusive rights only on copying/reproduction of the item or act protected (i.g. copyright) and those that grant a right to prevent others from doing something. The difference between these it that a copyright would prevent someone from copying the design of something, but could not stop them from making that design if they had no knowledge of the original held by the copyright holder. Patents and trademarks on the other hand, can be used to prevent that second person from making the same design even if they had never heard of or seen the claimed "property". Those rights must be applied for or registered and are more expensive to enforce.

HISTORY OF IPR

The early history of patents dates from the 15th century in England and Venice.

Copyright was not invented until after the advent of the printing press and wider public literacy. In England the King was concerned by the unfair copying of books and used the royal prerogative to pass the Licensing Act 1662 which established a register of licensed books and required a copy to be deposited with the Stationers Company. The Statute of Anne was the first real act of copyright, and gave the author rights for a fixed period. Internationally, the Berne Convention in the late 1800s set out the scope of copyright protection and is still in force to this day.

The term intellectual property appears to have originated in Europe during the 19th century. French author A. Nion mentions "propriété intellectuelle" in his Droits civils des auteurs, artistes et inventeurs, published in 1846, and there may well have been earlier uses of the term.

In 1847, a U.S. circuit court defined intellectual property as "the labors of the mind productions and interests as much a man's own...as the wheat he cultivates." Woodbury & Minot, Rep. Cases Circuit Court of U.S., I. 56.

Worldwide, however, use of the term was uncommon until its use in the Geneva-based World Intellectual Property Organization (WIPO), which was established in 1967.

With the French Revolution, which followed the American Revolution, there was controversy over the nature of copyright and patent protections in Europe; those who supported unlimited copyrights frequently used the term property to advance that agenda, while others who supported a more limited system sometimes used the term intellectual rights.

RECENT TRENDS IN IPR

Recently the general trend in exclusive rights law has been expansion: to cover new types of subject matter such as databases, to regulate new categories of activity in respect of the subject matter already protected, to increase the duration of individual rights, and to remove restrictions and limitations on these rights.

Another effect of this trend is an increase in the term of the government-granted rights, and an expansion of the definition of "author" to include corporations as the legitimate creators and owners of works. The concept of work for hire has had the effect of treating corporation or business owner as the legal author of works created by people while employed.

Another trend is to increase the number and type of what is claimed as "intellectual property". This has resulted in increasingly broad patents and trademarks: for instance, Microsoft attempting to trademark the phrase, "Where do you want to go today?". Trademarks in EU and US law can now encompass smells (e.g. of cut grass for tennis balls), shapes (e.g. of a soft drinks bottle), colors (e.g. red for fizzy drinks), words (e.g. COCA-COLA) and sounds (Intel has registered a five-note-melody with the USPTO. The granting of patents for life forms, software algorithms and business models stretches the initial concept of giving the inventor limited rights to exclude the use of his invention.

Some argue that these expansions harm an essential "bargain" driven between public and copyright holders: as most "new" ideas borrow from other ideas, it is thought that too many "intellectual property" laws will lead to a reduction of the overall creative output of a society. The expansion of exclusive rights is also alleged to have led to the emergence of organizations whose business model is to frivolously sue other companies.

The electronic age has seen an increase in the attempt to use software-based digital rights management tools to restrict the copying and use of digitally based works. This can have the effect of limiting fair use provisions of copyright law and even make the first-sale doctrine (known in EU law as 'exhaustion of rights') moot. This would allow, in essence the creation of a book which would disintegrate after one reading. As individuals have proven adept at circumventing such measures in the past, many copyright holders have also successfully lobbied for laws such as the Digital Millennium Copyright Act, which uses criminal law to prevent any circumvention of software used to enforce digital "rights management" systems. Equivalent provisions, to prevent circumvention of copyright protection have existed in EU for some time, and are being expanded in, for example, Article 6 and 7 the Copyright Directive. Other examples are Article 7 of the Software Directive of 1991 (91/250/EEC), and the Conditional Access Directive of 1998 (98/84/EEC).

At the same time, the growth of the Internet, and particularly distributed search engines like Kazaa and Gnutella, represents a challenge for exclusive rights policy. The Recording Industry Association of America, in particular, has been on the front lines of the fight against what it terms "piracy". The industry has had victories against some services, including a highly publicized case against the file-sharing company Napster, and some people have been prosecuted for sharing files in violation of copyright. However, the increasingly decentralized nature of such networks makes legal action against distributed search engines more problematic.

IPR AND GLOBALIZATION

Twenty first century will be the century of knowledge, indeed the century of mind. Innovation is the key for the production as well as processing of knowledge. A nation's ability to convert knowledge into wealth and social good through the process of innovation will determine its future. In this context, issues of generation, valuation, protection and exploitation of intellectual property (IP) are going to become critically important all around the world. Exponential growth of scientific knowledge, increasing demands for new forms of intellectual property protection as well as access to IP related information, increasing dominance of the new knowledge economy over the old 'brick & mortar' economy, complexities linked to IP in traditional knowledge, community knowledge and animate objects, will pose a challenge in setting the new 2lst century IP agenda. Intellectual property will no longer be seen as a distinct or self-contained domain, but rather as an important and effective policy instrument that would be relevant to a wide range of socioeconomic, technological and political concerns. The development of skills and competence to manage IPR and leverage its influence will need increasing focus; in particular, in the third world.

Intellectual property rights are being harmonized worldwide. As per the obligation under the Trade Related Intellectual Property Systems (TRIPS) agreement, developing countries are now implementing national systems of intellectual property rights following an agreed set of minimum standards, such as twenty years of patent protection; the least developed countries have an extra 11 years to do so. One of the third world concerns is that while a fully harmonised system of IPR is being advocated, today's advanced economies had refused to grant patents throughout the 19th and early 20th centuries. They formalized the enforced intellectual property rights gradually as they shifted from being net users of intellectual property to bring net producers. Indeed, France, Germany and Switzerland, who are leading developed countries today completed, what is now standard protection, only in the 1960s and 1970s.

An ideal regime of intellectual property rights strikes a balance between private incentives for innovators and the public interest of maximizing access to the fruits of innovation. This balance is reflected in article 27 of the 1948 Universal Declaration of Human Rights, which recognizes both that "Everyone has the right to the protection of the moral and material interest resulting from any scientific, literacy or artistic production of which he is the author" and that "Everyone has the right.... to share in scientific advancement and its benefits". The burning question seems to be balancing the interest of the inventor and that of the society in an optimum way.

Further, there is a feeling that without good advice on creating national legislation that makes the most of what TRIPS allows, and under pressure to introduce legislation beyond that required by TRIPS, many countries have legislated themselves into a disadvantageous position. The TRIPS agreement entered into force in most developing countries in January 2000; the least developed countries have until 2006. With implementation still under way and industries still adjusting, little empirical evidence is available on the effects of the legislative change.

The battle today is between those that are not equal, economically and institutionally. TRIPS, like other World Trade Organization agreements is an agreement on a legal framework. Its implications will be decided by resolving disputes. That makes case law and the power of the parties involved of great importance. The third world has a clear disadvantage here.

In the developing world, the impact of TRIPS will vary according to each country's economic and technological development. Middle-income countries like Brazil and Malaysia are likely to benefit from the spur to local innovation. Countries like India and China, which are endowed with a large intellectual infrastructure, can gain in the long term by stronger IPR protection. However, least developed countries, where formal innovation is minimal, are likely to face higher costs without the offsetting.

Facilitating the access of the third world countries to technologies required by them constitutes one of the key elements in accelerating the pace of their economic and social development. Such access is generally the result of licenses and technology transfer agreements. The fact of the matter is that the prospective technology seekers in developing countries face serious difficulties in their commercial dealings with technology holders in the developed countries. These difficulties arise for a variety of reasons. Some arise from the imperfections of the market for technology. Some are attributed to the relative lack of experience and skill of enterprises and institutions in developing countries in concluding adequate legal arrangements for the acquisition of technology. Some arise due to government practices, both legislative and administrative, in both developed and developing countries, which influence the implementation of national policies and procedures designed to encourage the flow of technology to, and its acquisition by, developing countries.

There are concrete examples to show that technology transfers to the third world have not taken place when they were needed most. The 1990 Montreal Protocol on Substances that Deplete the Ozone Layer ran into conflicts over commitments to ensure fair and favourable access for developing countries to chlorofluorocarbon (CFC) substitutes protected by intellectual property rights. The 1992 Convention on Biological Diversity aims to ensure fair and equitable use of genetic resources partly through technology cooperation, but its technological provisions have received little attention. The 1994 TRIPS agreement calls for technology transfer to the least developed countries, yet that provision has scarcely been translated into action.

The transfer and dissemination needs of the developing countries have to be seen from the point of view of the capacity of those in need of accessing the technologies, particularly where the cost of technology may be prohibitive due to economies of scale and other reasons. In such cases, in order to implement the related provisions of the TRIPS Agreement, commercially viable mechanisms will have to be found.

PROTECTION & PROMOTION OF COMMUNITY RIGHTS

One of the concerns of the developing world is that the process of globalization is threatening the appropriation of elements of the collective knowledge of societies into proprietary knowledge for the commercial profit of a few. An urgent action is needed to protect these knowledge systems through national policies and international understanding linked to IPR, while providing its development & proper use for the benefit of its holders. We need a particular focus on community knowledge and community innovation. To encourage communities, it is necessary to scout, support, spawn and scale up the green grass root innovation. Linking innovation, enterprise and investment is particularly important. New models and new thinking on IP will have to be envisioned to accomplish this.

The local communities or individuals do not have the knowledge or the means to safeguard their property in a system, which has its origin in very different cultural values and attitudes. The communities have a storehouse of knowledge about their flora and fauna-their habits, their habitats, their seasonal behaviour and the like-and it is only logical and in consonance with natural justice that they are given a greater say as a matter of right in all matters regarding the study, extraction and commercialization of the biodiversity. A policy that does not obstruct the advancement of knowledge, and provides for valid and sustainable use and adequate intellectual property protection with just benefit sharing is what we need.

The existing IPR systems are oriented around the concept of private ownership and individual innovation. They are at odds with indigenous cultures, which emphasize collective creation and ownership of knowledge. There is a concern that IPR systems encourage the appropriation of traditional knowledge for commercial use, and that too without the fair sharing of benefits of the holders of this knowledge. They violate the indigenous cultural precepts by encouraging the commodification of such knowledge.

The issues of the economics of community knowledge are truly complex. While it is true that many indigenous cultures appear to develop and transmit knowledge from generation to generation within a system, individuals in local or indigenous communities can distinguish themselves as informal creators or innovators, separate from the community. Furthermore, some indigenous or traditional societies are reported to recognize various types of intellectual property rights over knowledge, which may be held by individuals, families, lineages or communities. Discussion of IPRs and traditional knowledge should draw more on the diversity and creativity of indigenous approaches to IPR issues.

The issue of 'protection' of traditional knowledge needs to be looked at from two perspectives, the "protection" may be granted to exclude the unauthorized use by third parties of the protected information. On the other hand, the

"Protection" is also means to preserve traditional knowledge from uses that may erode it or negatively affect the life or culture of the communities that have developed and applied it. Further, the protection also promotes self-respect and self-determination.

While recognizing the market-based nature of IPRs, other non-market-based rights could be useful in developing models for a right to protect traditional knowledge, innovations and practices. To date, debate on IPRs and biodiversity has focused on patents and plant breeders' rights. Provisions under undisclosed information or trade secrets could be invoked to protect traditional knowledge not available in the public domain. Geographical indications and trademarks, or sui generis analogies, could also be the alternative tools for indigenous and local communities seeking to gain economic benefits from their traditional knowledge. The potential value of geographical indications and trademarks is in protecting plants and germplasms that are specific and unique to geographical regions. They could protect and reward traditions while allowing innovation. They will emphasize the relationships between human cultures and their local land and environment. They are not freely transferable from one owner to another. They can be maintained as long as the collective tradition is maintained.

Giving legally recognized ownership of knowledge to communities through sui generis IPRs has several benefits. It will raise the profile of that knowledge and encourage respect for it both inside and outside the knowledge holding communities. This will enthuse the younger members of such communities to contribute to the further development of that knowledge. Furthermore, prospects of economic returns for the use of that knowledge by others will act as a further incentive for the community members to respect their knowledge and continue to engage in practices in that knowledge. Prior protection will also provide disclosure, use and proliferation of such knowledge, which might have otherwise been eroded.

IPR RELATED TO MEDICINE

Traditional Medicine (TM) play a crucial role in health-care of serves the health needs of a vast majority of people in developing countries. Access to "modern" health care services and medicine may be limited in developing countries. TM becomes the only affordable treatment available to poor people and in remote communities.

World Health Organisation (WHO) defines traditional medicine as "the sum total of all the knowledge and practices, whether explicable or not, used in diagnosis, prevention and elimination of physical, mental or social imbalance and relying exclusively on practical experience and observations handed down from generation to generation, whether verbally or in writing". Health care providers worldwide including major pharmaceutical giants are turning to incorporate many of these into their mainstream activities. As traditional medicines are largely based on medicinal plants, indigenous to these countries, where the system has been in vogue for several centuries, the effort is on accessing them either directly or through the use of modern tools of breeding and cultivation, including tissue culture, cell culture and transgenic technology. IP issues linked to such endeavours remain unresolved.

The protection of TM under intellectual property rights (IPRs) raises two types of issues. First, to what extent it is feasible to protect, existing IPR system. Certain aspects of TM may be covered by patents or other IPRs. There have also been many proposals to develop sui generis systems of protection. Such proposals are based on the logic that if innovators in the "formal" system of innovation receive a compensation through IPRs holders of traditional knowledge should be similarly treated.

World Intellectual Property Organization, (WIPO) has been sensitive to these concerns. At a conference held in October 1998, under the aegis of the WIPO an agenda for the future of IPR in the field of traditional medicines was prepared, which prioritized activities in this area, namely, development of standards for the availability, scope and use of IPRs on traditional medicine in Asian countries, systematic documentation of traditional medicine for protection purposes, regional and inter-regional information exchange and compilation of the requisite data bases, etc. This agenda needs to be moved forward.

The codification of TM varies significantly. A distinction can be made, particularly in Asia, between the codified systems of 'traditional medicine' and non-codified medicinal knowledge, which includes "folk", "tribal" or "indigenous" medicine. Thus, in India, folk traditions are handed over orally from generation to generation. The "folk" medicine is based on traditional beliefs norms and practices based on centuries old experiences of trials and errors, successes and failures at the household level. These are passed through oral tradition and may be called, "people's health culture", home remedies or folk remedies. TM may be possessed by individuals. In some cases, for instance, healers use rituals as part of their traditional healing methods, which often allow them to monopolize their knowledge, despite disclosure of the photochemical products or techniques used. The codified tradition consists of medical knowledge with sophisticated foundations expressed in thousands of manuscripts covering all branches of medicine. Examples are ayurveda, siddha, unani and the Tibetan tradition.

The grant of patents on non-original innovations (particularly those linked to traditional medicines), which are based on what is already a part of the traditional knowledge of the developing world have been causing a great concern to the developing world. It was CSIR that challenged the US patent No. 5,401, 5041, which was granted for the wound healing properties of turmeric.

The consensus statement of Global Health Forum I, February 2000, said "The move to globalize the protection of intellectual property is not politically sustainable without, at the same time, making the delivery of health technology more equitable". On April 23, 2001 the United Nations Commission on Human Rights called on governments to ensure the accessibility of pharmaceuticals and medical treatments used to treat pandemics such as HIV/AIDS, as well as "their affordability for all," in accordance with international law and international agreements. The resolution also calls on governments "to safeguard access to such preventive, curative or palliative pharmaceuticals or medical technologies from any limitations by third parties." However, the recent landmark event on medicines HIV/AIDS in South Africa has raised new questions in this regard.

The adoption of the TRIPS Agreement has entailed significant changes for the protection of pharmaceutical products and processes. The Agreement not only made product patent protection binding to all Member countries (article 27.1); it also strengthened, inter alia, process patents (articles 28 (b) and 34), narrowly defined the conditions for establishing exceptions to patent rights (article 30), and limited the possibility of applying especial modalities of compulsory licenses to pharmaceuticals (e.g. as provided for in Canada until 1993).

A key question is whether the TRIPS regime has led to an increase in the prices of patented medicines. Although many researchers argue that that there is no clear relationship between the patents and the prices of medicines, there is a strong evidence that average pharmaceutical product prices decline in the face of entry by generic substitutes. Competition is important to keep prices down.

There are a number of options available within TRIPS to ensure affordable access. Compulsory licensing, parallel imports and differential pricing between developed and developing countries have been suggested as instruments to improve access within the broad framework of TRIPS. But it is not clear as to the kind of legal instrument that could be used to enforce differential pricing and segment markets. It is also not clear as to whether TRIPS regime is compatible with national exhaustion or international exhaustion. There is an additional problem with differential pricing in those developing countries, which have capacity for producing generics. They will slap on anti-dumping duties because of the pressure from domestic industry. Under the differential pricing regime, one will have to decide as to how to organize competition based on negotiated prices. There is also a fear that if one segments markets in pharmaceuticals in this manner, there will have for international competition in other sectors.

The full implementation and application of the TRIPS Agreement will entail welfare losses to varying extent depending on the economic status of individual countries. The question is about the extent of this loss and what should be done to mitigate the adverse consequences.

PROCESS OF RE-EXAMINATION OF US PATENTS

There is a general perception that the process of fighting an erroneous patent is long, arduous and very expensive. This is true as exemplified by the Eastman Kodak-Polaroid patent war, which was settled after several years for about a billion dollars. However, the process of re-examination of a US patent, a route that was adopted by CSIR to challenge the turmeric and the Basmati patent, is relatively straightforward. It cost CSIR approximately Rs. 5 lakhs to win the turmeric case.

As per the provision of re-examination of granted US patents, any person may file a request for re-examination of a patent. Corporations and/or governmental entities are included within the scope of the term 'any person'. Even the patent owner can ask for a re-examination, which would be limited to an ex-parte consideration of prior patents or printed publication. It is also possible for the Commissioner to initiate re-examination at the Commissioner's own initiative under 37 CFR 1.520. Re-examination can be initiated by the Commissioner on a very limited basis such as where a general public policy question is at issue and there is no interest by 'any other person'.

The provisions for re-examination are as follows:

1. Anyone can request re-examination at any time during the period of enforceability of the patent.
2. A substantial new question of patent ability must be presented for re-examination to be ordered.
3. Prior art considered during re-examination is limited to prior art patents or printed publications applied under the appropriate parts of 35 U.S.C. 102 and 103.

4. If ordered, the actual re-examination proceeding is ex-parte in nature.
5. Decision on the request must be made within three months from initial filing and remainder of proceedings must proceed with 'Special dispatch'.
6. If ordered, a re-examination proceedings will be conducted to conclusion and issuance of certificate.
7. The scope of a claim cannot be enlarged by amendment.
8. All re-examination and patent files are open to the public.

After the filing of the re-examination request, the US PTO will decide within three months whether a 'substantial new question of patent ability' has been raised by the request. If so, a decision ordering the re-examination to proceed will be issued. After the order to proceed is issued, there is a period of two months during which the patent owner can file a statement or amendment in response to the issue raised in the request. If the patent owner does this, the requester will have a period of two months to file a response. This response represents the last opportunity for the requester to participate in the re-examination. Ordinarily, the patent owner does not file any paper, so that the only opportunity for the requester to present his views is in the initial request papers. After the deadline has passed for the patent owner to file a statement (or after any statement and response by the requester have been filed), the Examiner conducts the re-examination in a manner similar to a regular patent prosecution. The final re-examination, certificate is then issued.

NON-GOVERNMENTAL ORGANISATIONS TO PROTECT TNTELLECTUAL PROPERTY

The notion of protecting intellectual works is much older than copyright or patent law. There have long existed socially-enforced systems for protecting intellectual works. These include the ancient scholarly taboo against plagiarism, along with other informal systems such as the code of non-infringement, used by clowns to recognise each clown's exclusive rights to their unique style of makeup, costume and persona. In the case of 'The Code' of the clowns, the universality of the custom lends credence to the clown's belief that this protection is 'stronger' than that provided by trademark and copyright law. Regardless of this, some clowns do trademark, copyright or patent "clown material" perhaps as protection from infringement by those outside the clown community.

More recently, "intellectual property" law has been brought to bear on holders of domain names contested by third parties, particularly when a domain name infringes on a trademark ("domain squatting"). The domain name registries, many of whom are not governmental organisations, have had to find a solution to this and therefore have dispute resolution systems which operate in parallel with national laws. The majority of the generic top level domain names (.com, .net etc.) use the ICANN model known as the Uniform Dispute Resolution Policy (UDRP). Other registries have their own different systems, such as Nominet UK's "Dispute Resolution Service" for the UK registry.

IPR IN RELATION TO DEVELOPED & DEVELOPING WORLD

International agencies will have to make an effort to bridge the gap between the developed world and the third world. Some laudable efforts are afoot in this direction. WIPO is setting up WIPONET to narrow the information access gap that exists between the developed countries and developing countries; improve the flow of information concerning intellectual property rights among WIPO member states, regional intellectual property offices and the International Bureau; to improve access to and exchange of intellectual property information in terms of costs and access time; to improve intellectual property information dissemination; to consider the information needs and filing requirements of applicants and develop electronic services keeping in mind the need to provide benefits to applicants and intellectual property offices, and to other interested parties; to help guide the International Bureau to leverage information technologies and to improve the retrieval of intellectual property information through further development of international classifications of patents, trademarks and industrial designs as efficient search tools.

The developing countries faces several other challenges. Weak physical infrastructure in terms of inadequate IP offices, as explained above, is just one aspect; but inadequate intellectual infrastructure, poor public awareness and lack of government policies that are not in tune with the times are some other hurdles. Many R&D institutions and industrial firms in the developing world have so far focussed on imitative research or reverse engineering, and have depended heavily on borrowed technology and, therefore, not created productive national IP portfolio. Apart from manpower planning for IPR protection setting up of patent training institutes and specialized courses, a judicious management of patent information is needed is the need of the hour. This will require well-structured functioning of information creating centres, information documenters and retrievers, information users and information technology experts.

Inadequate preparedness of many national IP offices in most of the developing countries is a serious concern. The problem areas pertain to manual and paper based operations, static manpower resources, rapid increase in the number of applications filed in recent years leading to inordinate delays in granting IPRs, non-uniformity in the examination, poor quality of search resulting in fresh objections even after the first examination report, inadequate search facilities and tools and lack of digital data & networks. Most seriously, IT has not yet been inducted in the IP administration in most cases. The question of capacity of the Third World IP Offices to handle complex IP issues is a serious one. In the year 2000, the World Intellectual Property Organization received 30 patent applications, which were over 1,000 pages long, with several reaching 140,000 pages. It is clear that the patent offices in the developing countries may not even have a capacity to handle this.

Internet can play a key role in the protection and promotion of traditional knowledge of the communities (while bringing in added economic value to these communities). An example is the recent experiment in India of the design of an e-commerce portal for Indian craftsmen and artisans, which will link individual craftsmen directly to designers and markets. It will be possible through this portal for a garment buyer in any part of the world to approach any craftsman directly, select a pattern, a weave and a fabric and place his order with him. This will mean not only a multiple increase in the craftsman's income but also his direct interaction with the market. This will unleash the creative skills to meet the demands of his market, and further enhance the innovation capacity. New challenges in IP protection will emerge as internet becomes a major facilitator in commercialization of traditional knowledge.

ECONOMIC ASPECTS

Exclusive rights such as copyrights and patents secure their holder an exclusive right to sell, or license rights. As such, the holder is the only seller in the market for that particular item, and the holder is often described as having a monopoly for this reason.

However, it may be the case that there are other items of "intellectual property" that are close substitutes. For example, the holder of publishing rights for a book may be competing with various other authors to get a book published. In such cases, economists may find that another market form, such as oligopoly or monopolistic competition better describes the workings of the markets for expressive works and inventions. This is one reason to prefer the term exclusive rights over monopoly rights.

The case for "intellectual property" in economic theory notes certain substantial differences from the case for tangible property. Consumption of tangible property is rivalrous. For example, once one person eats an apple, no one else can eat it; if one person uses a plot of land on which to build a home, that plot is unavailable for use by others. Without the right to exclude others from tangible resources, a tragedy of the commons can result.

The subjects of intellectual property do not share this feature of rival ness. For example, an indefinite number of copies can be made of a book without interfering with the use of the book by owners of other copies. When combined with a lack of exclusive intellectual property rights, this non-rivalrousness and non-excludability combine to make them public goods and susceptable to the free rider problem. A rationale for "intellectual property" therefore rests on incentive effects to overcome the free rider problem. This case asserts that without a subsidy that is afforded by exclusive rights, there is no direct financial incentive to create new inventions or works of authorship. However, as Wikipedia and Free software demonstrate, works of authorship are written without direct financial incentives. Moreover, many important works were created before copyright was invented. One might argue that much more invention occurred after patents came into existence; however, one could also argue that patents were brought into law as the power and influence of industrial interests grew.

Some hold that the three most common instruments provide "exclusive rights to use" different things: copyright covers original expressive works, patent covers solutions or ideas, and trademark covers means to uniquely identify a producer or other source of reputation. This view asserts that the three instruments have different histories, different intents, and allow three different kinds of incentives. Yet, the WIPO, the interest hody which introduced the term treats this like a dogma:

The status of "IP" is disputed in India, China and other developing nations. The United States and the United Kingdom are the only two nations who consistently receive net balance of payment benefits from "IP". These nations are the chief promulgators of "intellectual property" systems.

The direct incentive beneficiaries of exclusive rights have an interest in expanding their rights and benefits. Many pool their resources to form organizations that attempt this such as the Business Software Alliance (BSA), which purports to represent the interests of the commercial software industry while the Recording Industry Association of America (RIAA) represents the interests of the commercial music publishing industry. As policy expands in accordance with the notion of "intellectual property", in the interests of those who benefit directly from its; economic incentives, it tends to reduce the rights of its primary beneficiaries, the general public.

A more recent notion, proposing to expand the scope of exclusive rights to include databases, has been introduced by the EU in 1996. This is the idea of protecting the information contained in a database against re-utilisation and extraction of substantial parts. This would be an additional right predicated on a substantial investment that would exist alongside the copyright in the database structure. This notion was opposed by the United States Supreme Court in 1991 in the Feist Publication finding, which said that exclusive rights cannot cover the factual elements of any copyrighted work, that copyright does not derive from the effort expended in the production of the work, and that in the case of a collection of information, only the originality that may be found in the selection and arrangement of the information is governed by copyright. This case holds that the purpose of exclusive rights policy is to provide information to the public, and this consideration takes priority over concerns such as investment. A study has found that the introduction of exclusive rights to databases in the EU did not do any good to the economy.

Under the notion of "intellectual property" the public is increasingly prevented by law from benefiting from the use of published information without complying with the conditions set by the rights holder. The cost for this to the public is not easy to quantify.

The cost is distributed widely and unequally based on the need for the product. Ironically the direct incentive beneficiary organizations are a good source for these data. The BSA-reports a study that claims "while $80 billion in software was installed on computers worldwide last year, only $51 billion was legally purchased" (Source: BSA). The BSA says "software pirates" avoided a cost of $29 billion while the rest that obey the policy and do not purchase or make use of the work bear a real and substantial opportunity cost that is yet uncounted. However, it is questionable whether Microsoft would lower their price if it would earn $10 billion more on licensing from countries such as Russia, Thailand, India and China where most of this "piracy" happens.

But Microsoft is dumping its selling price on competition from GNU/Linux, for example with government clients. Because of this competition, Microsoft will also be forced to release an update to Internet Explorer to the public for its current product, which it originally planned to release with its next operating system.

CONCLUSION

The industrial property systems were set up centuries ago for inanimate objects and that too in formal systems of innovation. The time has come to revisit them. The emerging challenge is to look at the systems that will deal with animate objects (such as plants and animals) and with informal systems innovation (such as those by grass root innovators like farmers, artisans, tribes, fishermen and so on). The standard intellectual property systems will certainly not suit such innovators and their innovations. We, therefore, need innovation in the intellectual property system itself! The issue of whether TRIPS should fundamentally belong to WTO is under discussion. Other issues such as the desirability of uniformity of patent term need for new reforms to exclude certain sectors from TRIPS, lowering the minimum standards, differential treatment depending the state of economy of a developing country, etc. are also under discussion.

It is important is to recognize that the principal objective of the GATT/WTO system is to promote free trade. This can be done if competitive opportunities are provided across the nations on a non-discriminatory basis. The TRIPS provisions should be interpreted. In other words, the emphasis should be on promotion of competition, and not its restriction. The TRIPS provisions have to be interpreted in this context alone, and especially with an aim of laying down the foundation of a fair trade system. It is hoped that the third world concerns enumerated in this paper will be addressed by a dialogue to create a new 'TRIPS plus', getting a new meaning of 'TRIPS plus equity and ethics'.

REFERENCES

Roger E. Schechter, John R. Thomas, Intellectual Property: The Law of Copyrights, Patents and Trademarks, West Wadsworth, 2003.

Michael Perelman, Steal This Idea: Intellectual Property Rights and the Corporate Confiscation of Creativity, Palgrave Macmillan, 2002, ISBN 0312294085.

Stephan Kinsella, "Against Intellectual Property", Journal of Libertarian Studies, Vol. 15, No. 1, pp. 1-53, 2001.

Arthur Raphael Miller, Michael H. Davis, Intellectual Property: Patents, Trademarks, and Copyright, West Wadsworth; 3rd edition, 2000.

TRADE RELATED INTELLECTUAL PROPERTY RIGHTS: A CRITICAL ANALYSIS

*C.M. Rajpraveen**

INTRODUCTION: A HISTORICAL PERSPECTIVE:

Intellectual property rights may basically be defined as information with value. Conventions regarding intellectual property rights (IPR's) have traversed through various milestones namely–the Brussels conventions in 1911, Hague conventions in 1925, London convention in 1958, Lisbon convention in 1958, and Stockholm convention in 1967. The World Intellectual Property Organization (WIPO) existed before the establishment of the WTO i.e it became functional in 1970 and in the same year the UNO provided special stat us. The WIPO implemented 2 important conventions namely: (i) the Paris convention for the protection of industrial property (patents, industrial designs, etc) in 1883 in which 11 countries took part and ii) the Berne convention for the protection of literary and artistic works (copyright) in 1986.

The trade related intellectual property rights agreement covers the following seven properties namely:

(i) Copyright and related rights;
(ii) Trademarks, including service marks;
(iii) Geographical indications;
(iv) Industrial designs;
(v) Patents;
(vi) Layout – designs (topographies) of integrated circuits; and
(vii) Undisclosed information, including trade secrets.

---

* Lecturer, Dept. of Political Science Mangalore University, Mangalagangothri.

Beside these seven properties, TRIPS also envisage a special form of protection namely Sui generis for plant breeder's rights and the protection of layout designs of integrated circuits.

INTERIM ARRANGEMENT

WTO agreements provide one year to developed countries to enact their laws and practices for confirmation to the TRIPS regulations. Developing countries are provided five years to effect the necessary changes to their patency regimes. Least developed countries have been provided eleven years. The other conditions are that the country must accept the filing of patent applications from the beginning of the transition period in case of pharmaceuticals and agricultural chemical products, though the granting of the patent was not needed until the end of the stipulated duration. However a provision was made whereby subject to certain conditions, the government was permitted to allow the relevant pharmaceutical or agricultural chemical to be marketed during the transition period - if need be under the provision of exclusive marketing right (EMR).

MAJOR ASPECTS OF THE INDIAN PATENT ACT, 1970

Following are some of the major aspects of this act.

1. Only process patents in fields of food, medicine, drugs, and chemical substances. Product patents in all areas other than those mentioned elsewhere.
2. Many products are not patentable i,e agricultural products including seeds and plants, animals and all life forms including microorganisms. It also includes biological and microbiological process.
3. No Sui generis system existing to protect rights of inventors.
4. Process for treatment of human beings and animals are not patentable.
5. Patent expiry period is 5 to 7 years in case of patents food, medicine, drugs, and chemical substances and 14 years in case of the other patents.

6. In respect of patents for food, medicines, drugs, and chemical substances, licenses of right (automatic license) are deemed to have been endorsed after three years.
7. Infringement proceedings are permitted under Indian patent law.
8. There is ceiling on the royalty or fee that the patent holder can demand from a license.[1]

TRADE RELATED INTELLECTUAL PROPERTY RIGHTS PROVISIONS AND INDIA

Patents and designs have been protected in India since 1872 and trademark since 1940. Patent and design act 1911 is an important improvement or a milestone as far as the intellectual property rights is concerned. India has also been a participant at the Paris and Berne conventions regarding protection of intellectual property rights. The intellectual property rights cases in India have been dealt with according to the provisions as mentioned in the Indian patent act 1970. However in accordance with the provisions as mentioned in the TRIPS provisions, India has an obligation to modify its IPR regime accordingly. A general transitory period of 5 years was given to member countries and an extra 5 more years was also given to allow competing patent protection of agriculture and chemical product, until, 1 January 2005 under WTO provisions. It is important to note that India did not grant product patent protection when the TRIPS, agreement came into force (January1, 1998). Nonetheless India has been given 10 years to introduce product patent.[2]

Presently the government of India has passed 2 amendment bill of Indian patent 1970 act in order to comply to the obligations as required under the TRIPS agreement. The first patent amendment bill passed in parliament in 2000 permitted exclusive marketing rights (EMR) for importing and selling of product to any member countries of the world trade organization. But some products had been exempted under this EMR system. Secondly a legislation regarding patent amendment was passed by the parliament in 2000. This bill provides for compulsory licensing.[3] But no provision for the requisite product patent has been made in this amendment bill because the government of India has been provided time till 2005 to make the necessary changes. Furthermore, the amendments to the Indian patent act, 1970 merits more consideration because the Indian government has tabled before the house of the parliament, three others bill namely:

(a) Act of geographical indication, 1999;

(b) Varieties protection and farmers rights act 2000; and

(c) Bio- diversity bill 2002. [4]

THE INDIAN PATENT ACT AND TRIPS PROVISIONS: A COMPARATIVE STUDY

Diverse fields		*Indian patents act*	*TRIPS Provisions* [5]
(i)	Definition of innovation	Narrow	Broader
(ii)	Microorganisms	Not patentable	Patentable
(iii)	Plant variety protection	Not available	Available
(iv)	Drugs and pharmaceuticals	Only process patents	Processes and products
(v)	Importation permissible	Without prior permission.Amounts to infringement not accepted as working of patent	Importation
(vi)	Compulsory licensing only in	Both exclusive and non exclusive, special circumstances	Non - exclusive
(vii)	License of right	Provision exists.	No provision
(viii)	Term of patent	14 years for patents other than food and drugs; for food and drugs7 years from date of filing of patent or 5 years from date of grant	Unilaterally 20 years
(xi)	Burden of proof	On the plaintiff	On the defendant

IMPLICATIONS OF THE AMENDMENTS TO THE INDIAN PATENTS ACT, 1970

For quite sometime now, apprehensions had been expressed whether it would be possible for the government of India to succeed in making major amendments to the Indian patent act of 1970 that would establish the regime of product patents for pharmaceuticals and chemicals. It is appropriate that the Manmohan Singh government passed the litmus test by virtue of it complying with the TRIPS (Trade Related Intellectual Property Rights) obligations/provisions of the world trade organization. This achievement is all the more significant because major international powers namely the United States and the European Union were eagerly waiting to see if New Delhi would miss the bus so that it would enable them to create mischief in other trade issues particularly textiles. But it did not so happen.

The amendments to the Indian patents act, 1970 was not a smooth affair. The existing political situation in the country (i.e. the Manmohan Singh led) United Progressive Alliance government is to a very large extent dependent on the support of the left parties namely the CPI (M), the CPI, the RSP and various others to ensure that the coalition government survives. Against such a backdrop, the UPA Government that is in power in India clearly sensed that the combined opposition scuppering its amendments to bring about product patents from January 1, 2005. Throughout these developments, one aspect that strongly guided the left parties was to inject a strong dose of public policy concerns.

The final bill, which has now become the amended Indian Patent Act of 1970, has not yet been made public. Still, in what appears to be a significant turnaround, the Indian government announced New Delhi's compliance with the TRIPS obligations from January 1, 2005.

In the following pages, an attempt will be made to examine and analyse and critically estimate as to what exactly is the nature of the impact or how the three important sectors namely pharmaceuticals (and chemicals), agriculture and bio-technology which I have chosen to highlight are affected by the amendments that have been made to the Indian Patent Act of 1970 so as to enable them to comply with the TRIPs obligations that has been so formulated by the World Trade Organisation.

TRIPS AND ITS IMPACT ON THE PHARMACEUTICALS SECTOR

Pharmaceutical industry is one of the fastest growing industries of the recent times. The global pharmaceutical industry is estimated to be of 550 billion U.S dollars, which is growing at the rate of 13.5 per centannually. Exports and imports make up to around 45% of total market with export comprising 22.5% and import comprising 23.9%. The growth appears to be phenomenal for countries like India with increasing purchasing power and awareness about healthcare.[6]

Pharmaceuticals consist of both bulk drugs and also formulations.[7] Driven by research and development, the industry strongly requires intellectual rights protection/ safeguards in order to survive and achieve profits. It is important to take cognisance that the drug discovery process is a complex one which involves huge financial resources and risk. Further, it is also necessary to mention the strengths, weaknesses, opportunities and the new threats facing this sector.

Strengths, Weaknesses, Opportunities and Threats of the Indian Pharmaceutical Industries

A brief mention is made here of the aforementioned aspects.

Strengths:

1. Highly skilled and low-cost talent;
2. Low cost of pre-clinical research;
3. Diverse medicinal systems;
4. Experience with natural products.

Weaknesses:

(i) Lack of medicinal chemistry and biology skills.

(ii) Hidden costs;

(iii) Unacceptability of clinical data;

(iv) Regulatory bottlenecks.

Opportunities:

(a) Size of domestic market
(b) Growing global recognition;
(c) Opportunity in generics;
(d) Contract research and manufacturing.

Threats:

(a) New patent regime
(b) Competition from MNCs
(c) Unstable policy environment.

In a move to placate the international pharmaceutical industry, which made the patents issue a central plank for its future investments in India, the government had turned a nelson's eye to the battles waged earlier during the Uruguay round of trade negotiations that established the world treaty organization in 1995, and subsequently at the WTO. It is necessary to take cognizance that the patent protection which ensured unaffordable prices for new medicines until then was confined to a small section of rich countries. However, the Uruguay Round agreement ushered a sea-change in the protection of IPRs. It should also be noted that neither the U.S has an easy way. The U.S encountered stiff resistance against its battle-like campaign to widen the global cover for IPRs, from a few countries-India, Brazil, Argentina and so on. These developing countries vehemently argued that patent rules and provisions have no place in the conduct of global trade because such rights would undermine public policies in the poor countries, which are afflicted highly by various diseases and to top it all a large majority of people residing in these countries earn less than a dollar on any given day. However, the U.S along with its partners, Switzerland, the European Union and Japan have been largely successful in bringing about what is generally referred to as the norms and conditions to implement IPR rules in various areas. Nonetheless, developing countries too claimed credit for introducing strong compulsory licensing provisions that offered a cushion to balance the excessive protection rights of a patent holder.

RAMIFICATIONS OF THE NEW PATENCY REGIME

The ramifications of the new patency regime may well be understood against the backdrop of a ruling by the Madras High Court in a case involving the multinational pharmaceutical company, Novartis. Upholding the plea of Novartis, the court ordered Indian companies to stop manufacturing an anti-cancer medicine as it was found to be violating the provisions of the exclusive marketing rights. Such a measure would seriously affect those suffering from cancer and its immediate impact is that the cancer patients who were hither-to not paying more than Rs. 10,000/- for the same drug manufactured by the Indian companies will have to shell out Rs. 1.20lakh for a month's treatment if they are keen to stay alive. From this it becomes crystal clear that the new patency regime will greatly benefit the pharmaceutical companies.

Another drug Ranitidine that fights ulcers do not cost more that Rs. 6 for ten tablets of 150gm each. But the same drug costs Rs. 864 in the United States of America. Likewise, Atenol, a medicine that is prescribed for those suffering from heart diseases, the price in India is Rs. 7.50 for ten tablets of 50gm each, whereas it costs Rs. 101 in the U.S.. Another anti-cancer drug Boposide that is injected in the human body costs Rs. 190 in India whereas the same medicine is sold at Rs. 6210 in America. Thus the drug is available at a price that is 32 times costlier. Similarly for the cholesterol reducer, Atorvastatin, the price difference between India and America is 28 times.[8]

The Indian pharmaceutical Alliance has warned that the domestic production capacity worth Rs. 3,000 crore will come to a standstill following the patent amendment.[9] This will necessarily result in the shooting-up of the prices of medicines and drugs for life threatening and chronic diseases. Such a situation will soon arise because a majority of the popular, cheaper and locally manufactured medicines that were being produced in the country from 1970 onwards will need to be withdrawn. Although such an eventuality will not happen over night, but as the life of the existing drugs fizzles out, the Indian manufacturers will be forced to stop manufacturing these cheap drugs. Such a situation will eventually pave the way for multinational companies or their subsidiaries to take complete control over manufacture of the common medicines.

LOOKING FOR A BREATHER

The government is taking refuge behind a compulsory licensing clause that enables it to stop a multinational company from producing an essential drug if it is not reaching the masses in case of an epidemic or a national health emergency. Although article 31(b) of TRIPs Agreement permits grant of compulsory license if the effort of obtaining production licence from a patent holder on reasonable commercial terms does not fructify, in reality the provision does not mean much once the domestic generic manufacturers pull down the shuters.[10] Under such a circumstance, the poor will be left to survive on their own.

CRITICISMS TO THE CHANGES TO THE PATENCY ACT, 1970

The leading international humanitarian agency, 'Doctors without borders' (Medicines Sans Frontieres (MSF) in French) have criticized the proposed amendments to Indian Patents Act of 1970. According to Rovan Gillies, the president of the MSF's international council in Geneva the proposed amendments–which aims to grant product patents to latest drugs patented by international pharmaceutical companies such as Pfizer, Merck Glaxo Smithklime "will drastically restrict, perhaps even prevent, the production and supply of anti-retroviral drugs for HIV/AIDS treatment in poor countries." Further the MSF chief in a letter addressed to the president of India said the ordinance to amend the patent act will "prevent the production and supply" of vital HIV/AIDS therapy by Indian pharmaceutical companies to other developing countries.[11] MSF estimates that 50 per centof 700,000 people receiving anti-retroviral medicines to contain HIV/AIDS, take Indian Generic medicines produced by companies such as Cipla and Ranbaxy.[12]

Humanitarian pressure groups like the MSF want the government to take full advantage of the flexibilities permitted in the TRIPS agreement. They argued that the amendments are being introduced to marginalize the robust generic drugs industry. Further the MSF president expressed the view that: "we hope that India will continue to demonstrate the kind of international leadership it has shown with the WTO Doha Declaration on TRIPS and public Health."[13]

Lawyer Lawrence Liang of the Alternate Law Forum says: "Strangely, the Indian government has gone even further than required by the WTO TRIPs agreement. For instance, under the new law, compulsory licensing is allowed only three years after the patent is granted".[14] (To prevent patent holders from abusing their monopoly when production does not meet demand or is too highly priced, patent law allows others to take permission from the patent owner and manufacture the same drug by paying royalty, which is fixed by the government.) Another lawyer Viswas Devaiah says: "Indian pharmaceutical companies believe that by the year 2008 many drugs will be out of the patent and they will be able to manufacture generic versions."[15] Further he said: ".....the 'new use' clause means that a minor enhancement to an existing medicine for heart disease could still mean a new patent being granted effectively extending the validity of the patent beyond the original 20 years. Again this is something not required by the TRIPs agreement."[16]

Tahir Amin perceives "the devils in the details in this law: namely total ownership and monopoly rights are enhanced greatly."[17]

BIO-TECHNOLOGY AND THE TRADE RELATED INTELLECTUAL PROPERTY RIGHTS

Biotechnology is a generic name of all technologies that have resorted to genetic manipulation. It can be defined as the use and manipulation of living organization for the purpose of commercialization and includes the use of tissue culture, cell fusion, embryo transfer and recombinant of DNA technology. The area that has evoked most concern is recombinant DNA technology or genetic engineering, which enabled the creation of novel communication through transfer of genetic material.

In biotechnology section, about 68% companies are involved in health care, 8% in agriculture sector, 15% in industry and 9% in environmental application.[18]

INDIA AND BIO-TECHNOLOGY

1. Today India's share of the global biotech market 2% and $2.5 billion. Until now Indian biotechnology industry is in infancy stage but many new small biotechnology companies are emerging in would business area. For instance, Santha Biotech, a small biotech company launched the hepatitis caccine shamac.
2. India has a large technical resource base and a number of research institutes such as the Council for Scientific And Industrial Research (CSIR), Indian Institute of Science (IISc), Indian Council for Medical Research (ICMR).
3. Indian companies have started production of HYV (High Yielding Variety) seeds. The production of genetically modified seeds has increased in the last few years. Monsanto is one of the MNC that has set up a subsidiary unit in India for production.
4. In India 80% of our population are not aware about TRIPs provision. It is the responsibility of the government and the various governmental agencies to impart information to the farmers.
5. More worrisome is the speed at which MNC are getting patents over genes etc. For example, Monsanto own all genetically modified varieties of cotton as well as 228 other cotton gene sequencing. The U.S based MNC Dow has applied for patents for 655 maize gene sequence, DU pont for 587. Thus top 5 MNCs account for 85% of all such application of patent.

TRADE RELATED INTELLECTUAL PROPERTY RIGHTS AND INDIAN AGRICULTURE

India has a tremendous wealth of agricultural ideas, techniques, products and processes and many of its knowledge and practices relating to agriculture has been passed on from generation to generation. These traditional knowledge and practice have found many modern applications. Thus it is felt that India will gain to a large extent from the TRIPs provisions. However, India's rich reservoir of traditional knowledge and practices are under serious threat from MNCs and undesirable elements who are waiting for an appropriate time to patent our knowledge and practices in western countries. India should act fast and take necessary steps so as to protect them. Proper documentation of these knowledge and practices seems to be the measure that needs to be taken immediately.

On August 9, 2001 the Lok sabha passed the plant variety protection and farmers rights bill. This bill recognizes the farmer not just as a cultivator but also as a conservator of the agricultural gene pool and a breeder who has bred several successful varieties. The bill provides for such farmers varieties to be registered with the assistance of non-governmental organizations in order to safeguard them from being scavenged by formal sector breeders. In addition, the rights of the rural communities are acknowledged as well.

Section 39, clause (iv) which basically states as to what constitutes a farmer's right now reads: "the farmer.....should be deemed to be entitled to save, use, sow, exchange, share or sell his farm produce including seed of a variety protected under this act.....;

Provided that the farmer shall not be entitled to sell branded seed of a variety protected under this act...".[19] Thus, both the farmers and breeders rights are protected. Moreover, the breeder is rewarded for his innovation by having control of the commercial market place but without being able to threaten the farmer's ability to independently engage in his livelihood and would also immediately benefit the livelihood of other farmers.

Clauses in the Plant variety Protection and Farmers Rights Bill that needs changes:

(i) Benefit-sharing;

(ii) Protection against bad seed;

(iii) Protection against innocent infringement;

(iv) Exemption from fees.[20]

In addition there is much in the bill that needs a closer re-examination. For instance, it has areas of concern like the special treatment given to essentially derived varieties (EDVs), which more often than not will be GM varieties. In order to ensure transparency, EDVs too should be considered on par with the conventionally bred varieties.

OTHER AREAS OF CONCERN

Given the present situation the one and the only international platform is the International Union for the Protection of New varieties of Plants (UPOV), which is essentially a western platform regulating plant breeders rights for the industrial nations, it becomes a matter of great concern to India to decide as to which international platform it will use to interact among the comity of nations. This issue has acquired added importance because GENE CAMPAIGN strongly apposes India having any correspondence with the UPOV because UPOV does not address India's needs and moreover its working is totally alien to the conditions of agricultural practices that is prevailing in the countries of the South. It is strongly believed that developing countries must create their own platform which will provide, apart from breeder's rights, farmers rights also, and get ready to work towards food and nutritional security in these countries. A major drawback of the UPOV system is that there is no concept of farmer's rights in it which necessarily implies that rights are granted only to the breeders which in the present situation are the seed companies.[21]

As an alternative to UPOV, Gene Campaign together with the centre for environment and agriculture development has chalked out a treaty called the convention of farmers and breeders (CoFaB). CoFaB has an agenda of its own and it reflects the strengths of the developing countries, seeks to secure and strengthen their interests in agriculture and fulfill the food and nutritional security goals of their people.

CONCLUSION

Compulsory licensing has been made subject to market demand not being completely met. The issue of how determines where the non-manufacturing countries can issue compulsory license. This issue is of prime concern to India and Brazil who produce low cost drug. TRIPs agreement has profound implication for public policy. It directly affects prices of medicines, technology, agriculture, environment and many other areas. At present valuable traditional knowledge of developing countries is not protected under the TRIPs and many time exploited by the developed nations without any safeguards. World Development Report 1998-99 mentions the case of Madagascar's unique Rose plant, used for manufacturing of two anti-cancer drugs which has generated more than $100 million sales for a global company, but Madagascar got no financial return. Indian drug industry should follow a different model from western model. India must pay attention to alternate system of medicine which has a rich tradition and heritage. Indian industry can and is better placed to develop products based on Indian systems of medicine like Unani, Ayurveda etc., which would be more acceptable to the people worldwide. TRIPs agreement provides for transfer of technology. But in actual practice this provision is of very little use to the less developed countries because of their low technological knowledge base. In sharp contrast, OECD(Organization for Economic Co-operation and Development) countries despite having only 14% world population accounts for 86% patents across the world and has more than 8 lakh patent applications. In India, processing of patent applications has enormous delay. There is dearth of an effective structure of intellectual property rights. There is need of a IPR appellate body to be set up under trade mark act. It will greatly benefit registration of trademark and issues relating to geographic indication.

NOTES

1. Deepak Srivastava, "Globalisation, Privatization and WTO", (New Delhi: Sarup & Sons, 2003.), pp. 98-99.

2. Ibid., p. 97
3. Compulsory licensing means a government allows someone else to produce the patented product or process without the consent of the patent author.
4. (a) The bill pertaining to act of geographical indication, 1999 covers control and protection given to all varieties of basmati rice, Assam tea etc.

   (b) With regards to the varieties protection and farmers rights act 2000 India adopted 'sui genris' system. This bill recognized the right of farmer to store and sell seeds and reproduced same seeds.

   (c) Bio-diversity bill 2002: The objective of this bill is suitable use of India's bio-resources that would aid conservation and simulating provides remuneration to local communities for protecting special and traditional knowledge.
5. Ibid., no. 1, p. 100.
6. Ajai S. Gaur et.al., "Strategic Roadmap for Indian Pharmaceutical Industry in the Post 2005 era", Indian Journal of Marketing, Vol. 35, No. 1, January 2005, p. 3.
7. Bulk drugs are active pharmaceuticals ingredients (API), whereas formulations are dosage form of drugs which are prescribed by doctors. Most of the formulations are sold only under prescription; however, there are a few which the consumers can purchase directly. These are called over the counter (OTC) products.
8. Deccan Herald, 16 April, 2005.
9. Ibid.
10. Ibid.
11. Deccan Herald, 17 March, 2005.
12. Ibid
13. Ibid
14. Deccan Herald, 8 April, 2005
15. Ibid
16. Ibid
17. Ibid
18. Srivastava, no. 1, p. 102.
19. Suman Sahai, " Plant Variety Protection and Farmess Rights law", *Economic and Political Weekly,* Vol. 36, No. 35, September 2001, p. 3338.

20. For More Details Relating to there Four Points, Please Refer : Ibid., pp. 3339-40.
21. Ibid, p. 3341.

BIBLIOGRAPHY

A. BOOKS

1. Carbaugh, Robert J., *"International Economics"*, 8th ed., (Singapore: Thomson) 2002.
2. Gerber, James, *"International Economics"*, (Reading, Masaochusetts: Addison Wesley Longman, Inc.), 1999.
3. Mithani, D.M., *"International Economics"*, (New Delhi: Himalaya Publishing House), 1999.
4. Sabanna, Talwar, *"WTO and the Agriculture"*, (New Delhi: Serials Publications), 2005.
5. Srivastava, Deepak, *"Globalisation, Privatization and WTO: with Reference to India"*, (New Delhi : Sarup & Sons), 2003.

B. NEWSPAPER ARTICLES

1. DH News service, *"Patents: Patients to bear the brunt: Drugs to cost More"*, Deccan Herald, 8 April, 2005.
2. DH News Service *"Changes to patent Act will cost poor dear"*, Deccan Herald, 17 March, 2005.
3. Ravikanth, D., *"Litmus Test on Patents Act"*, Deccan Herald (Mangalore), 28 March, 2005.
4. Sharma, Devinder, *"When Death becomes Cheap: Patent law Amendment"*, Deccan Herald, 16 April, 2005.

C. JOURNALS AND PERIODICALS

1. Agrawal, Pradeep et. al., *"TRIPs and India's Pharmaceuticals Industry", Economic and Political Weekly* , Vol. 36, No. 39, September 29, 2001.
2. Gaur, Ajai S. et. al., *"Strategic Roadmap for Indian Pharmaceutical Industry in the Post 2005 Era"*, Indian Journal of Marketing, Vol. 35, No.1, January 2005.
3. Rao, Hanumantha C.H., *"WTO and Viability of Indian Agriculture", Economic and Political Weekly*, vol. 36, no.36, September 8, 2001.
4. Sahai, Suman, *"Plant Variety Protection and Farmers Rights law" Economic and Political Weekly*, Vol. 36, No. 35, September 1, 2001.

THE IMPACT OF TRIPS ON AGRICULTURE

*R. Meenakshi**

INTRODUCTION

The contribution of knowledge as a factor of production is being increasingly given central importance in economic development. The past decade has seen a rising storm of international debate and legal challenge over the patenting of Traditional Knowledge (TK) and its products of agriculture. Two important developments have altered the processes by which improved crop varieties and related technologies are being discovered, commercialized and diffused to farmers. The first is the expansion and strengthening of Intellectual Property Rights (IPR) that applies to processes and products. The second is the development of methods and techniques in genetic manipulation, generally described as bio technology. Although both have been underway for more than two decades, their importance to Government, Non Government and private entities in the crop seed industry has increased in recent years. Analysis of these two developments should recognize that they are part of processes affecting other sectors outside agriculture and may actually change the nature of agriculture. Economists have an important role to play in fashioning policy measures dealing with both IPR and with biotechnology product regulations. These policy measures may be particularly important for developing countries where experience has been limited.

IMPORTANCE OF INTELLECTUAL PROPERTY

IPRs are intangible rights which grant an exclusive right to impede others to freely exploit an invention or creation.

* Reader, Department of Economics, Sri Sarada College, Salem

Intellectual property protection is the key factor for economic growth and advancement in the high technology sector. They are good for business, benefit the public at large and act as catalysts for technical progress. Whether IPRs are good or bad thing, the developed world has come to an accommodation with them over a long period. Even if their disadvantages sometimes outweigh their advantages, by and large the developed world has the national economic strength and established legal mechanisms to overcome the problems so caused. Insofar as their benefits outweigh their disadvantages, the developed world has the wealth and infrastructure to take advantage of the opportunities provided. It is likely that neither of these holds true for developing and least developed countries. The importance of IPRs can be gauged from the fact that most globally competitive corporations strategically protect their intellectual properties in all potential markets/ countries by filing patents, trademark protection or other IPR arrangements. For Indian enterprises to compete globally, recognition and reward of innovations and inventions is imperative. IPRs provide one of the major instruments for doing so.

TRADE RELATED INTELLECTUAL PROPERTY RIGHTS (TRIPS)

In agriculture sector, the role of IPRs is becoming even more important because so far much of the R and D have been concentrated in public sector and private sector R and D is only emerging slowly. However, for technology development with in the country as well as for its acquisition from abroad or transfer to other countries, IPRs may play an important role. The provisions of TRIPs agreed upon by most countries of the world as the consequence of GATT and WTO require individuals and institutions engaged in inventive activity to protect the same through a harmonized patent law within a specified period depending upon the economic situation of the country concerned. Knowledge of various kinds of IPRs equips a manager and organizational leaders to not only develop mechanisms within the firms to protect the IPRs but also to acquire external intellectual property through licensing.

Although the TRIPs agreement contemplates a transition period of ten years for India as a developing country to introduce product patent protection in area of technology not so protected in its territory like agri-chemicals, the obligation to grant exclusive marketing rights for patents at any time after entering into WTO agreement effectively neutralizes this transition period. The issue of development of proprietary patents by enterprises based on the Traditional Knowledge of indigenous communities, nurtured through generations, without obtaining prior informed consent or without coming into any agreement on benefit sharing, have been viewed as unjust practices by countries such as India, which are store houses of such indigenous knowledge.

WHAT DOES TRIPS DO?

TRIPs is intended to maximize the contribution of intellectual property systems to economic growth through trade and investment by:

- Establishing minimum standards for protection of IPRs in the national systems of WTO members
- Prescribing agreed elements of an effective mechanism for administration and enforcement of intellectual property rights.
- Creating a transparency mechanism-each WTO member is required to provide details of its national intellectual property laws and systems, and to answer questions about its intellectual property systems.
- Creating a predictable, rules-based system for the settlement of disputes about trade-related intellectual property issues between WTO members.
- Allowing for mechanisms that ensure that national intellectual property systems support widely accepted public policy objectives, such as stamping out unfair competition, facilitating transfer of technology, and promoting environmental protection.

TRIPS AGREEMENT

The importance of intellectual property in India is well established at all levels-statutory, administrative and judicial. India ratified the agreement establishing the World Trade Organization (WTO). This Agreement contains an Agreement on Trade Related Aspects of Intellectual Property Rights (TRIPs) which came into force from 1st January 1995. It lays down minimum standards for protection and enforcement of IPRs in member countries which are required to promote effective and adequate protection of IPRs with a view to reducing distortions and impediments to international trade.

Thus the obligations under the TRIPS Agreement relate to provision of minimum standard of protection within the member countries' legal systems and practices. The Agreement provides for norms and standards in respect of following areas of intellectual property:

- Copyrights and related rights
- Trade Marks
- Geographical Indications
- Industrial Designs
- Lay out Designs of Integrated Circuits
- Protection of Undisclosed Information (Trade Secrets)
- Patents
- Plant varieties

India is also a member of the World Intellectual Property Organization (WIPO), Geneva. The objectives of WIPO are to promote respect for use of intellectual property throughout the world through cooperation among Member States and to ensure administrative cooperation among the intellectual property unions. The protection is promoted through Conventions and Treaties administered by it. The major ones are:

- **Paris Convention** for the protection of industrial property rights in inventions, trademarks and industrial designs, etc.

- **Berne Convention** for the protection or copyright in literary, musical and artistic works, etc.

SPECIAL AND DIFFERENTIAL TREATMENT FOR DEVELOPING COUNTRIES

Developing and Less Developed Countries have been given special and differential treatment as below:

- Developing countries are not required to reduce certain domestic support measures which are an integral part of their development programs. (This includes investment subsidies to agriculture and agriculture input subsidies to low-income or resource-poor producers).
- Developing countries have a higher de minimis level with respect to trade distorting domestic support.
- During the implementation period, developing countries are not required to undertake commitments on subsidies to reduce the costs of marketing exports of agricultural products or internal transport subsidies for export products, provided these are not applied in a manner that would circumvent reduction commitments.
- Developing countries are not bound to consider the food security concerns of other members when applying an export prohibition or restriction on foodstuffs unless they are net exporters of the foodstuff concerned.
- The required cuts for tariff and trade-distorting support in case of the developing countries are lower, by one third, than the rates applicable for developed countries.
- Less Developed Countries are not required to undertake reduction commitments in agricultural tariffs, domestic support or export subsidies.
- Developed countries are to take appropriate action as provided within the *Decisions on Measures Concerning the Possible Negative Effects of the Reform Program on Least Developed and Net Food-Importing Developing Countries.* The committee on Agriculture is to monitor the follow-up to this decision.

- The agricultural continuation negotiations will take into account, amongst other things, special and differential treatment for developing countries.
- Special and Differential treatment includes specific provisions in favour of developing countries concerning public stock holding for food security purposes and domestic food aid.
- The "special treatment" clause, for specified members to maintain agriculture-specific non-tariff measures during the period of tariff reduction, provides for more favourable treatment for developing countries.
- Requests by Less Developed Countries and net food-importing developing country members for technical and financial assistance, for the improvement of their agricultural productivity and infrastructure, will be given full consideration in the context of member's aid programmes.

INDIA'S INTERNATIONAL OBLIGATIONS ON IPRS

India is entitled for most of the provisions of TRIPs. An important exception is the introduction of product patents in areas of technology not covered so far. At present the Patents Act, 1970 does not allow the patenting of plants or animals or micro-organisms. Although it does not contain any such specific exclusion, the definition of an invention seems to exclude these. Even microbiological processes are excluded if they involve a method of agriculture or horticulture; as such methods are specifically excluded. However, such applications have sometimes been granted patents, at least since the mid-80's as is evidenced by the process patent granted to Agracetus, a US company, on genetically engineered cotton cells and lines. This patent was later revoked in public interest by the government of India. India is thus, obliged to either introduce patents for new plant varieties or have an effective law to protect them. In addition India must make available strong patents on microbiological and non-biological processes for the production of plants and animals. India must also bring the protection of trademarks and geographical indications. While IPRs such as copyrights, patents, and trademarks are centuries old, the extension of IPRs to living entities and attendant knowledge/technologies occurred only relatively recently.

Many biotechnological products and processes are easier to copy than in other areas of technology. Seed can be replanted, genes can be cloned based on sequence information, and methods can be copied following established protocols. This makes enforcement of IPR harder to keep up. The most common IPRs in agro biotech are patents, material transfer agreements (MTAs) and Plant Breeders' Rights (PBRs). Patents provide the strongest protection for know-how and genetically modified plants. A patent may protect a process used to obtain transgenic plants as well as the plants themselves and uses thereof. While PBRs are generally the best way to protect individual plant varieties they are not applicable to essentially derived varieties, e.g. a variety into which one gene construct has been introduced by genetic manipulation while maintaining the rest of the genome practically unscathed. Plants are not patentable subject matter in many countries, although in the USA plants are patentable. Signatories of the Agreement on Trade Related Aspects of Intellectual Property Rights (TRIPs) are expected to provide IP protection for inventions in all fields of technology and that includes genetically modified plants also. How this is done in detail is a matter of national legislation and international agreements. Genetic engineering provides materials and methods to introduce genes into many varieties of one species or into completely different species.

IPR AND BIODIVERSITY

Genetic diversity in agriculture enables poor farmers to select varieties of plants and animal breeds that are best adapted to changing environmental, economic and social pressures. Over centuries a huge range of seed varieties has been developed at local levels, many of which are unique to a small area and produce local food crops that are not extensively traded.

Furthermore, in the poorest and most marginal locations, traditional diets often contain a finely balanced mixture of domestically produced crops and plants and fruits found in the wild as well as cultivated by them. Agricultural biodiversity is crucial for livelihood and nutritional security of the poor.

A wider genetic base is the pedestal on plant breeding and farming. Maintenance of plant genetic diversity is a shared heritage and responsibility of all humankind. Historically, we have used about 5,000-plant species world wide to meet food and other needs, which in itself is a fraction of the world's flora and fauna. Today, only about 150 plant species are important in meeting the food needs of humans' worldwide. Hence, greater dependence on fewer plant species, 20 to 30 in global contexts gradually, has resulted in the loss of native genetic resources which are otherwise essential as building blocks of genetic diversity.

The technological bind of improved varieties with support from intellectual property protection leads to the elimination of the resource upon which they are based. The narrowness of the genetic base is responsible for greater risk of crop failure as occurred in the wheat stem rust of 1954 or the southern corn blight of 1970 in the US. The Irish potato famine in the 1840s is a classic example of genetic vulnerability.

IPR AND SEED TECHNOLOGY

In most developing countries, the use of certified seed of modern varieties is either recommended by extension services, linked to credit facilities, or is obliged by the processing industry. The marketing of seed of traditional varieties may also be reduced by mandatory registration of varieties.

In the UK farmers' varieties of seeds sold in brown bags are illegal as they are not on the National seeds list. It's ironic that farmers' natural right to save, exchange and sell seeds becomes a legal privilege to be granted to them by the governments if they so choose to in their national laws, under the TRIPs agreement and sui generis laws of the UPOV 1991 kind.

The argument that farmers can use improved and proprietary varieties of seed and it is only a question of their choice overlooks the genetic richness of the seeds being used by subsistence farmers. For many companies seed is seed–one variety fits all. Yet the gene banks of international agricultural research centres have built up over the past 25 years large stocks of local farmer varieties collected from all over the world. Plant breeders have used these collections, which represent the natural biological diversity of crops, as the raw material for fashioning new crop varieties. In fact an FAO official states that "Every major commercial crop grown in developed countries today originated in what are now termed developing countries, restoration of seed would be one small way to repay what is by any measure a very large debt."

Agribusiness domination of the global seed market and aggressive campaigns to promote broad patenting rights for biotech seeds and plants, challenge traditional farming practices such as seed saving and seed sharing. Until recently, certain concepts were universally accepted among farmers.

- First, out of economic necessity, farmers had the right to save, replant, and resell seeds to other farmers willing to buy seeds with desirable characteristics.
- Second, the genetic composition of seeds, rather than the seed itself, was considered part of a common heritage and widely shared among farmers.
- Third, seeds were not seen as a commodity; rather, the right to use and reproduce seeds was inherent in the first purchase of the seed.
- Until the nineteenth century, seeds were seen as a public commons which were bred and then freely distributed by the public sector.

Strong IP protections for genetically modified seeds are partly responsible for the rapid growth and ingenuity of new seed varieties. Though TRIPS resulted in great benefits for science and large agribusinesses, developing nations do not stand to gain nearly as much from groundbreaking technological advances. An imbalance exists between the benefits derived by the developed nations and the toll taken on the developing and underdeveloped with respect to knowledge transfer.

TERMINATOR CROPS

Terminator or Traitor seeds are genetically modified to be sterile and not usable for replanting. As a consequence, farmers using these seeds would be forced to purchase new grain every sowing season. This makes quite clear how dangerous Terminator technology is, primarily for the 1.4 billion people worldwide who heavily rely on farm-saved seed and who could not afford to buy new seed every year. Moreover, this technology could be used to develop plants which may be dependent on chemical treatment in order to become fertile or healthy giving Gene Giants the power to control agriculture and thus food supply worldwide. Multinational Biotech Companies are well aware of the commercial possibilities of this technology and a number of Terminator patents have been filed so far. Syngenta, the result of a merger between Astra Zeneca and Novartis, has at least six patents protecting Terminator technology including a patent for the creation of plants with destabilized immune systems.

The terminator technology is an "invention" which genetically engineers crops to kill their own seeds in the second generation, thus forcing farmers to buy seed every year, through which Monsanto creates a coercive market. In an occasional paper of the Edmonds Institute, Dr. Martha Crouch, a leading genetic engineer who had worked in the early stages of the development of the terminator technology but who left genetic engineering because of its high social and ecological costs has described how the Terminator terminates. The Terminator system has three systems.

1. A gene for a toxin that will kill the seed late in development, but that will not kill any other part of the plant.
2. A method for allowing a plant breeder to grow 8 several generations of cotton plants, already genetically-engineered to contain the seed-specific toxin gene,

without any seeds dying. This is required to produce enough seeds to sell for farmers to plant.

3. A method for activating the engineered seed-specific toxin gene after the farmer plants the seeds, so that the farmer's second generation will be killed.

These three tasks are accomplished by engineering a series of genes, which are all transferred permanently to the plant, so that they are passed on via the normal reproduction of the plant. The plant grows normally from germination, through growth of stems, leaves, roots and all the way through flower formation, pollination and most of seed development. Then on cue, the Terminator produces a lethal dose of toxin to kill the embryo. The next generation seed would thus be killed. Hence there is widespread feeling that the terminator technology must be terminated due to the reason that it has ethical impact, socio-economic impact, ecological impact and jeopardizes food safety.

IPR AND BIOPIRACY

There is an apprehension that patenting of organisms encourages 'biopiracy'. A rational definition of 'biopiracy' would focus on activities relating to access or use of genetic resources in contravention to national regimes based on the CBD. Accordingly, a legitimate claim of 'biopiracy' will involve unauthorized access to a controlled genetic resource. In practical terms, this means that (a) the activity in question occurred after the CBD came into force (December of 1993), and (b) the acts consist of a party gaining access without the consent of the source country, or in contravention to laws or regulations governing access to or use of genetic resources that the country has established. This concept of biopiracy stands in sharp contrast to the claims of biopiracy that are made with ever-increasing frequency by certain groups. For these groups, biopiracy consists of an innovator gaining access (legitimate or otherwise) to some genetic resource, making an invention, and filing a patent application. Indeed, some groups make lists of 'examples' of biopiracy that consist merely of patent applications.

It is hard to see how the filing of a patent application can, in itself, amount to 'biopiracy'. The filing of a patent application presumes that something beyond the information relating to the genetic resource has been developed; namely, an invention. By attacking the innovative process itself, including efforts to obtain intellectual property protection for inventions arising out of use of genetic resources, these groups will ultimately prevent or deter parties from even attempting to create benefits that could be shared under the CBD model.

Finally, we do not accept the application of this term to cases where indigenous knowledge is used to make a further invention: for example, by isolating the active principle from a medicinal herb. Of course, the CBD may require equitable sharing of the benefits from such an invention; if this does not take place, this could then reasonably be termed 'biopiracy'. However, the wrong does not lie in filing the patent application, but in failing to deal fairly with the parties that helped create the opportunity for innovation.

There are a number of concerns in respect to the potential impacts of the patenting of food and farming crops on agricultural livelihoods and the ability of poor people to feed themselves in developing countries. Another strong argument for considering the exclusion of patenting of genetic resources for food and agriculture is what some call bio-piracy, 'licensed theft', or privatisation of common, cultural or indigenous knowledge relating to the economic and other benefits of plants.

Bio-piracy is a term used to express the expropriation and licensing of genetic resources which are common property (freely available) in developing countries, without any recognition or recompense to the countries or communities who have traditionally used and developed them. UNDP's Human Development Report 2000 refers to TRIPs as entailing the "silent theft of centuries of knowledge from some of the world's poorest communities in developing countries". These patents are increasingly being subject to successful legal challenge. Arguments regarding the negative impacts of IPRs (including plant breeders' rights - PBRs) over biodiversity conservation, specifically in the area of agro biodiversity, also point out to:

- A tendency to homogenize agricultural diversity;
- Displacement of native and traditional crops;
- Restriction to exports of traditional medicinal plants (thereby impacting *in situ* conservation efforts);
- Restrictions on saving, using and selling farm saved seeds by small farmers and indigenous communities, among others.
- Furthermore, patents have been critiqued as legitimizing "biopiracy", enhancing the concentration of research and development capacities in hands of private sector conglomerates.

CASE STUDIES

There have been several discussions over the consequences of IPR in agriculture, and in areas where knowledge is said to have been traditionally handed down the generations. However, a proper IPR regime can help protect not only the foreign inventors, but also the domestic players. Following is a summary of the present status of IPR in some of the most prominent instances.

Turmeric

In 1993, two American scientists of Indian origin filed a patent for use of turmeric to heal wounds. Initially the specification contained information on the prior knowledge of the various uses of turmeric and it also acknowledged that the pharmaco-kinetics involving the safety toxicity dosage and biological properties of turmeric are well known. It also said the main object of the invention is the use of turmeric powder at the site of injury by topical application and/or oral intake. The US Patent Office in 1995 granted the patent claim, reversing its earlier ruling that had held the invention not novel. Council of Scientific and Industrial research, Government of India (CSIR) challenged it, providing 32 references from ancient texts to show prior knowledge on the use of turmeric as a powder. The US Patent office reexamined the claim, maintained that the invention lacked novelty and revoked the patent.

Neem

There are more than 40 patents, mainly for Neem pesticides, held by laboratories in the US and Europe. A US company, was granted a patent for Neem as a pesticide. India couldn't challenge it because the patent was for a formulation which increased the shelf life of Neem extract. It was a valid patent and so protests had no effect. Indian scientists had been experimenting with this but since they had not applied for a patent for this process, they couldn't challenge it. Incidentally, even India has granted more than 80 patents on Neem, 48 of them of Indian origin. None of these patents have prevented Indians from using Neem nor has anyone paid royalty.

Cotton

In October 1992, another US Company got a patent for rights on all forms of genetically engineered cotton, no matter what techniques or genes are used to create them. It was challenged in court and the US patent office revoked it in 1994.

Medicine for Jaundice

A US virologist obtained a patent for a formulation of phyllanthus amarus, a plant used for centuries in south India for the treatment of jaundice. On the face of it, this does not satisfy the criterion of novelty, but he obtained the patent for viral hepatitis, not mentioned in earlier texts. So his innovation satisfied the criterion of novelty.

Basmati

In September 1997, a US Company obtained a patent for calling aromatic rice grown outside India as Basmati and selling it under any brand name. It has already been selling brands like Kasmati and Texmati claimed to be Basmati type rice. With the patent, this company will be able to label its exports of rice also as Basmati.

Company claimed basmati is a generic term and that it had invented certain novel Basmati lines and grains which make possible production of high quality, high yielding Basmati rice worldwide. It claimed to have isolated specific scientific parameters like length-width ratio, starch index, percentage increase on being cooked etc. Otherwise authentic Basmati is said to be available only from India and Pakistan due to the unique and complex combination of environment, soil, climate, sowing practices and genetic variety. The US Company claimed that the invention was based on the surprising discovery that certain Basmati plant and grain characteristics and aspects of the growing environment for traditional Basmati rice lines were not critical to the perceived quality of the product.

Geographical Indication

Actually this is not an issue of patents but geographical indication. This relates to the area of production of a premium product, like champagne, can only be from the Champagne district of France even if those grapes are grown elsewhere and Feta cheese is goat cheese only from Greece. India still doesn't have any law relating to geographical indication but is expected to use this line of defense to argue its case. Darjeeling tea and other similar products could benefit from this, just as Champagne has.

Bean Biopiracy

In 1999 a US company won both a patent and a Plant Variety Protection Certificate for its bean variety called 'Enola'. In the same year two US companies importing Mexican beans were challenged with legal suits brought in by the former accusing the later of violating the company's patent monopoly.

The former company purchased bean seed in north-west Mexico, in 1994. Back home in the US they sorted out the yellow beans and let them propagate. They then continuously sorted out beans of colours other than yellow until they claimed to have created a new plant variety and applied for patent protection. Technically, the necessary prerequisites for a patent are novelty, usefulness and non-obviousness. Paradoxically, the US Patent & Trademark Office saw all these points fulfilled and granted the patent. Farmers in North-West Mexico saw this quite differently. They argued that they have been harvesting these yellow beans for generations. This claim was supported by the International Centre for Tropical Agriculture (CIAT) in Colombia, which confirmed that the bean variety in question is 'in trust' germplasm under a UN Agreement of 1994. 'In-trust' germplasm must not be part of a patent and is kept in the public domain. Experts agree that a certain colour of the seed does not represent an innovative process which can be patented, because uniqueness is not provable. Hence this patent "is technically and morally unacceptable". It was found out that export sales for the Mexican yellow beans dropped by 90%, harming local farmers considerably. Meanwhile, the CIAT has legally challenged the 'Enola bean'-patent on the basis of its research with samples in its gene bank of designated germplasm. CIAT found out that six samples of this gene bank were quite identical to the patented crops, which proved that the 'Enola-beans' were not new. It is to be hoped that this case and its publicity will mark a turning point for the way biopiracy is dealt with.

RECOMMENDATIONS

It is critical that the potential benefits of GM technology become available to developing countries. Therefore where appropriate:

- Farmers must be allowed to save seeds for future use (re-use seed) if they wish to do so;
- Publicly funded research should investigate the value and limitations of re-using seed and the results of this research should be made freely available to interested parties;
- Broad intellectual property claims, without a true invention being made, should not be granted because they stifle research and development;
- Possible inconsistencies among international conventions, such as those that pertain to patent rights and the

Convention on Biological Diversity, should be identified and clarified;

- Research institutions should establish partnerships among industrialized and developing countries so that the benefits of GM research, applications and licensing will become much more widely available; and
- An international advisory committee should be created to assess the interests of private companies and developing countries in the generation and use of transgenic plants to benefit the poor not only to help resolve the intellectual property issues involved, but also to identify areas of common interest and opportunity between private sector and public sector institutions.

CONCLUSION

Production, protection, commercialisation and incorporation of intellectual property in development of national developmental strategies, will be crucial in defining the role India will play in world markets on one hand and overcoming deprivation and hunger with in the country on the other. India should not view the challenges posed by WTO as if it will remain always an importing country and that it has no substantive intellectual property to offer to world market. The knowledge intensity of Indian agriculture has to go up if it has to become competitive globally and at the same responsive to the urges of local communities which conserve agro-biodiversity that made green revolution possible. The provision of TRIPS needs to be strengthened to include:

- Micro organisms but exclude life forms;
- Registration system of grassroots innovations (this registration system should be like product patent for a fixed period);
- Widespread patent search facility for educational and entrepreneurial networks and centers so that quality of research and education can be competitive;
- Just as a global registry has been proposed for wines under TRIPS, India must insist that similar global registry must exist for green small innovations too.

To summarise the situation, developing countries are in a serious situation if they try to comply with the obligations imposed on them by the TRIPS Agreement. There is an urgent need for a reform of TRIPS although in some cases a different interpretation of the regulations would be sufficient in order not to discriminate against developing countries, their economies and their people.

REFERENCES

Gupta, Anil, "Management of Intellectual Property Rights in Agricultural Sector", Indian Institute of Management, Centre for Management in Agriculture, Ahmedabad.

Vaidya, Vandana, Advocate/Patent Agent, "Intellectual Property Rights-A Boon to Indian Companies".

Diaz, Carolina Lasen (2005), "Intellectual Property Rights and Biological Resources–An Overview of Key Issues and Current Debates", Wuppertal Institute for Climate, Environment and Energy.

Louwaars, N.P., Tripp, R., Eaton, D., V. Henson-Apollonio, Mendoza, R. Hu, Muhhuku, M.F., Pal, S. & Wekundah, J., (2005), "Impacts of Strengthened Intellectual Property Rights Regimes on the Plant Breeding Industry in Developing Countries-A Synthesis of Five Case Studies", A Study Report Commissioned by the World Bank.

Liberty Features, A Report from Liberty Institute, New Delhi, 1999.

Kothari, Ashish and Anuradha, R.V., (1999), "Biodiversity and Intellectual Property Rights: Can the Two Co-Exist?" Journal of International Wildlife & Policy.

Ramasamy, C., Raveendren, N. & Ajjan, N. "Indian Agriculture and Management in the Context of World Trade Organization" A Report from Tamil Nadu Agricultural University.

Veena, Nalini, Ajith and John, "Impact of WTO Development and Situation of Indian Agriculture" A CED Documentation-compiled for Jan Sangati Kendra.

Dawkins, Kristin, Thom Michelle and Carr, Carolyn, "Intellectual Property Rights and Biodiversity", Institute for Agriculture and Trade Policy.

"Intellectual Property Rights and Biodiversity: Processes and Synergies", (2003), Background paper for Workshop on TRIPs and CBD, Global Biodiversity Forum, Cancun, Mexico, September 5-7, 2003.

Tripathi, Ruchi, "Implications of TRIPs on livelihoods of farmers in developing countries", Action Aid, Berne, Switzerland.

Mayer, Jorge E., (2003), "Intellectual Property Rights and Access to Agro Biotech by Developing Countries", Ag Biotech Net, Vol. 5, March 2003, Review Article.

Stein, Haley, (2005), "Intellectual Property and Genetically Modified Seeds: The United States, Trade, and the Developing World", Northwestern Journal of Technology and Intellectual Property.

Habian, Erich, "Intellectual Property Rights for the Rich and the Poor?", The Impact of TRIPS on Developing Countries.

INTELLECTUAL PROPERTY RIGHTS AND ITS RELATIONSHIP WITH TRADE

*R. Hiremani Naik**

INTRODUCTION

The modern company is now more then ever confronted by rapid changes in technology and competition. Intellectual property is an area of the law that is central to the protection of, and competition in, technology. Whether we like it or not, intellectual property is being created in our company's workplace all the time, and is continually arising in the workplace around us. To navigate this minefield a deeper understanding intellectual property is crucial. Knowledge and proper use of intellectual property will ensure the protection and maintenance of Competitive edge, company image and reputation.

WHAT IS INTELLECTUAL PROPERTY?

Intellectual property is intangible property that arises out of creative endeavour (some forms of which must be registered to prevent loss). For example, intellectual property includes: patents for inventions; registered designs for new shapes and patterns; trade marks for various types of signs; copyright for literary and artistic works; confidential information/trade secrets, and know-how; plant breeders rights for new plant varieties; and integrated circuit protection. There are three important registrable forms of intellectual property, namely, patents, trade marks and designs. On the other hand, copyright and confidential information, arise automatically with the creation of a work and do not require separate registration.

* Reader, Dept. of Commerce, Karnatak University, K.R.C. P.G. Centre, B.R.-Hatti-Belgaum-591156, Karnatak.

PATENTS

Generally, patents protect ideas or concepts that can be practically implemented. For example, patents can protect mechanical apparatus, chemical, agricultural and biotechnological processes and products, electrical and products and processes; besides computer software and living organisms. Overall, to be patentable, an invention must be the right subject matter, and be new and inventive. The patent monopoly provided by Governments enables the protection not only of the particular form of the idea, but of all equivalent forms (i.e. Protection of the concept). Hence, it is vital that the concept that the be defined broadly in an effort restrict competitors from using the, technology. A company should note that many inventions arising in the workplace are either overlooked or pursued independently by the employee-inventor. An adequate IP policy and review process with a patent authority can prevent a company's valuable technology from being wasted.

TRADE MARKS

Trade marks include marks, signs which enable one trader to distinguish its goods/services from those of another. Where possible, trade marks should always be registered, because of many advantages associated with registration. They are, automatic-wide coverage, notice of rights to the public, easier enforcement than an equivalent common law action, and the acquiring of a listable asset. We are all familiar with word trade marks. For example, the well-known Coca Cola® bottle shape functions as a trade mark and has been registered. However, to achieve registration the mark must be distinctive (i.e. Not descriptive of the product/service and not likely to be legitimately needed by the other traders in describing their business). Companies should therefore ensure that distinctive trade marks (e.g. Invented words, symbols etc) are selected for their business otherwise problems with registration and enforcement will enforcement will confront them. A great misunderstanding in relation to trade marks arises in the context of business and company names. Companies should be aware that business and company name registrations confer no rights. It is only through the use of these names that common law rights arise, although these rights are often substantially weaker than those conferred by a trade mark registration.

REGISTERED DESIGNS

Registered designs protect the shape of or pattern applied to an article. Unlike patents, registered designs do not protect the concept behind an article's shape or the pattern applied thereto and often-small variations in another article's shape or pattern can fall outside the scope of registered design protection. However, registered designs can be extremely effective in some situations (e.g. Where an article must be made with a particular shape).

COPYRIGHT

Copyright is not a registrable right and subsists automatically when a copyrightable work is created (e.g. The simple act of writing a letter, making a sketch, or directing an inter-office memo generates material that is automatically the subject of copyright). Copyright typically arises in relation to original literary, dramatic, musical, and artistic works, including works of artistic craftsmanship. Industrially generated copyright and the ownership thereof can be extremely important for manufacturing companies (e.g. Plans, blueprints, technical drawings and computer software). Companies should be aware of the problem that can arise in relation to a work that is commissioned by the company of an independent contractor (e.g. a graphic designer or a computer programmer). According to law, the creator/author of the copyright work owns the copyright. Generally, if the company pays a contractor to create a copyright work, the contractor still owns the copyright and all that the company is provided with is a royalty-free licence to use the copyright work for which it was created. However, if the copyright work has other applications (e.g. a computer programme prepared for a company has applications in another unrelated industry), then the company may well have no licence to exploit the copyright work in the other industry (i.e. Exploitation could occur only with the author's consent and the author may demand significant remuneration before providing consent). Companies should always ensure that the company's employees are covered by adequate employment contracts that vest ownership of employee- generated copyright with the company.

CONFIDENTIAL INFORMATION

Confidential information, trade secrets and know-how remain valuable when they are kept secret. Again, the company should ensure that an appropriate policy and proper agreements to cover both the company's employees and external dealings the company makes are in place.

HOW IS INTELLECTUAL PROPERTY TRADE RELATED

Much of the value in traded goods and services resides in its intellectual property content. For raw commodities this can be negligible, although many primary producers use the intellectual property system to derive higher value from their products: Dargeeling tea, bearing a famous trade mark and certified as organic, would be more valuable than undifferentiated bulk tea sold as a row commodity. For highly trade transformed manufactures-such as computers and motor vehicles-the relationship is even more complex, as these normally comprise bundles of intellectual property rights, some formally recognized such as registered trade marks, and some implicit, such as know how and trade secrets. The growth of electronics of commerce has further shed light on the 'trade-related' quality of intellectual property. It has underlined that intellectual property rights can be the subject of trade in their own right. From the practical perspective of the consumer, 'purchasing' a software application or a musical work on line from a web site is slightly different from purchasing the same product on CD or in a package. However on-line transaction involves no physical trade in goods. The essence of the transaction in the transfer of certain rights to use the copyright products. Yet this is an important and growing kind of international trade. Similarly, many innovative companies rely largely or entirely on licensing their intellectual property to other enterprises in export markets, again without the transfer of goods and often without any specific service being provided with the technology being licensed for a fee. Intellectual property also has a role in transfer of technologies, as investment in new industries often depends on confidence in the protection of the intellectual property rights that emphasizes availability of new technologies. The need for a balanced approach is underscored by concerns that misuse of intellectual property right protection and enforcement mechanisms, or abusive commercial practices involving intellectual property rights, could unduly restrain legitimate trade. For example, a competitor could undermine a legitimate trader's product launch by bargaining power given by the patent to demand that a person using the technology must also exclusively purchase the patent owner's goods and services in another area. Trade rules can take account of the need to restrain these kind of abusive practices as part of an equitable intellectual property system.

WHY IS INTELLECTUAL PROPERTY PROPERLY RELEVANT TO GLOBAL EXPORTS

Global's export profile increasingly features knowledge-intensive, sophisticated and distinctive products and services that rely on effective and affordable intellectual property right protection. Revenues to global innovators from direct licensing of intellectual property rights abroad are steadily rising. This makes the international intellectual property system a valuable instrument for promoting global trade and investment interest. However, protection of intellectual property rights in export markets can be a complex, expensive and risky enterprise. Up-front costs are particularly high, given the pressing need to secure intellectual property right early in the life cycle of a new product. Harmonisation of the national intellectual property laws in export markets within the agreed international frameworks is necessary to reap the benefits of intellectual property protection within the practical reach of enterprises, especially smaller enterprises or those in the process of establishment.

MANAGING INTELLECTUAL PROPERTY

The current business should effectively manage an intellectual property and innovation policy. Such management may be as regularly instructing the search and registration as a trade mark of the name of new products or services. Alternatively, it may involve the management of substantial international intellectual property portfolios. Regardless of the size of the company, there are a few golden rules which each company could follow to prevent valuable innovations from being squandered.

- To ensure new ideas and innovations are kept confidential, at least until suitable protection is secured.
- To restrict publication of new ideas even after protection has been secured, until the release of idea in the market.
- To ensure that employees understand their confidential obligations which are bound to the company by appropriate agreements and do not share their brilliant ideas to the public at large.
- To ensure that ideas and innovations are protected broadly and in relevant countries/ jurisdictions after ascertaining the breadth of protection is: (a) suitable to our commercial needs; and (b) align with our commercial strategies and direction.
- To ensure that any modifications, improvements and/ or developments of ideas and innovations are monitored, reviewed and, if necessary, further protected.
- To ensure that company owns any innovative input that such people/firms make for us, while soliciting input from external consultants, designers etc.
- To continually monitor the market the market and ensure that existing protection for ideas and innovations is still relevant.

- To systematically search the scientific literature, especially patent literature, and use international patent and trade mark searching agencies to monitor what our competitors are doing and to ensure that our competitors are not copying/infringing upon our ideas, or attempting to design or engineer around them.
- To make sure that all deadlines (especially in relation to the protection and maintenance of intellectual property) are diarised.
- To make sure that we fully understand the costing associated with protecting the ideas, including the cash flow.
- To consult and instruct the legal advisers early in the innovation procedure.
- To have an intellectual property policy which clearly specifies the steps and procedures for our company's innovation, how individuals are remunerated, the duties of various positions within the organization etc.
- To systematically use and archive standard agreements such as employer/employee agreements, agreements between contractors/designers, licensing agreements etc.

CONCLUSION

While much progress has been made in the areas of trade mark law, much remains to be done towards harmonization and the consistent treatment by domestic and foreign trade mark owners. The scope of what can be protected is an example of where improvement can be made. Originally, only trade marks where protected. Of late the protection for service marks has been introduced in many countries. Trade mark owners and practitioners who wish to obtain protection for such service are required to file in respect of the goods to be sold. Trade mark infringement and piracy in certain regions of the world has become exceedingly volatile issue. This is not because there has not always been piracy, but rather because of increase global economic activity and the increasing economic importance of some of the regions in which piracy and infringement are rife. Over the past years, piracy has costed foreign intellectual property owners billions of dollars in lost sales and can even cause political tension between nations. In many ways, the development of trade mark law has followed the development of commerce, and can be expected to do so, given its importance as a tool for protecting commerce. Harmonization of national trade mark laws and the introduction of international intellectual property treaties has progressed significantly. It is possible, however he or she may do business. Intellectual property is now the most sophisticated juggernaut for competition and thus its vital that it be properly understood and managed. All companies should have an appropriate management policy and action plan for the protection and commercialization of company-generated intellectual property.

REFERENCES

Chartrand, H.H., Intellectual Property in the Global Village, Government Information in Canada, Vol. 1, No. 4, 1995.

Andean Community, Decision 351: Common Provisions on Copyright and Neighboring Rights, December 17, 1973.

Chaffe, Z., Jr., Reflections on the law of Copyright: I & II, *Columbia Law Review,* Vol. 45, Nos. 4 & 5, July and September 1945 in Berrings, R.C. (ed), Great American Law Reviews, Legal Classic Library, Birmingham, 1984.

Chartrand, H.H., Compleat Multilateral Copyright & Related Agreements, Conventions, Covenants & Treaties 1998, Complier Press, Sasktoon, 1998.

Malhotra, Y., Knowledge Assets in the Global Economy: Assessment of National Intellectual Capital, Journal of Global Information Management, July-Sept, 2000, 8 (3), 5-15.

ASSESSING THE IMPLICATIONS OF INTELLECTUAL PROPERTY RIGHTS ON AGRICULTURE, BIOLOGICAL RESOURCE AND INDIGENOUS PEOPLE

*I. Sundar**

INTRODUCTION

Intellectual property rights are legal and institutional devices to protect creations of the mind such as inventions, works of art and literature and design. They also include marks on products to indicate their difference from similar others sold by competitors. Further IPR has been directed to include not only patents, copyright, industrial designs and trademarks, but also trade secrets, plant breeders' rights, geographical indications and rights to layout designs of integrated circuits. Intellectual property right consists of three important regimes. The first one is the widening of proptectable subject matter. The parameters of protectable subject matter have been widened and there has been a tendency to reduce. The extensive of copyright and patent protection of computer programmes, the application of patent protection to cover business methods, life forms, cell lines and DNA sequences and the removal of exclusion on product patents for drugs are the noteworthy examples. The second regime is the creation of new rights. It includes plant breeders' rights, rights to layout-designs of integrated circuits and rights related to copyrights such as performer rights. The third IPR regime is the progressive standardization of basic features of IPRS. It could be noted that patent regulations increasing by provide 20 years

* Senior Lecturer in Economics, Directorate of Distance Education, Annamalai University, Annamalai Nagar-608 002.

protection term; require prior art searches and examinations for novelty, inventive step and industrial applications, assign rights to first application rather than the first inventor and provide protection for inventions in all industries and fields of technology. However, there is a growing concern on implications of IPRS on various aspects of human life. This paper analyses implications of IRS in three different areas viz., agriculture, environmental resource and indigenous people.

AGRICULTURE

There is a debate with respect to implications of IPRS on agriculture in general and agriculture in developing countries in particular. In developed countries plant breeders have sought IPR protection for new plants including new foodstuffs through the system known as Plant Breeders Rights. There is a need to analyse the international acceptance of common standards of plant breeders rights through the international convention for the protection of new varieties of plants. Initially they are developed to meet the conditions in the advanced industrialized countries may have the effect of undermining the food security of communities in developing countries. This papers makes a comprehensive analysis of implications of intellectual property rights on agriculture.

Traditional crop varieties developed over many generations by indigenous farmers are an important component of global crop genetic resources for use by both industrial and indigenous agriculture. Currently there is a debate between advocates of indigenous farmers' rights in their traditional varieties and the dominant world system, which vests IPRs to crop genetic resources only in users of those resources for industrial agriculture. While indigenous people at the individual and group levels do have a broad range of IPRs in their traditional varieties, they define and use them differently from the industrial world. Therefore industrial world IPRs are generally inappropriate for protecting the IPRs of indigenous farmers, but some could be used effectively, To meet indigenous farmers' need for protection, new approaches are being developed that embed indigenous farmers' rights in traditional varieties in cultural, human, and environmental rights. More research on the cultural, social, and agronomic roles of traditional varieties, ongoing negotiation of the meaning of key concepts such as 'crop genetic resources', 'rights', and 'indigenous', and an emphasis on a common goal of sustainability will help to resolve the debate (Cleveland, D.A., and S.C. Murray, 1997).

Property rights are assured by the collective standing behind one's claim to the benefit stream generated by property. Changing technology and institutions have interacted throughout history to create property rights from what had previously been public goods. The discovery of knowledge about DNA and the useful products that can be created through the applications of that knowledge has generated conditions that have led to intellectual private property claims on many new processes and products. Large multinational life science companies seeking to capitalise on these developments have purchased many heretofore independent seed companies, leading to a high level of concentration in the seed industry. These issues are treated differently in various countries and many developing countries have limited capacity to deal with them.

Today half the world relies on a few basic crops for its food and over 830 million people go hungry every day. Taking this reality as its starting point, it is observed that the impact of bio-patenting on food security for poor countries and communities. It is argued that trade policy and food security are matters of justice and human rights, not just economics. Trade rules, especially those relating to IPRs, must be fair and equitable and must promote rather than hinder human development. Hence one raises concerns about the rise in monopoly power accompanying bio-patents which it is felt is more likely to stifle innovative approaches to the problem of world hunger than it is to provide a solution. These days 'biopiracy' is taking place on staple food crops important to the South. Plant genetic material is moving into private ownership–against the wishes of many developing countries. The world's agri-business and biotechnology industry own most of the patents on staple food crops. Patents on rice, wheat, sorghum, cassava, maize, millet, potato, soybean and wheat are falling into company hands. The higher prices of patented seeds and accompanying royalties are likely to outweigh any possible benefits of generally modified plants to poor farmers. This raises questions for food security. Of grave concern to Action Aid is evidence that biotechnology patents are being granted which could allow companies based in the developed nations to substitute crops grown in the developing countries. With advances in mapping the 'genome' or entire genetic code of the world's staple food crops, this trend to patent is set to continue. We are in the midst of an explosion of activity in this area. Despite some work by the public sector, it is clear that private corporations are racing to complete the majority of this 'mapping'. Never in history has so much information about the genetic make-up of plants been available. If patents are granted on 'prize' genes from staple food crops, the losers are likely to be poor farmers in the developing countries (Baxter, B., S. Mayer and A. Wijeratna 1999).

The international protection of IPRs has been a contentious issue between developed and developing countries. Protection of IPRs in agricultural biotechnology is the latest manifestation of the dispute with both developed and developing countries accusing each other of piracy (Watal, J. 2001). Trade Related Intellectual Property Rights was only grudgingly agreed to by developing countries at the Uruguay Round. The WTO allows trade retaliation to be used for violations of TRIPS commitments. It is observed that developed countries will not receive the protection they desire and, hence, there may be a mutual interest in re-opening negotiations related to patenting genetic material (Kerr, W.A., J.E. Hobbs and R. Yampoin, 1999).

TRIPS has been denounced by developing countries, which have relied heavily on indigenous biotechnology from several decades in the area of high-yielding seeds, bio-pesticides and fertilizers, herbal medicines and household consumables. Hence, there is a need to analyse the social, economic and preservation implications of TRIPS for biological resources (Mangeni F. 2001). Establishing IPRs to products derived from genetic resources is necessary but not sufficient for bioprospecting and the long-term survival of these resources. Developing countries must also develop suitable institutions and policies governing the use of their resources and enabling local communities to receive benefits of biodiversity conservation and prospecting (Bhat, M. G. 1996 and Escudero, S. 2001).

Presently, IPR law is the mechanism that determines international protection and control over biotech innovations and genetic resources. The IPR paradigm employs western definitions of property in order to provide a framework in which to allocate rights. This has resulted in serious distributive problems. Until international IPR law increases awareness of the importance of the public domain in preserving genetic diversity, protecting the global food supply, and safeguarding genetic resources, IPR law will under-value and under-compensate the contributions and agricultural concerns of the developing countries that safeguard the vast majority of the world's plant genetic resources (Ewens, L.E. 2000).

Seeds and planting materials are central to the agricultural industry that feeds us all. Yet, until recently, there has been little interest in analysing the legal and political processes through which IPRs are constructed for these biological materials. The emergence of the new biotechnologies and of large corporations that produce both seeds and chemicals for the agriculture industry is a significant recent phenomenon. In spite of their dependence on the plant genetic resources of the South, the economic and political power of these corporations and of Northern governments has ensured that they continue to enjoy free access to these resources (Kloppenburg, J., Jr. 1988).

A patent recently granted on a technology which produces sterile seeds has revived the discussion on the consequences of in-built biological protection against seed saving. Seed companies see this as an incentive to develop new varieties. But what will be the consequences for farmers in developing countries if they cannot re-use their harvest as seed material?

(Lehmann, V. 1998). Hence, they should have serious concern on this issue. There is a growing dominance of the global seed industry by a small number of life-science corporations such as Monsanto. In spite of the optimistic claims of such companies, there is little discussion of how the application of agricultural biotechnology to agricultural trade policy's emphasis on monoculture production will reverse the loss of plant diversity essential for reinvigorating plant breeding programmes (Suppan, S. 1998).

GENETIC AND BIOLOGICAL RESOURCES

There is a growing concern on implications of intellectual property rights on agro-biodiversity. Hence, there is a need to address issues like. Do intellectual property rights encourage the spread of monocultural agriculture, consisting of genetically modified crops. And if so does this cause erosion of bio-diversity: Is the increasing production and sale of seed agro-chemical packages like transgenic crops sold with pesticides and herbicides for which they have build in resistance harmful to bio-diversity. And if so are intellectual property rights an inducement for companies to produce these kinds of package: Do intellectual property rights conflict with certain provisions and objectives of the convention on biological diversity such as national sovereignty, benefit sharing, technology transfer and the interest of holders of traditional knowledge? A more direct way that intellectual property rights (IPRS) may encourage allegedly environmentally unfriendly research and development is that IPRS are sometimes said to stimulate. Industries restructuring in ways that make such research and development more alternative to industry than it would otherwise be (Llewelyn, M. 2000).

It has been observed that genetically engineered herbicide resistance has some serious negative environmental effects. The use of herbicide resistant transgenic plant may encourage excessive use of herbicides which may kill other plant varieties are species accelerate the development of resistance among pests and create the possibilities of herbicide resistant genes crossing over to other plants including the weeds being targeted. This could create super weeds which would render the herbicide ineffective in the long run and cause ecological impacts that cannot be easily predict. Hence there is a need of a property understanding of implications of IPRS on bio-diversity and environment is an essential aspect of this paper.

The erosion of genetic resources continues at an alarming pace. Simultaneously, technologies which develop and make use of these resources outpace the ability of laws and societies to understand and cope with them. Spurred by technological advances, appreciation of the monetary and non-monetary value of genetic resources has grown, leading to increasing conflict over rights and responsibilities for these resources. Developments in international and national law and policy over the past 5 years have significantly changed the policy of environment relating to the management and control of genetic resources. The task of discerning all the issues of relevance to the conservation and management of genetic resources and then integrating them into consistent policy is extremely complex. Hence, there is a need of proper analysis of developments in the past 5 years, identifying cross-cutting issues and trends that have emerged including farmers' rights and interests of indigenous and local communities, benefit-sharing, access to genetic resources, patenting and industry trends, and sui generis protection of plant varieties (Bragdon, S.H. and D.R. Downes 1998).

It is significant to note that two types of legal regime have emerged to regulate the allocative aspects of the trade in biogenetic resources and products derived from them: access and benefit sharing laws and IPRs (Monagle, C. 2001). Hence, there is a need to describes both, but IPRs are emphasized because: (1) the acquisition by firms of patent and plant variety right portfolios appears to influence the unequal allocations of benefits obtained from industrial use of biogenetic resources; (2) the number of countries allowing strong IPR protection for life-science products and technologies is increasing rapidly. The effect may be to reinforce this asymmetry of benefit allocations; (3) patents and plant breeders' rights have been accused of encouraging biodiversity-erosive breeding and cultivation practices; and (4) just as inappropriate IPRs may harm the interests of developing countries, well-designed IPR systems could conceivably be highly beneficial, helping such countries to add value to their biogenetic wealth. Unfortunately, the global IPR system has become increasingly inflexible in recent years, reducing such opportunities for developing countries (Dutfield, G. 1999).

Plant genetic resources are crucial for world agriculture, food security and the global economy. They are vital for the pharmaceutical industry and important assets of biodiversity-rich developing countries. The patents and intellectual property rights (IPRs) associated with the development of new products are critical to trade in these resources. Hence, efforts examine the relevant international agreements: the convention on biological diversity TRIPS and the UPOV Convention. It provides an account of how to integrate the requirements of the CBD into an equitable global IPR regime, taking into account ethical concerns, environmental and social impacts, technology transfer and traditional knowledge (Dutfield, G. 2000).

Because TRIPS and the CBD embody and promote conflicting objectives, systems of rights and obligations, many states are questioning which treaty takes precedence over the other. It is argued that the CBD has primacy over the WTO in the areas of biodiversity and traditional knowledge, that the review of TRIPS allows states to exclude all life forms and related knowledge from IPR systems, and that the a priori collective rights of indigenous peoples and local communities over their biodiversity and related knowledge must be recognized (Gaia Foundation and Genetic Resources Action International 1998). The debate over TRIPS and the CBD has exposed a series of fault lines dividing technology-rich industrialized countries located in the temperate zone of the Northern Hemisphere, and the biodiversity-rich developing countries located primarily in the tropics and Southern Hemisphere. Hence, there is a need to analyse two of the most visible North-South conflicts, and examine the treaty provisions that have given rise to these conflicts and the two specific issues that are at their root. New institutions like the CBD and the 'green' World Bank reflect attempts to regulate international flows of 'natural capital' by means of an approach. It is called 'green developmentalism' underpinned by a post-neoliberal environmental-economic paradigm, according to which nature is constructed as a world currency and ecosystems are recoded as warehouses of genetic resources for biotechnology industries. (McAfee, K. 1999).

Genetic resources have the property that access to one unit is sufficient for the purpose of propagating millions of copies of them. This leads to market failure with potentially significant consequences for environmental protection. A solution to correcting this market is proposed which consists of the grant of a new property right (genetic resource right) akin to and inspired by IPRs. The solution has the attractions of addressing the problem of forest degradation, of being a market-based solution and of providing a simple means of securing international cooperation which would not necessarily rely on public financial transfers (Subramanian, A. 1992).

Biotechnology industry interests normally call for an extension of patents to plants and animals as a requirement to stimulate investments in biotechnological research, and to insure the wide distribution of the benefits from such research. So it is one the other hand questioned whether such an extension will serve this purpose. If IPRs must be extended to living organisms, hence it argued that another legal form would be needed (Busch, L. 1995).

The public distancing of bioscience companies from the image of corporate concerns taking precedence over public and environmental safety has meant a renewed focus on more traditional methods of producing new plant varieties. There is a clear need, if the bioscience industry is to survive, for it to regain public confidence as well as that of the marketplace. One of the key factors in this lack of confidence is the insistence on patent protection for all aspects of genetic research. The need to reclaim confidence cannot and should not be simply seen in terms of human genetic research, but also in respect of all biosciences. The failure within Europe to reach agreement on the issue of the provision of patent protection for genetic material should serve as evidence that it is time for those who have sought to gain acceptance of the patent system as an appropriate means of protecting biological material to admit defeat. While the exclusions remain they leave the system open to abuse through encouraging legal sleight of hand. It is time for the situation to be clarified. In respect of plants, this could be achieved either by removing the exclusion or by banning patent protection for all plant material leaving the plant variety right as the sole means of protection (Llewelyn, M. 2000).

Over the last two decades, the biotechnology industry has been stretching the interpretation of patent law in order to obtain IPRs over genetically engineered living organisms. Such patent rights, coupled with moves to gain exclusive access to the biodiversity of the South, are leading to a new global order. Hence, opposition to such 'biotechnological imperialism' is gaining in momentum (McNally, R. and P. Wheale 1996).

INDIGENOUS KNOWLEDGE

Indigenous knowledge has been subjected to massive and increasing bio-piracy by companies from the pharmaceutical, seed and agrochemical industries. It has been tend to increase exponentially each year. Bio-piracy is said to be unauthorized extraction of traditional knowledge or biological resources and the patenting of inventions that derive from such knowledge or resources without provision of benefit sharing with the providers (Drahos, P. 2000). In this context two questions can be considered to discuss the relationship between IPRS especially patents and the rights of holders of traditional knowledge, innovations and practices. First do IPRS have characteristics that are inherently unjust or which leads to injustice to traditional knowledge holders. Second to extent can IPRS be used to protect rights of indigenous people. Hence, a proper analysis is needed in this context.

The importance of protecting traditional knowledge is increasingly recognised. Developing countries seek to ensure that the benefits of cumulative innovation associated with traditional knowledge accrue to its holders while enhancing their socio-economic development. They also aim at preventing the improper appropriation of traditional knowledge (United Nations Conference on Trade and Development 2000).

The contemporary evolution of intellectual property is largely in response to pressure exerted by commercial interests, causing a conceptual fault line which emphasises existing exclusionary tendencies. If examined from the ostensibly unrelated perspectives of indigenous people and the digital age difficulties, the conceptual challenge becomes clear. However, the EU provides an ideal opportunity to encourage a conceptual re-alignment consistent with the emergence of other international legal standards (Tunney, J. 1998).

There is a need to consider how the nature of indigenous knowledge relates to IPRs. In particular, one has to analyse the nature of indigenous knowledge of medicinal plants and its role in the search for new drugs in order to address three issues: (i) whether the contribution of indigenous knowledge to a final drug is the sort of contribution that would allow one or more indigenous persons to be considered a joint inventor; (ii) whether publication of information concerning indigenous plant use would bar the availability of a patent; and (iii) whether IPRs are the most appropriate vehicle for addressing problems of compensation in the exploitation of genetic resources (Huft, M. 1995).

IPRs for ethnobiological knowledge have been proposed as a way to compensate indigenous people (Moran K.S.R. King and T.J. Carlson 2001). Four obstacles are critical: whether general and collective knowledge can be protected; whether certain indigenous groups can claim exclusive control over knowledge and resources; the uncertain status of indigenous peoples; and the lack of a well-developed market for biological resources or traditional knowledge (Brush, S.B. 1993).

Although IPRs currently provide limited incentives to communities, it is argued that some form of IPRs could be a valuable tool for communities to use to control their traditional knowledge and gain greater shares of the benefits (Downes, D.R. 2000). CBD Parties are urged to explore possible modifications to existing IPRs, or the creation of sui generic rights, that could accomplish these goals. Convention on biological diversity proposed various recommendation including: exploring the use of geographical indications, trademarks and authors' moral rights; supporting the establishment of national and international registries of traditional knowledge; and considering a requirement for patent applicants to disclose traditional knowledge and its origin as well as the origin of genetic resources used in the invention (Downes, D. 1997). In recent years there has been an increase in activism in the area of IPR protection for indigenous peoples' knowledge and cultural expressions. Up to now copyright courts have refused to allow indigenous communities to enforce their rights in such expressions (Blakeney, M. 1998).

The digital revolution has dramatically increased the ability of individuals and corporations to appropriate and profit from the cultural knowledge of indigenous peoples, which is largely unprotected by IPR law. In response, legal scholars, anthropologists, and native activists now propose new legal regimes designed to defend indigenous cultures by radically expanding the notion of copyright. Unfortunately, these proposals are often informed by romantic assumptions that ignore the broader crisis of intellectual property and the already imperiled status of the public domain (Chapman, 2000). Hence, there is a need of a skeptical assessment of legal schemes to control cultural appropriation–in particular, proposals that indigenous peoples should be permitted to copyright ideas rather than tangible expressions and that such protection should exist in perpetuity. A proper attention is needed to the pronounced tendency of intellectual property debates to pre-empt urgently which is a reflection on the political viability of special rights regimes in pluralist democracies and on using copyright law to enforce respect for other cultures (Brown, M.F. 1998).

IPR law contains an in-built bias that protects the intangible assets of companies while failing to recognise traditional knowledge as protectable subject matter. The rapid globalisation of high-level IPR minimum standards is certain to exacerbate the situation. The main reason why IPRs are unfair is not that they are explicitly discriminatory, but that they treat all knowledge in the world as the intellectual commons except that which is protected under patent or other mainstream IPRs. This situation is unjust to indigenous people and contrary to the interests of everybody except those who profit from exploiting traditional knowledge unfairly (Dutfield, G. 2000).

The scientific and commercial interest in traditional knowledge and resource management practices have been greater, these days, however, human cultural diversity is eroding at an accelerating rate. Concerned scientists are calling for the documentation of such knowledge before it disappears. But some indigenous peoples' organisations worry that documentation initiatives are likely to be top-down and exploitative (Dutfield, G. 1999). The development in international law by which local communities and developing countries could increase their own control over others' use of their resource-related innovations. Exactly how these norms should be implemented in domestic law, however, is far from clear. In this context it is argued that one plausible means of implementation would be through policies to increase the participation of indigenous communities in resource management decision-making. Another possible means would be through the creation of national sui generis IPR laws to protect indigenous and local knowledge. At least in theory, vesting IPRs in indigenous and local communities over their innovations would assist them to stop undesired use of their knowledge and compel compensation when it is used (Halewood, M. 1999).

After centuries of disparagement, indigenous people suddenly find their millennial wisdom coveted by outsiders and they are demanding that mechanisms be established to effectively protect their rights. The problem is how. Hence one has to analyze the legal avenues open to indigenous peoples to defend their cultural heritage, and seeks to elucidate the advantages and disadvantages of the various approaches so far advocated. It aims not to determine indigenous policy but to help them define their own local, national and international proposals to secure their futures, in accordance with their right to self-determination and to exercise their customary law (Simpson, T. 1997).

CONCLUSION AND POLICY IMPLICATIONS

It could be seen clearly from the above discussion that intellectual property rights have some positive implications as well as some negative implications particularly or developing countries, indigenous people and indigenous communities. In order to overcome the negative implications of intellectual property rights on indigenous knowledge system and developing countries, the following policy measures can be considered.

MEASURES TO PROMOTE SUSTAINABLE DEVELOPMENT

In order to promote indigenous ways of sustainable development the following measures can be considered.

1. There is a need to adopt laws and policies, which promote and protect indigenous people's rights including the recognition of the right to self-determination.
2. Enhance indigenous people's participation in the development of sustainable development plans and policies in various levels.
3. Mechanisms and resources to allow for meaningful participation of indigenous people should be clearly defined. Ensuring food security and sustainability should be integral to these.
4. Recognition of the vital contributions of indigenous human to sustainable development should be created which ensure their equal participation in formulating implementing and evaluating policies and policies from the level.
5. Supporting capacity building activities to allow indigenous people to be more effective and creative in influencing

policies, designing and implementing sustainable development plans.

6. The transfer of destructive technology to indigenous people should be prevented and support for the development of appropriate and environmentally sensitive technology should be promoted.
7. Research and education programmes should be strengthened to achieve wider and improved understanding of local people's knowledge perspectives and practices on sustainable development.
8. Building of genuine partnership to implement conservation programmes that fully promote and advance the rights and welfare of indigenous people development of partnership mechanism between government and indigenous people for sustainable development.
9. Recognition of land rights, water rights and rights of indigenous people to have control over their culture.
10. Recognition and support for indigenous resource management practices such as forest protection and conservation, sustainable agriculture, hunting and fishing practices etc.
11. Regulation activities of multi-national corporations in indigenous people's lands including bringing in destructive technologies.

REFERENCES

Baxter, B., S. Mayer and A. Wijeratna, (1999), "Crops and Robbers: Biopiracy and the Patenting of Staple Food Crops. Preliminary Findings of an Action Aid Investigation". London, Action Aid.

Bhat, M.G., (1996), "Trade-related Intellectual Property Rights to Biological Resources: Socio Economic Implications for Developing Countries." Ecological Economics 19: 205-17.

Blakeney, M., (1998), "Communal Intellectual Property Rights of Indigenous Peoples in Cultural Expressions." Journal of World Intellectual Property 1(6): 985-1002.

Bragdon, S.H. and D.R. Downes, (1998), "Recent Policy Trends and Developments Related to the Conservation, Use and

Development of Genetic Resources". Issues in Genetic Resources No. 7. Rome, International Plant Genetic Resources Institute.

Brown, M.F., (1998), "Can Culture be Copyrighted?" Current Anthropology 39(2): 193- 222.

Brush, S.B., (1993), "Indigenous Knowledge of Biological Resources and Intellectual Property Rights: the Role of Anthropology." *American Anthropologist* 95(3): 653-686.

Busch, L., (1995), "Eight Reasons why Patents Should Not be Extended to Plants and Animals." *Biotechnology and Development Monitor* 24: 24.

CIDSE International Cooperation for Development and Solidarity (2000).

Champman, A., (2000), "Approaching Intellectual Property as a Human Right: Obligations Related to Article 15 (1) (c)". Geneva, United Nations Committee on Economic, Social and Cultural Rights.

Cleveland, D.A. and S.C. Murray, (1997), "The World's Crop Genetic Resources and the Rights of Indigenous Farmers." *Current Anthropology* 38 (4): 477-514.

Downes, D., (1997), "Using Intellectual Property as a Tool to Protect Traditional Knowledge: Recommendations for Next Steps". Washington DC, Center for International Environmental Law.

Downes, D.R., (2000), "How Intellectual Property Could be a Tool to Protect Traditional Knowledge". Columbia Journal of Environmental Law 25: 253-281.

Drahos, P., (2000), "Indigenous Knowledge, Intellectual Property and Biopiracy: is a Global Bio-collecting Society the Answer?" European Intellectual Property Review (6) : 245-250.

Dutfield, G., (1999), "Protecting and Revitalising Traditional Ecological Knowledge: Intellectual Property Rights and Community Knowledge Databases in India". Intellectual Property Aspects of Ethnobiology. M. Blakeney. London, Sweet and Maxwell: 101-122.

Dutfield, G., (1999), "Sharing the Benefits of Biodiversity: Access Regimes and Intellectual Property Rights". Science, Technology and Development Discussion Paper No. 6.

Dutfield, G., (2000), "The Public and Private Domains: Intellectual Property Rights in Traditional Knowledge." Science Communication 21(3): 274-295.

Dutfield, G., (2000), Intellectual Property Rights, Trade and Biodiversity: Seeds and Plant Varieties. London, Earthscan and IUCN.

Escudero, S., (2001), "International Protection of Developing Countries and Geographical Indications", South Centre.

Ewens, L.E., (2000), "Seed Wars: Biotechnology, Intellectual Property, and the Quest for High Yield Seeds". *Boston College International and Comparative Law Review* 23 (2): 285-310.

Fowler, C., (1994), *Unnatural Science: Technology, Politics and Plant Evolution*. Yverdon, Gordon and Breach.

Gaia Foundation and Genetic Resources Action International (1998), "TRIPS versus CBD: Conflicts Between the WTO Regime of Intellectual Property Rights and Sustainable Biodiversity Management". Global Trade and Biodiversity in Conflict, Issue 1. London & Barcelona, Gaia Foundation and GRAIN.

Gupta, A.K., (1996), "Rewarding Creativity for Conserving Biodiversity in the Third World". Presented at AIPPI Forum on Ethical and Ecological Aspects of Intellectual Property Rights, 10-14 September, Interlaken.

Halewood, M., (1999), "Indigenous and Local Knowledge in International Law: A Preface to *sui generis* Intellectual Property Protection." McGill Law Journal 44: 953-996.

Herdt, R.W., (1999), "Enclosing the Global Plant Genetic Commons". Paper Prepared for Delivery at the China Center for Economic Research, May 24.

Huft, M., (1995), "Indigenous Peoples and Drug Discovery Research: a Question of Intellectual Property Rights." *Northwestern University Law Review* 89(4): 1678-1730.

Kerr, W.A., J.E. Hobbs and R. Yampoin, (1999), "Intellectual Property Protection, Biotechnology and Developing Countries: will the TRIPS be Effective?" AgBioForum 2 (3 & 4): 203-211.

Kloppenburg, J., Jr., (1988), *First the Seed: The Political Economy of Plant Biotechnology*. Cambridge, Cambridge University Press.

Lehmann, V., (1998), "Patent on Seed Sterility Threatens Seed Saving". *Biotechnology and Development Monitor* 35: 6-8.

Llewelyn, M., (2000)., "The Patentability of Biological Material: Continuing Contradiction and Confusion." European Intellectual Property Review 22(5): 191-197.

Mangeni, F., (2001), "Technical Issues on Protecting Plant Varieties by Effective Sui Generis Systems", Occasional Paper no. 2, Geneva, South Centre.

McAfee, K., (1999), "Selling Nature to Save it? Biodiversity and Green Developmentalism." *Environment and Planning D: Society and Space,* 17: 133-154.

McManis, C.R., (1998), "The Interface Between International Intellectual Property and Environmental Protection: Biodiversity and Biotechnology." *Washington University Law Quarterly,* 76: 255.

McNally, R. and P. Wheale, (1996), "Biopatenting and Biodiversity: Comparative Advantages in the New Global Order." *The Ecologist,* 26(5): 222-228.

Mongale, C., (2001), "Biodiversity and Intellectual Property Rights: Reviewing Intellectual Property Rights in Light of the Objectives of the Convention on Biological Diversity". Gland and Geneva, WWF and CIEL.

Monran, K., S.R. King and T.J. Carlson, (2001), "Biodiversity Prospecting: Lessons and Prospects", Annual Review of Anthropology 30: 505-526.

Simpson, T., (1997), Indigenous Heritage and Self-determination: The Cultural and Intellectual Property Rights of Indigenous Peoples. Copenhagen, International Work Group for Indigenous Affairs.

Subramanian, A., (1992), "Genetic Resources, Biodiversity and Environmental Protection: An Analysis, and Proposals Towards a Solution." *Journal of World Trade* 26: 105-109.

Suppan, S., (1998), "Biotechnology's Takeover of the Seed Industry". Minneapolis, Institute for Agriculture and Trade Policy.

Tunney, J., (1998), "European Union, Intellectual Property, Indigenous People and the Digital Age: Intersecting Circles?" European Intellectual Property Review, 20 (9): 335-346.

United Nations Conference on Trade and Development (2000), "Systems and National Experiences for Protecting Traditional Knowledge, Innovations, and Practices". Background Note by the UNCTAD Secretariat". Geneva, Switzerland.

Watal, J., (2001), Intellectual Property Rights in the WTO and Developing Countries London, The Hague and Boston, Kluwer Law International.

INTELLECTUAL PROPERTY RIGHTS - PROTECTION AND ENFORCEMENT

S. Sri Krishna and S. Anil Kumar***

The WTO's Agreement on Trade-Related Aspects of Intellectual Property Rights (TRIPS), negotiated in the 1986-94 Uruguay Round, introduced intellectual property rules into the multilateral system for the first time. The TRIPS Agreement has an additional important principle: intellectual property protection should contribute to technical innovation and the transfer of technology.

India showed signs of resistance to quick enforcement of international intellectual property right (IPR) protection laws as demanded by the developed countries, particularly the US. China could get away on grounds that it is not a member of the World Trade Organisation (WTO), but India was required to comply. Under the terms of the WTO, India is required to implement WTO-standard IPR protection laws by 2005. It must be acknowledged that there has been remarkable progress in IPR protection the field of software and cinema products.

India's general argument was that it does acknowledge in principle the case for strict IPR protection, but this can be done only in phases suited by its own ground reality. The reality is that absence of international IPR protection for some decades has spawned employment for millions, so an overnight clampdown on IPR violators would foment social unrest.

However, under pressure from its own domestic industry and the United States, India strengthened its copyright law in

* Professor & Head Department of Political Science & Public Administration, No.I, Prakasam Nagar Sri Venkateswara University, Tirupati - 517 502, (A.P.), INDIA.

** Lecturer and Head, Department of Political Science, Nalanda College, Proddatur, Andhra Pradesh, INDIA.

May 1994, placing it at par with international practice. The new law, which entered into force in May 1995, fully reflects the provisions of the Berne Convention on copyrights, to which India is a party. Based on its improved copyright protection, India's designation as a "priority foreign country" under the United States' Special-301 list was revoked and India was placed on the "priority watch list." Copyright enforcement is also rapidly improving.

Classification of copyright infringements as "cognisable offenses" expands police search and seizure authority. While the formation of appellate boards under the new legislation should speed prosecution, local attorneys indicate that some technical flaws in the laws, which require administrative approval prior to police action, need to be corrected.

Trademark protection is considered good by the US authorities, and could be raised to international standards with the passage of a new trademark bill that codifies existing court decisions on the use and protection of foreign trademarks, including service marks. The bill was first introduced in 1995 but failed to win parliamentary approval. Passage of the trademark bill is expected in 1998. Enforcement of trademark owner rights had been weak in the past, but is steadily improving as the courts and police respond to domestic concerns about the high cost of piracy to Indian rights' holders.

India's patent protection is weak and has especially adverse effects on international pharmaceutical and chemical firms. Estimated annual losses to the US pharmaceutical industry due to piracy are $450 million, but Indian authorities have a different point of view. India's patent act prohibits product patents for any invention intended for use or capable of being used as a food, medicine, or drug or relating to substances prepared or produced by chemical processes. Consequently, many drugs invented by foreign companies are widely reproduced.

Processes for making drugs are patentable, but the patent term is limited to the shorter of five years from the grant of patent or seven years from the filing date of the patent application. Product patents in other areas are granted for 14 years from the date of filing. However, as a signatory to the Uruguay Round of GATT, including its provisions on Trade Related Intellectual Property Rights (TRIPS), India must introduce a comprehensive system of product patents no later than 2005.

The Indian government has formed an advisory committee to recommend changes in the 1970 Indian Patents Act. A temporary ordinance for patent protection implementing the "mailbox" provisions of the WTO TRIPS agreement and providing for exclusive marketing rights was issued in December 1994. However, the ordinance lapsed and the parliament has yet to pass a new patent bill implementing the provisions of the ordinance. In July 1996, the U.S. initiated WTO dispute settlement procedures over India's failure to implement its TRIPS obligations. The final panel report on this case was issued in August 1997, and ruled that India had failed to meet its obligations under the TRIPS agreement. Indian officials have pledged to introduce another bill in parliament which, if passed, will put India in compliance with its TRIPS obligations.

The bottomline is that India considers itself a responsible member of the WTO which suggests that international class IPR protection should be in place by 2005. Besides, given India's determination to emerge as a power in the global software industry, it is most likely that all IPR protection laws will be instituted and enforced by 2005. Note that Bill Gates, the chief executive officer of Microsoft Corporation, has distinguished India as a most promising base for software development. If such an IPR-conscious business leader like Gates is of this opinion, one can only conclude that India's IPR scene is no deterrent to foreign companies.

Copyright: The TRIPS agreement ensures that computer programs will be protected as literary works under the Berne Convention and outlines how databases should be protected.

Trademarks: The agreement defines what types of signs must be eligible for protections trademarks, and what the minimum rights conferred on their owners must be.

Geographical Indications: A place name is sometimes used to identify a product. This "geographical indication" does not only say where the product was made. More importantly, it identifies the product's special characteristics, which are the result product's origins.

Industrial Designs: Under the TRIPS Agreement, industrial designs must be protected for at least 10 years.

Patents: The agreement says patent protection must be available for inventions for at least 20 years. Patent protection must be available for both products and processes, in almost all fields of technology. A patent owner could abuse his rights, for example by failing to supply the product on the market. To deal with that possibility, the agreement says governments can issue "compulsory licenses", allowing a competitor to produce the product or use the process under license.

Integrated Circuits Layout Designs: The basis for protecting integrated circuit designs ("topographies") in the TRIPS agreement is the Washington Treaty on Intellectual Property in Respect of Integrated Circuits, which comes under the World Intellectual Property Organization. This was adopted in 1989 but has not yet entered into force. The TRIPS agreement adds a number of provisions: for example, protection must be available for at least 10 years.

Having intellectual property laws is not enough. They have to be enforced. This is covered in Part 3 of TRIPS. The agreement says government have to ensure that intellectual property rights can be enforced under their laws, and that the penalties for infringement are tough enough to deter further violations.

Technology Transfer: Developing countries in particular, see technology transfer as part of the bargain in which they have agreed to protect intellectual property rights. The TRIPS Agreement includes a number of provisions on this.

ANTI DUMPING, SUBSIDIES, SAFEGUARDS, CONTINGENCIES, ETC.

Binding tariffs, and applying them quality to all trading partners (most-favored nation treatment, or MFN) is key to the smooth flow of trade in goods. The WTO agreements uphold the principles, but they also allow exceptions – in some circumstances. Three of these issues are:

- Actions taken against dumping (selling at an unfairly low price).
- Subsidies and special "countervailing duties" duties to offset the subsidies.
- Emergency measures to limit imports temporarily, designed to "safeguard" domestic industries.

ANTI-DUMPING ACTIONS

If a company exports a product at a price lower than the price it normally charges on its own home market, it is said to be "dumping" the product.

WTO focus is on how governments can or cannot react to dumping–it disciplines anti-dumping actions, and it is often called the **"Anti–Dumping Agreement"**. WTO agreement allows governments to act against dumping where there is genuine ("material") injury to the competing domestic industry.

Anti-dumping action means charging extra import duty on the particular product from the particular exporting country in order to bring its price closer to the "normal value" or to remove the injury to domestic industry in the importing country.

Anti –dumping measures expire five years after the date of imposition, unless an investigation shows that ending the measure would lead to injury.

SUBSIDIES

This agreement addresses two things: it disciplines the use of subsidies, and it regulates the actions countries can take to counter the effects of subsidies. It says a country can use the WTO's dispute settlement procedure to seek the withdrawal of the subsidy or the removal of its adverse effects. Or the country can launch its own investigation and ultimately charge extra duty (known as "countervailing duty") on subsidized products that are found to be hurting domestic producers.

The agreement defines two categories of subsidies: prohibited and actionable

Prohibited subsidies: subsidies that require recipients to meet certain export targets, or to use domestic goods instead of imported goods. They are prohibited because they are specifically designed to distort international trade, and are therefore likely to hurt other countries' trade.

Actionable subsidies: in this category the complaining country has to show that the subsidy has an adverse effect on its interest. Otherwise the subsidy is permitted.

Countervailing duty (the parallel of anti-dumping duty) can only be charged after the importing country has conducted a detailed investigation similar to that required for anti-dumping action.

Least-developed countries and developing countries with less than $1,000 per capita GNP are exempted from disciplines on prohibited export subsidies. Other developing countries are given until 2003 to get rid of their export subsidies.

SAFEGUARDS

A WTO member may restrict imports of a product temporarily (take "safeguard" actions) if its domestic industry is injured or threatened with injury caused by a surge in imports. An import "surge" justifying safeguard action can be a real increase in imports (an *absolute increase*); or it can be an increase in the imports' share of a shrinking market, even if the import quantity has not increased.

When a country restricts imports in order to safeguard its domestic producers, in principle its must give something in return. The agreement says the exporting country (or exporting countries) can seek compensation through consultations.

NON-TARIFF BARRIERS AND RED TAPE

A number of agreements deal with various bureaucratic or legal issues that could involve hindrances to trade.

- Import licensing.
- Rules for the valuation of goods at customs.
- Pre-shipment inspection; further checks on imports

- Rules of origin; made in .... Where?
- Investment measures.

IMPORT LICENSING

The Agreement on Import Licensing Procedures says import licensing should be simple, transparent and predictable. For example, the agreement requires governments to publish sufficient information for traders to know how and why the licenses are granted.

The above listed are the developments that happened in Doha on the founding agreements of WTO that were signed in 1995. Each and every following ministerial attempts to expand the scope of WTO to include the issues other than Tariff However the developed nations do not with to discuss the agricultural subsides while the developing countries do not wish to discuss the agricultural investment issues. In the case of non-agricultural issues the developed nations are insisting on the faster reduction in tariff barriers however this is not acceptable by the developing countries. In the case of GATS the developing countries was liberalization of Mode 4 however the developed countries want the restrictions of the professionals who work in the developing countries to be removed and better repatriation laws.

REFERENCES

Correa, Carlos A., "Implementing the TRIPs Agreement", Third World Network, Penang, Malaysia, 1998.

Gupta, K.R., World Trade Organisation (Successor of GATT) and in India, Atlantic Publishers and Distributors, New Delhi, 1996, pp. 23-24.

Stuart, S. Malawer, "The US and WTO: Lessons Learned from Trade Legislation and Global Governance", Esserman and Howe, pp. 185, 2003.

Deardorff, Alan, "Welfare Effects of Global Patent Protection", Economica, Volume. 59, pp. 35-51, 1992.

John, O., McGinnis and Mark L. Movsesian, "Against Global Governance in the WTO", *Harvard International Law Journal*, Volume. 45, 2004.

Satapathy, C., "WTO Agreement on Anti-Dumping: Misuse and Case for Review", Economic and Political Weekly, Volume XXXIV, No. 32, August 7-13, 1999.

Subramaniam, A. and Wattal, J., "TRIPs as an Enforcement Device in the WTO for Developing Countries", Journal of International Economic Law, 2000.

IPR REGIME IN INDIA: POST WTO SCENARIO

*S.B. Somannavar**

INTRODUCTION

Intellectual property rights (IPRs) remain an active subject in international policy debates. Technology experts in developed countries argue that stronger IPRs are needed in developing countries in order to provide better incentives for innovation and international technology transfer. The recent introduction of global minimum standards for IPRs, through the Agreement on Trade-Related Intellectual Property Rights (TRIPS) in the World Trade Organization, raises many questions about the relationship among IPRs, technology transfer, and economic growth [Guifang Yang, KPMG, Atlanta and K.E. Maskus, 2003]. The present study has four sections. Section I is an introduction. Section II deals with IPRs and the world situation. Section III brings out IPRs and the post WTO scenario in India. Section IV is the conclusion.

Intellectual Property is "information and original expression which derives its intrinsic value from creative ideas". (Steve Pike, Anna Rylander and Goran Roos., 1977). It is the *information with commercial value.* (Sveiby., 2000). Countries have made laws to foster innovation by regulating the copying of inventions, identifying symbols and creative expressions. These laws encompass four distinct types of intangible property viz., patents, trade marks, copyrights and trade secrets which are collectively called intellectual property. (Charrand, H.H., 1995).

* S.G.L. in Economics, K.L.E. Society's Lingaraj College, Belgaum – 590 001, Karnataka.

Intellectual property shares many of the features associated with real and personal property. IP is an asset which can purchased, sold, exchanged or gratuitously given away like any other form of property. Further, the IP owner has the *right to prevent* the unauthorized use or sale of the property. It distinguishes itself from other forms of property in that it is *intangible* and therefore cannot be defined or identified by its own physical parameters. [Mascus, K.E., 1998].

IPR deals with the following knowledge activities: creating, generating and accessing, trading and applying knowledge. IPR promotes synergy between industrial production, human resources and research resources.

IPR-WORLD SITUATION

The difference in the relevant laws in different countries complicates the legal issues which arise at each of the four stages in the *IP life cycle viz., creating, protecting, utilizing, and enforcing* the intellectual property. This has necessitated the establishment of global standardization of IP laws. Further, the development of new areas within IP tests the flexibility of old rules necessitating new ones. The WTO and the World Intellectual Property Organization (WIPO) and other international bodies are working towards *global standards in IP laws* and ensuring the same by *appropriate changes in the national laws.*

The important aspects of IPR are built into WTO through TRIPS (Trade Related Intellectual Property Rights). TRIPS lays down the following: 1] rules for granting IPR 2] enforcement of the rights 3] capability building and 4] technology and knowledge sharing.

TRIPS Agreement provides norms and standards in respect of: 1] copyrights and related rights e.g. story, poem, film, musical record, 2] trademarks e.g. name, word etc. 3] geographical indications e.g. made in India 4] industrial designs e.g. lathe machine 5] layout designs of integrated circuits e.g. SSI, MSI 6] protection of undisclosed information [trade secrets] e.g. formula, process 7] patents and 8] plant varieties.

The technology generation and innovative activities are highly concentrated in few developed countries. Just 10 countries account fro the major technological activity in the world and account for 84% of resources spent on R & D annually and they control 94% of technological output in terms of patents taken out in the U.S., and receive 91% of global cross royalties and technology license fees. The control over technology is reflected in their 74% share of global outflows. The strengthening of IPR regime will benefit only these countries. However, in recent years, countries like Taiwan, South Korea, Israel, Hong Kong, South Africa and India have started obtaining U.S. patents in increasing numbers. [Thompson, 1996].

IPR – INDIA'S POSITION

The Indian Patents Act of 1970 continued to govern the IPR regime in India over the past 30 years except for the recent amendments brought to provide exclusive marketing rights (EMRs) in tune with India's obligations under WTO's TRIPS Agreement. India joined the Paris Convention and the Patent Co-operation Treaty only in 1999.

The Patenting process in India is a lengthy one. Any invention that fulfils the pre-requisites viz., novelty, inventiveness (non-obviousness) and usefulness is eligible for grant of a patent. Patents along with designs and trademarks are controlled by the Controller General of Patents, Designs and Trade Marks (CGPDTM) Mumbai, under the Ministry of Industries. The patents can filed at one of the branches of the Patent Office in 4 regions i.e. the Head Office at Kolkata, or the Regional Branches at Chennai, Mumbai and New Delhi. The Indian Patent Act of 1970 specifies that residents of India have to first apply for a patent in India and must then for six weeks before filing a corresponding patent application in any foreign country (Subramanian, A. 1999]. It takes six years to complete the processing of patents in our country, where as in USA it takes one to one and a half years to get a patent. The Head Office is located in New Delhi and there are 40 patent branch offices in different parts of the country. At present, the pending applications for patents are about 20-25 thousands. With just fourty patent branch offices, a maximum of three thousand applications could be cleared annually.

The most important research organization which leads the Indian patenting process is the Council of Scientific and Industrial Research (CSIR), New Delhi. It is the world's largest publicly funded R & D organization, having a chain of 40 world class R & D establishments with field stations. These centers are manned by 10,000 highly qualified scientists and engineers with 13,000 auxiliary staff. Its patrons and partners hail from 50 countries with annual turnover of about US $ 83 million. The following table shows the post WTO patenting by CSIR:

Table 1
Post WTO Patenting by Council of Scientific and Industrial Research

Year	*Indian – Patent*	*Foreign – Patent*
1996–1997	92	15
1997–1998	155	24
1998–1999	134	38
1999–2000	112	35

Source: Council of Scientific and Industrial Research, New Delhi.

The CSIR has initiated an aggressive programme. But the Industries and Academic Institutions are yet to take off. CSIR now stands at No. 2 position in patent applications (89 as against 921 of China).

In the Post–WTO scenario of the world and India, a student of modern law is going to be none but a corporate lawyer.

Corporate companies having spent huge amount of capital on R & D must own all the works created by their employees and independent contractors. Only then, the company can take full and complete licenses in capitalizing on such intellectual property. To accomplish this, it is necessary for the companies to understand the regulations pertaining to "what can be protected and how?" within their respective countries. Further, the companies must obtain signed (legally binding) agreements from all the employees and outside consultants, assigning any and all such IP rights to the company.

To seek the protection of the IP, the company must be aware of the different national IP laws. The company must weigh the potential value of an IP right against the probability of realizing that value and the costs involved in securing, enforcing and maintaining that right for a defined period of time frame. There are no hard and fast rules which determine the potential value of a given IP right. Because, what is valuable to one individual or company may be worthless to another. However, there are certain obvious factors which contribute to the potential value of IP including the potential value of exclusive or other rights, assignments or licenses or cross-licenses, enforcements against in fringers, and as collateral for securing financing.

IP deals with the prevention of others from unauthorized use and exploitation of the protected property. IP may be misappropriated in many ways. The IP law must ensure both civil remedies and criminal sanctions, if warranted, to ensure appropriate punishment and deterrence from the wrongful activity.

The scope and definition of Intellectual Property is constantly changing with the inclusion of new areas under the gambit of Intellectual Property. WTO, WIPO and other international bodies have recognized the need for global standards in Intellectual Property Laws and therefore, they are working towards ensuring the same. [McCalman, Philips. 1999].

IP related laws cannot remain static in a world where economic development is becoming increasingly technology-based. IP laws are going to be more stringent and stricter in the days to come, offering more opportunities and challenges. Companies hoping to compete will need to be aware of the legal issues and policies relating to IP in each country in which they will potentially claim IP protection.

Regulation of IP rights gives inventors, scientists, writers, artists, business persons and others enforceable property rights in their creations and makes it possible for creators to recoup their investment in the creative process, encourage them to devote their time and efforts for developing new works, products and services. [May, Christopher, 2000].

CONCLUSION

Though India, an economically developing country, as far as Intellectual Capital is concerned, it is treated as a developed country world over. It is a recognized fact that the best Intellectual Capital is available in India. Few examples are: More than 15% of Pharmaceutical R & D scientists in the US are of Indian origin, Majority of the Scientists in the US Defence Research Establishments are Indians, the entire Health System of UK is controlled by Indians. [Fikkert, Brian. 1993].

Hence, the most pertinent dilemma facing us is that why we are lagging behind? The most important reasons seem to be: 1] the slow of liberalisation 2] vast bureaucracy yet controlling everything even after two and half decades of economic reforms 3] poor quality of patent awareness among the Indian entrepreneurs 4] patent illiteracy even among the educated representatives of the people and 5] the lack of transparency in governance.

The plausible reply to the question raised in the preceding paragraph lies in: 1] faster liberalisation process 2] speedy privatisation of all economic activities except the most important aspects of social sector 3] launching WTO awareness campaign even at the grass root level 4] creation of strong and vigorous R&D activity in the industrial sector 5] imbibing the spirit of competition with quality and 6] the sense of national pride.

REFERENCES

Chartrand, H.H., (1995), "Intellectual Property in the Global Village", *Government Information in Canada,*Vol. 1, No. 4.

Fikkert, Brian, (1993), "An Open and Closed Technology Policy? The Effects of Technology Licensing, Foreign Direct Investment and Technology Spillovers on R & D in Indian Industrial Sector Firms", *PhD. Dissertation,* Yale University.

Guifang Yang, KPMG, Atlanta and K.E. Maskus, (2003), "Intellectual Property Rights, Licensing and Innovation", *World Bank Policy Research Working Paper,* 2973.

Mascus, Keith E., (1998), "The International Regulation of Intellectual Property" *Welwirtschaftliches Archiv,* 134 (2).

May Christopher, (2000), "A Global Political Economy of Intellectual Property Rights: The New Enclosures"? London and New York, Routledge.

McCalman, Philips, (1999), "Reaping What You Sow: An Empirical Analysis of International Patent Harmonization". *Journal of International Economics*, 55.

Steve Pike, Anna Rylander and Goran Roos, (1977), "Intellectual Capital Management", *CMA, Canada*, Vol. 12, December.

Subramanian, A., (1999), "India as User and Creator of Intellectual Property: The Challenges Post Seattle", *Paper presented at a Conference, WTO 2000*, The World Bank, New Delhi.

Sveiby, (2000), "Knowledge Management the Viking Way", *www. sviby.com.*

Thompson, Mark A. and Rushing Francis W., (1996), "An Empirical Analysis of the Impact of Patent Protection on Economic Growth", *Journal of Economic Development* 21 (2), December.

INDIA AND WTO: WHAT INDIA SHOULD DO?

*P.L. Sablok and Geetanjali Sharma**

On January 1, 1995, just after the most comprehensive but the most contentious GATT trade round was concluded, the first and the most powerful world trade regulating agency, named, World Trade Organization (WTO) came into existence[1]. India is one of its 132 founding members. The WTO is the umbrella organization responsible for overseeing the implementation of all agreements that have been negotiated just before it came into existence or those that will be negotiated in future. The WTO is expected to provide a forum for further negotiations on matters already covered by the agreements as well as new issues. It is also responsible for settlement of disputes among its members. Finally, periodic review of the trade policies would also be initiated under the auspices of WTO.

Before the WTO came into existence, until 1994[2], international trade in merchandise was guided by the rules and provisions of the General Agreement on Tariffs and Trade (GATT). The GATT rules, however, did not work effectively to absorb the complexities of world trade which had been growing steadily since the Bretton Woods days, both in terms of commodity coverage and the nature of regulators applied by the regional trade blocks and "big players of the trade game". Moreover, the GATT umbrella did not cover trade in services which was assuming extreme significance to a number of countries, partly because transnationalization of finance and capital was increasing under global restructuring of commodity production, and partly because the expanding volume of merchandise necessitated a larger to and fro flow

* School of Studies in Economics, Jiwaji University, Gwalior.

of trade in services. Agriculture too was outside the GATT purview[3].

It was thus natural that in the most intense 8-year long pre-WTO Uruguay Round, ending towards the end of 1994, the world economic community was called upon to take a very comprehensive view of trade and trade-related issues and to devise an equally comprehensive package of trade practices, rules and instrumentalities to be adhered to by the trading partners, to obviate unfair trade practices. On a broad plane, WTO had thus to encompass international trade in goods (including agricultural, commodities), services and Trade Related Aspects of Intellectual Property Rights (TRIPs)[4]. Gradually, the canvas of WTO negotiations expanded. In the 1999 Seattle Ministerial Conference, non-trade issues, most ostensibly those connected with environment, child labour and labour standards, were also raised, mostly by the developed western economies and the USA. In essence, such non-trade issues would make the concept of *market access* melt before its moreretrograde counterpart of *effective market access*. More issues, and a continuing review of the existing ones, e.g. Agriculture, Textiles, TRIPs, etc., are likely to come up in future. The political economy of such negotiations and reviews is bound to impose many new stresses, challenges and adjustment compromises on the developing world.

The most avowed goal of the WTO, as set out in the promoting documents, is to create a fair and equitable, rule-based multilateral trade system. The most appealing aspect is that the new multilateral trade regime would be transparent and nondiscriminatory. For the world trading community as a whole, every initiative on trade liberalization should ensure rewards in the form of large and expanding markets, and greater trade flows for all participating members. All quantitative restrictions (e.g. quotas, mandatory import licensing, other forms of restrictions, etc.) would be replaced by tariff, so as to make the process more transparent and open to international public scrutiny; all reductions and adjustments in tariffs would be effected through negotiations and are to be notified to the WTO. Most importantly, such reduced tariffs are to be compulsorily bound, by each member country, against subsequent increases. Then, all kinds of subsidies would be reduced/eliminated in due course, most substantially by the developed economies, so that the developing economies, under their sheer comparative cost advantage, could gain larger access to the markets in the developed world and so on.

Before we over to challanges of the WTO system, it is essential to make a note of the **overall guiding principles** that would govern the flow of international trade. The two most significant principles, ostensibly highly assuring to the so-called weak partners (developing and the least developed economies) are the Most Favoured Nation (MEN) Principle and the National Treatment clause[5]. Under the former, no discrimination is to be exercised among member countries, any trade concession offered by one member to another must be offered to all members. Under the later, imported products and domestic products are to be accorded the same treatment; moreover, besides import duty, no extra tax other than ones also levied on domestic products is to be imposed. Then, the multilateral trade system must be **predictable** foreign companies, investors and governments must feel assured that trade barriers (including tariffs, non-tariff barriers and other measures) would not be raised arbitrarily by any trading partner. Lastly, the new trade regime should work to a **greater advantage of the less developed countries**[6], they must be given more time to adjust, greater flexibility and some special privileges. In overall terms, it would appear that for the developing economies, the incentive to join the multilateral trade system would be no less justified than for the developed world. Jumping into international trade arena would look too good to ignore.

Let us now briefly look at some of the agreements. On a broad plane, the canvas of WTO agreements is spread over three compartments: goods, services and intellectual property rights. First, **Trade in goods**[7] of all descriptions (agricultural, industrial or others) is to be governed under GATT re-formulations. Second, **Trade in Services**[8] of all kinds (e.g.

business services including professional and computer, communication; construction and engineering; distribution, educational and environmental services; financial services (banking and insurance); health services; tourism and travel services; recreational, cultural and sporting services; transport services, and consultancy) is to be regulated under General Agreement on Trade in Services (**GATS**)[9]. Trade in services, thus, encompasses practically all varieties of services in use the world over (e.g. service supplied from one country to another such as telephone calls, or consumers making use of service in another country, such as tourism, or a foreign company setting up a subsidiary or branch such as a foreign bank, or individuals working abroad on a service contract such as Indian software professionals in USA and so on). Third, Trade Related Aspects of Intellectual Property Rights (**TRIPs**)[10] would set out the terms and conditions for the international flow of intellectual property. While GATT and GATs are based on three-part structures (namely, general principles, associate agreements on specific sectors/issues, and commitment of individual members), the TRIPS agreement contains only general principles expected to be followed by member countries.

WHAT INDIA SHOULD DO?

The previous section has given a brief profile of the historical background and overall guiding principles which have emerged in the new trading system under WTO. In this section we present a synoptic account of the approach that India needs to adopt in dealing with the challenges and the opportunities of the WTO System.

1. **Intensive Preparedness:** The most important failure of India in the context of the WTO system is that of preparedness for negotiations. Inadequacy of preparedness has been quite in evidence both in the context of Uruguay Round and the various Ministerial review meetings held thereafter in Singapore, Geneva and Seattle. Preparation for negotiation requires three basic things: (i) clarity in our perceptions regarding our goals and development

strategies. (ii) clarity in regard to the mapping of the strategic options available with us and the identification of bargaining points and negotiation strategies, and (iii) effective co-ordination with like minded countries and the negotiators, both in the developing and the developed world. It may be unfair if we pronounce that India has been failing on all three accounts in the various stages of negotiations in the past. There have been occasional strides of significant and successful initiatives in all these three aspects of the process of preparedness. However, lack of consistency in the pursuit of our efforts towards the logical conclusion of the process of negotiations has often caused us very heavily in terms of final achievements. Obviously, the process of preparedness requires high level of professional expertise with analytical and practical wisdom. There has to be a national debate on all the issues of negotiations and intensive research studies need to be launched on the various issues of negotiations well in advance of the launching of the negotiations process. There has to be a close nexus between the negotiators of the government on the one hand and industry and business circles, and academic and research bodies, on the other.

In India general awareness about the different Agreements of WTO, their implications, and knowledge about the new issues that are likely to come up in the various review meetings, are extremely poor and inadequate. The government machinery is often scary of throwing the issues for public debate on the apprehension that this may create embarrassment to the negotiating strategy to be adopted by the government negotiators. Unfortunately, it is not recognised that a widespread debate on the issues of negotiations and increasing awareness about the emerging challenges and opportunities would be useful to the government negotiators in acquiring greater clarity in the identification of the options open to them. In short, the first and the foremost thing that India should do is to strengthen the process of preparedness for the various issues of negotiations that continue to come forward in the WTO fora. The intensification of preparedness is also applicable to the forthcoming review meetings on Agriculture, Textiles, TRIPs and TRIMs.[11]

2. **Adopting an Integrated Approach of Implementation:** India, as a signatory to the WTO, has to honour its commitment and that too in right time. With a broad review of the pace at which implementation of the commitment is taking place, one would feel that we have not worked out an integrated programme of the implementation of our commitment in WTO. In fact, one should state that there has been a highly lop-sided framework of implementation of our commitments. In regard to our import liberalisation for increasing market access in our economy, we have reduced our tariff rates to a much greater extent that was warranted. This has implied a sudden exposure of domestic industry and agriculture to a big international competition. We have also not worked suitable tariff equivalents in cases of QR removal. The contours of integrated approach for implementation imply the following: (i) Take steps to strengthen the competitive capability of the domestic industry, trade and agriculture by providing suitable infrastructural support and incentives for inducting technological change and managerial efficiency. (ii) Free the domestic economic entities from the unwarranted domestic state interventions before exposing them to international competition. (iii) Adopt the policies of liberalisation and globalisation in a phased manner so that the domestic economic agents are able to compete with the outside entities on a level playing field.[12] An integrated approach to the tast of implementing our commitments under WTO would enable us to take advantage of the emerging opportunities of trade and minimising the adverse effects of threats of open competition from the more powerful entities from abroad.
3. **Strengthening the Agricultural Sector:** The agreement on Agriculture provides for new opportunities for increased trade in agriculture. However, ability to take advantage of these opportunities would depend upon the structural

strength of the agricultural sector. Unfortunately, in the emerging liberalised and globalised environment the domestic agricultural sector is becoming weaker and getting further marginalised. With the decline in the infrastructural investment by the state and with the withdrawal of various types of domestic incentives and also with the increased threat of dumping of agricultural goods in the liberalised framework, there is every danger of our agricultural sector shrinking further, thereby generating and further aggravating the huge problems of property, unemployment and rural deprivation. It is also worth recognising that despite the commitment to reduce subsidies, the countries in EU are continuing their agricultural subsidy programme, in some form or the other: Recent studies have demonstrated that EU countries are increasingly adopting the Green Box Measures of the Agreement which are exempted from the subsidy reduction commitments. In this background, continued increase in the exposure of domestic agriculture to international unfair competition would imply considerable damage to the domestic agricultural sector. It is, therefore, necessary that an integrated strategy for the agricultural sector is adopted in the context of the new trading system.[13]

4. **Prepare a Long-term Textile Strategy:** Textile sector is the most crucial sector of the Indian economy - almost next to the agricultural sector. Unfortunately, its importance is not well recognised either in the industrial circles or in the policy circles. It has the potential of remaining as the lead sector for income generation and employment creation. Skill-requirements of the sector are not very high. In recent years, however, the textile sector is shrinking in size and getting more and more marginalised. The Challenges of the textile sector would be immense in the post-MFA scenario in the first decade of the present new century. Unfortunately, there is no well-co-ordinated integrated national textile strategy to foster the competitive strength of the textile sector in the highly competitive quota-free international market system in the post-MFA period.

Textiles sector is in urgent need of modernisation technical change, restructuring and financial support. Facilities for training and retraining the labour for new more skilled job profiles need to be strengthened. Presently, the textile industry, both in the public sector and in the private sector, is in the deep mode of sickness and slackness. National Textile Corporation has failed to revive the sick units. We should not discard this sector as a sector to be phased out-as is being advocated by some market fundamentalists. A multi-pronged national textile strategy needs to be worked out keeping in view the long-term potential of this sector. In the WTO fora, all textile-producing and exporting countries of the developing world should join hands in for enforcing the early termination of the MFA system and for evolution of a rule-based global textile-restructuring programme.[14]

5. **Strengthen the Institutional Basis of the IPR Regime:** As per the commitment under the TRIPs agreement, India is all set to move towards a comprehensive IPR regime with product-patent system, and a rigorous copy-right-enforcement framework. The issues of widening the scope of patentable matter, protection and promotion of bio-diversity, protecting the farmers rights as against the plant breeders rights, etc. would continue to figure prominently at the national and the international fora. We need to develop greater clarity in regard to the identification of our long-term interests without creating large damages for the short-term ones. In this context, one important initiative that needs to be launched without further delay is that of strengthening our institutional facility for patent registration, copy-right protection and legal processes of dispute settlement. It is learnt that China has established a facility under one roof for dealing with all the aspects of the IPR regime. In contrast to this, our patent registration system is cumbersome. There is no R & D activity with linkages with industrial applications and patenting facilitation. Our music and entertainment industry can earn huge amounts of foreign exchange if our copy right regime

is tightened. We have not mapped our bio-diversity resources properly and inventory on the profile of community knowledge sector is non-existent. We need to invest more in bio-technology research to make it a lead sector of global strength. We have already opted for the option of Exclusive Marketing Rights (EMR route), in the transition period of moving towards Product Patent System in the case of pharmaceutical and agro-chemicals. We have, however, not tightened our internal systems for ensuring fair place to domestic producers and traders of these products. Our investment on R&D activity as a proportion of GDP, is one of the lowest in the world. Since technology would be the prime engine of growth and competitiveness in the coming years, a sound national technology promotion policy-both at the governmental and corporate levels-is called for.

6. **Foster the Health of the Domestic Banking and Insurance Sector:** In the midst of liberalisation of the services sector, the domestic banking and insurance sector is likely to be the worst affected sector. The domestic banking sector is burdened with many obligations and stipulations imposed on it under the framework of nationalisation and social banking. The entry of the foreign banks and the new private banks, that are not subjected to these obligations and stipulations, is bound to adversely affect the domestic banking industry which has served so well the national cause of mobilisation of domestic savings, from the far and wide corners of India, and that of intermediation for the diverse investment needs. Financial sector reforms need to be carefully nurtured, on the basis of the wisdom contained in the various expert committee reports. In the same manner, strategies of privatisation and globalisation of the insurance sector need to be pursued in an integrated manner in such a way that the indigenous industry-which has served the economy so well in the past - does not get wiped out in one stroke of policy.

7. **Strengthen the Institution for Antidumping Measures & Competition Policy:** Whatever be the noble intentions of

the WTO system, tendencies for the adoption of unfair business practices -such as dumping, anti-competition methods-are bound to flourish even in the new rule-based system. The WTO agreement on dumping and antidumping measures stipulates a rigorous framework for dealing with the problem of dumping. It is envisaged that antidumping measures can be initiated only when: (i) existence of dumping is identified; (ii) injury to industry is measured and; (iii) causal link between dumping and industrial injury is established. All these three steps require strong technical and analytical support from technologists, chartered accountants, industrial and marketing consultants, researchers and policy-makers. Where do we have such an integrated institutional framework for monitoring the dumping cases well in advance of the actual dumping and for identifying suitable antidumping measures well before the damage is done? It is learnt that in the USA, there is a strong contingent of several hundred experts whose job is only that of monitoring of dumping cases and recommending antidumping measures. Many of our market fundamentalists are confusing our policy makers by arguing that adoption of anti-dumping measures is market-distortionary. Many mistake the dumping situations as a reflection of inefficiency of our domestic industry and open their eyes late in the day when initial dumping has captured huge market-share at the cost of our domestic producers. China is well adept in this game of dumping and capturing market share. The pertinent point here is that we should establish a strong contingent of experts as well as an institution with a legal authority for not only monitoring the dumping cases but also for initiating antidumping measures, as per the provisions of the WTO Agreements.[15]

8. **Strengthen the Legal Expertise:** All the WTO agreements envisage close nexus between law and economics. Legal legislation and legal enforcement are an integral part of the WTO system. Legal battles will have to be fought not only at the national level but also in the courts of foreign

countries and in the international courts-often at huge costs which our poor domestic economic entities cannot often afford. It is well known that in recent times many patent disputes-neem, basmati rice, etc. and dumping cases had to be fought in the courts of the USA, at huge costs of resources. We should recognise that the level of expertise on WTO issues in our legal profession is rather very poor. WTO needs to be introduced as a subject in all our Law Institutes and also in our post-graduate economics curriculum. Consultancy organisations specialised in WTO matters need to be established and linkages with similar institutions in other countries need to be encouraged. There may be an urgent need for creating a national pool of legal and professional experts on WTO matters. Since the costs of dealing with the WTO matters is bound to remain very high, there is a case for setting up a national WTO legal Fund which could extend financial support to the litigants at a highly concessional rate of interest. Some select banks could be earmarked to set up soft-loan windows for financing WTO related legal dispute cases. In short, some innovative approaches are required to deal with this most crucial aspect of the challenges posed by the WTO system for India.

REFERENCES

WTO Report-Global Trade, WTO, 1995, p. 1.

WTO Report, ibid., p. 2.

WTO Report, ibid., p. 19.

Anderson K. The Greening of World Trade Issues, 1999, p. 51.

Anderson K. ibid., p. 65.

Anderson, K. ibid., p. 73.

WTO Trade Policy Review, WTO, 2001, p. 123.

WTO Trade Policy Review, ibid., 125.

WTO Trade Policy Review, ibid., 128.

WTO Trade Policy Review, ibid., 130.

Reddy, C.R., "WTO Stirs Again", The Hindu, May 11, 2000.

Gulati, A. and Kelly, Tim, (1999), "Trade Liberalization and Agriculture", Oxford University Press, 1999. p. 33.

Gulati, A., ibid., p. 57.

Panchmukhi, V.R., "Trade, Technology and Employment: Profile of Sustematic Dilemmas and Paradoxes" *Indian Journal of Labour Economics*, Vol. 34, No. 1, p. 63, Jan.-March 2000.

Panchmukhi, V.R., ibid, p. 77.

WTO AND INDIA: COMMITMENTS AND IMPACTS

H.H. Uliveppa and D.R. Alabal***

INTRODUCTION

In recent times, no other issue has generated so much heat than the likely repercussions of the New International Economic Order on world economy in general and developing countries in particular. According to the supporters, the Uruguay Round Agreement, the Marrakesh Declaration, and the ultimate setting up of the World Trade Organisation (WTO) are expected to bring about substantial gains in world trade and increased income from liberalisation, improved market access and greater export opportunities, besides greater predictability of the trading environment. The Government of India has also been harping on this tune. However, critics have pointed out that the entire negotiation process was ruthlessly dominated by the developed countries (particularly the USA) and the results that have emerged in the form of various WTO Agreements are highly tilted in their favour. The poor countries operated in the periphery, seldom consulted until the rich ones had completed negotiations among themselves. As noted by Kevin Watkins, "whatever the skills of negotiators from the south, for the most part they are like extras on the GATT stage: the show cannot go on without them, but nobody is remotely interested in what they have to say;" (Biplab Dasgupta–1998). In India, the last few years have seen much talk of globalisation, economic liberalisation and global integration. The completion

* Reader, Department of Economics, Karnatak University KRC-PG Centre, Belgaum - 591156.

** Faculty, Department of Sociology, Karnatak University KRC-PG Centre, Belgaum - 591156.

of the Uruguay Round of trade negotiations in April 1994, and the establishment of the WTO in January 1995, has further raised many issues regarding India's participation in trade in future, its integration with the world economy and the likely costs and benefits from this integration.

In principle, the more provincial question of national interest becomes irrelevant in the era of globalisation. This holds good only when domestic economic interests are not affected adversely by the globalisation. But in this age of neo-liberalism, when nation-states all over the world under the tutelage of the IMF, the World Bank and the WTO, are being forced to withdraw from their respective economies, it is not incongruous to think of national economic interests to safeguard their individual domestic interests.

Why is the question of India's 'national interest' so important especially in its relation with the WTO ? There are two reasons: viz. (i) firstly, because, the WTO has emerged as the world's most powerful trading authority. It has been invested with quite extensive authority along with powers of sanction against erring nations; features that its earlier predecessor called GATT lacked. The rules of international trade have, for the very first time, been significantly altered with the creation of the WTO. There is now a new and clear set of 'binding' rules for all its 147 member countries. The stress is on 'binding' because the final decision of the Dispute Resolution Board, a board whose task is to settle trade disputes between member countries, must be accepted by the disputants or they will face WTO endorsed sanctions. This is a very significant development as it dramatically increases the power of enforcement given to the WTO.

(ii) Secondly, because there is, at the core of the WTO, an 'asymmetry' with respect to the trading interests of third world nations like India and first world nations like the USA. In other words, the set of interests articulated by the third world countries are different from those of first world countries. The first world countries see the WTO chiefly as a vehicle for further enhancing and consolidating their global competitive edge. The third world countries, however, see the WTO more as a vehicle for helping to create rapid industrial development. They expect the WTO could facilitate favourable western investments and thus aid them in their efforts to succeed in their export-driven industrialisation. This asymmetry of interests between the first and third worlds has become the very bone of contention for future trade relations.

WTO has become a vehicle par excellence of a western dominated globalisation. It has become a jaw and teeth of international trade. Along with its two sisters, the World Bank and the IMF, it cajoles, persuades and sometimes threatens its member countries into accepting the demands of a new form of market driven liberalism (referred to as neo-liberalism) that is sweeping the world. The WTO, ten years into its founding, has acquired epical significance and very ambitious intentions. It has a sum total 15 separate areas of negotiations with 60 agreements in all. The trade areas are divided into 2 tracks : a GNG – Group of Negotiations on Goods; and GNS – Group of Negotiation on Services. Some of the key subjects in the WTO include Agriculture, Sanitary and Phyto-Sanitary Measures, Textile and Clothing, Anti-Dumping Measures, Trade in Services, Trade in Goods, Trade Related Intellectual Property Rights (TRIPs), Trade Related Investment Measures (TRIMs), Dispute Settlement Understanding.

The WTO basically seeks to bind and unify the world under its trading banner. Such binding will lead to dramatic restructuring of old economic relations within nations and thus create considerable churning. The more rapid, that is destructive or otherwise, is the pace of globalisation, the more troubling and unanswered are the questions. The symptoms of such angst and anxiety were clearly witnessed in the large scale street protests leading up to the WTO trade talks at Seattle during November 1999 and the Doha declaration-during November 2001. In this paper, an attempt is made, first of all to highlight the commitments made by the Government of India to the WTO, and then assessed the likely favourable and unfavourable effects of the new world economic order on the Indian economy i.e. now integration of the Indian economy into the global economy is likely to affect us which is nothing but the impact of WTO on India in brief.

INDIA'S COMMITMENTS TO WTO

(i) **Tariff Lines:** India, as a member of the WTO, has bound to 67 per cent of its tariff lines whereas only 6 per cent of the tariff lines were bound prior to the Uruguay Round. For non-agricultural goods, with a few exceptions, ceiling bindings of 40 per cent *advalorem* on finished goods and 25 per cent on intermediate goods, machinery and equipment have been undertaken. The phased reduction to these bound levels is being undertaken over the period from 1995 to 2005. In textiles, where reduction will be achieved over a period of 10 years, India has reserved the right to revert to duty levels prevailing in 1990; if the integration process, envisaged under the Agreement on Textiles and Clothing does not materialise in full or is delayed. Under the Agreement on Agriculture, except for a few items, India's bound rate ranges from 100 to 300 per cent and no commitments have been made regarding market access, reduction of subsidies or tariffs.

(ii) **Quantitative Restrictions (QRs):** QRs on imports maintained on B.O.P grounds were notified to WTO in 1997 for 2714 tariff lines at the eight digit level. In view of the improvements in India's B.O.P., the Committee on B.O.P. Restrictions had asked India for a phase out for the QRs. Based on presentations before this committee and subsequent consultations with main trading partners, India reached an agreement with these countries, except USA, to phase out the QRs over a period of six years beginning from 1997. But the USA preferred a dispute under the WTO's Dispute Settlement Mechanism. The Dispute Settlement Panel and the Appellate Body ruled in favour of USA and against India. As a result, India was required to phase out QRs in a period of less than six years; and hence the agreement was reached between USA and India which envisaged the phasing out of all QRs by India by April 1, 2001. Accordingly, India removed QRs on 714 items in the Exim policy announced on March 31, 2000 and on the remaining 715 items in the Exim policy announced on 31st March 2001. By their ruling against India, the Disputes Settlement Panel and the Appellate Body have overruled the decision of the committee on B.O.P. According to Biswajit Dhar (1999), this brings into clear focus the fact that the supposedly democratic structure of the WTO which operates through the various committees comprising of the member states can be undermined by the Disputes Settlement Panel. The experts, who adjudicate the disputes between the WTO member states, can even disregard the institutional basis of the organization while passing their judgments.

(iii) **TRIPs:** Following the complaints made by the USA and the European Union that India had failed to meet its commitments under Article 70.8 (requiring the setting up of the Mail Box System) and Article 70.9 (granting of Exclusive Marketing Rights), the ruling of two WTO Dispute Settlement Panels made it obligatory for the Government of India to make appropriate amendments to the Patents Act, 1970 by April 19, 1999. Accordingly, the Patents (Amendment) Act, 1999 was passed by the Parliament in March 1999 to provide for Exclusive Marketing Rights, and again was followed by the adoption of Patents (Amendment) Act, 2002, in May 2002. In respect of plant varieties, a decision has been taken to put in a place a *sui generis system* as it is perceived to be in our national interest. Regarding copyrights and related rights, the Copyright Act 1957 as amended in 1994 takes care of our interest and meets the requirements of the TRIPs Agreements except in the case of terms of protection of performers' rights. A bill to increase this term to 50 years was passed by parliament in December, 1999. In respect of lay-out designs, a legislation giving protection to them was introduced in the Rajya Sabha on December 20,1999 by the Department of Electronics. In the field of trade marks, the Trade and Merchandise Marks Act (TMMA), 1958 is in its essential features, in accordance with international law. A Bill passed by the Parliament in December, 1999 provides for protection to service marks. For geographic indications, there is specific law in India for this purpose. Case law, however, enables legal action for protection of geographical indications. The Government of India decided to enact a new law on the subject to take advantage of the provisions of the TRIPs Agreement, and a bill in this regard was passed by the Parliament in December, 1999.

(iv) **TRIMs:** Under the TRIMs Agreement, developing countries had a transition period of 5 years up to December 31, 1999 during which they could continue to maintain measures inconsistent with the Agreement provided these were duly notified. The Government of India notified two TRIMs, viz, that relating to local content requirements in the production of certain pharmaceutical products and dividend balancing requirement in the case of investment in 22 categories of consumer items.

(v) **GATS:** India has made commitments in 33 activities in response to the General Agreement on Trade in Services (GATS). Foreign service providers are allowed to enter these activities. According to the Government of India, the choice of the activities has been guided by considerations of national benefit, viz, the impact on capital inflows, technology and employment.

(vi) **Customs Valuation Rules:** India's Legislation on Customs Valuation Rules, 1998, has been amended to bring it in conformity with the provisions of the WTO Agreement on implementation of Article VIII of GATT, 1994 and the Customs Valuation Agreement.

BENEFITS EXPECTED TO INDIA

(i) Estimates of World Bank, OECD and the GATT Secretariat are such that the income effects of the implementation of the Uruguay Round package will add between 213 and 274 billion U.S. dollars annually to world income. As per the estimate of the GATT Secretariat, the overall trade impact is that the level of merchandise trade in goods will be higher by 745 billion U.S. dollars in the year 2005, than it would otherwise had been; and that the largest increase will be in the areas of clothing (60 per cent) , agriculture, forestry and fishery products (20 per cent) and processed food and beverages (19 per cent). According to the Government of India, since our country's existing and potential export competitiveness lies in these product groups, it is logical to believe that India will get large gains in these sectors. The Government believes that the trade gains may conservatively be placed at 2.7 billion U.S. dollars extra exports per annum assuming that India's market share in world exports improves from 0.5 per cent to 1 per cent, and that we are able to take advantage of the opportunities thus created. A more generous estimate ranged from 3.5 to 7 billion U.S. dollars per year (Govt. of India, Economic Survey 1994-95, P. 99).

(ii) Further expected that the phasing out of the MFA (Multi-Fibre Agreement) by 2005 will benefit India as the exports of textiles and clothings will increase. India estimated that more than one-third of its WTO benefits to accrue from the new Agreement on Textiles and Clothing (ATC) that replaced the MFA. While the developed countries had demanded a 15 year period, the developing countries including India had insisted on a 10 year period. The developing countries' demand in the Uruguay Round has been enthusiastically accepted by the developed countries. But the phasing out schedule favoured the developed countries as a major proportion of the quota regime to the extent of 49 per cent is going to be removed only during the tenth year i.e. by 2005, and hence it has not provided an immediate market access for the third world textiles exports. Because by the time the MFA is completely phased out in 10 years, the developed countries could gear themselves to effect improvement in quality, efficiency and competitiveness; and strengthen their textile industry in the phase out period. Further, when quotas are removed, they will be eliminated not only for India, but for everyone else. There will, therefore, be considerable competition from China, Vietnam, Pakistan, Bangladesh, Indonesia and Malaysia. So the question of India's benefit is basically depending upon improvement in the competitiveness of India's garment exports. In this respect, India should do farewell vis-à-vis its competitors by removing supply side constraints like higher costs and prices, poor quality and unreliability of the end-products. (Bibek Debroy, 1996, PP.80-84).

(iii) The third benefit that India expects relates to the improved prospects for agricultural exports as a result of likely increase in the world prices of agricultural products due to reduction in domestic subsidies and barriers to trade. While on the one hand earnings from agricultural exports are likely to increase, on the other hand India has ensured that all major programmes for the development of agriculture will be exempted from the disciplines in the agricultural Agreement. Thus, the operation of the public distribution system will not be affected by the provisions of the Agreement; agricultural subsidies granted by developing countries need not be withdrawn till such time they remain within the prescribed limits specified in the Agreement; and protection necessary for developing the agricultural sector in the underdeveloped countries might be continued. In fact, as stated above, India hopes that the reduction of subsidies in the USA and the European community will enable it to increase its earnings from agricultural exports.

(iv) Further more, India expected the benefits on the ground that the Uruguay Round Agreement has strengthened multilateral rules and disciplines. The most important of these relate to anti-dumping, subsidies and countervailing measures, safeguards, and disputes settlement. This is likely to ensure greater security and predictability of the international trading system; and thus create a more favourable environment for India in the New World Economic Order.

WTO AGREEMENTS: UN-FAVOURABLE IMPACTS ON INDIAN ECONOMY:

India believed that by joining WTO will increase the volume of trade substantially and as a result, India's export earnings will expand considerably. However, a careful analysis of the impact of WTO on India shows that the estimates of quantitative gains by India are suspect and projections may well prove wrong. There are meagre prospects of increase in agricultural exports from India due to the very limited extent of agricultural liberalisation. Moreover, there will hardly be any liberalisation of our textile exports till 2005, with most of the liberalisation expected to come at the end of this period. The gains expected by the Government of India on account of tariff reductions on goods may also not materialise as the number of goods of export interest to India is very small. Not only this, "there will be erosion of the preferences enjoyed by India, and India will most probably be graduated out of the generalised system of preferences (GSP)"; (Muchkund Dubey, 1996, PP. 12-13). The most serious unfavorable effects to India are likely to flow from the Agreements pertaining to the TRIPs, TRIMs and Services.

(A) TRIPs: The strong argument in favour of protection of intellectual property rights (patents, copyrights, trademarks etc.) is that it encourages innovation by rewarding the inventors with the grant of monopoly rights over the commercial exploitations of their inventions for a specified period. However, the efforts made under the Uruguay Round to make such protection more stringent under the TRIPs agreement are bound to favour a handful of developed countries; as just 10 countries are accounting for the bulk of all technological activity in the world. The top 10 countries account for as much as 84 per cent of global resources spent on R and D activity annually, they control 94 per cent of the technological output in terms of patents taken out in the USA, and receive 91 per cent of global cross-border royalties and technology licence fees. It is obviously these countries that are bound to corner most of the benefits flowing from TRIPs Agreement. Moreover, the Agreement itself is highly weighted in favour of the MNCs and the developed countries. Further, it is pointed out that protection of IPRs is, in itself, anti-competition and anti-liberalisation and goes against the spirit of opening up the world economy and global integration, which amounts to 'legalising' the 'monopoly' of MNCs. Thus protection of IPRs is , itself, a barrier to trade. The Agreement on TRIPs is likely to work against India as noted below:

Firstly, the TRIPs Agreement goes against the Patent Act of India, 1970 in almost all important areas. Because: (i) Under the Indian Patent Act only *Process Patents* can be granted in food, chemicals and medicines; whereas, TRIPs Agreement provides for granting *Product Patents* also in all these areas; (ii) Under the TRIPs Agreement methods of agriculture and horticulture and bio-technological process (including living organisms like plants and animals) are patentable, there cannot be any exceptions as under the Indian Act; (iii) TRIPs Agreement provides that the general term of a patent shall be 20 years; but the Indian Patent Act provides for a general term of 14 years for both product as well as process patents. In sectors like food, chemicals and medicines, process patents are granted for a duration of 5 to 7 years; (iv) In India, there are reasonable and effective provisions for the compulsory licensing of patents and also for the revocation of patents in public interest; whereas under TRIPs Agreement, there are no such provisions; (v) Under TRIPs no ceiling can be placed on royalty demanded on patents like in the Indian Patents Act; (vi) Importation will be treated as working of a patent in the TRIPs Agreement, contrary to the patent philosophy in India; and (vii) TRIPs also reverses the burden of proof. Under the Indian legal system, the patentee has to establish a prima facie case that his patent has been infringed. However, under TRIPs the patentee will just have to accuse a person or a company of patent infringement and the person or company will have to prove that he did not infringe the patent.

Secondly, under the Patent Act of 1970 in India, only process patents are granted to drugs and medicines. This means that an Indian company only needs to develop and patent its own process for producing a drug, it is not required to invent the drug itself. The company can then legally manufacture this drug, even if it is protected under a product patent abroad; and finally Indian drug companies are allowed to obtain "licences of right" which allow them to produce, regardless of the process used, inventions (again usually pharmaceuticals) patented abroad. Licences of right can be obtained only 3 years after the original patent is granted. The effects of these laws have been positive for India. Indian drug prices are considered to be among the lowest in the world; and this is not at the expense of quality. In addition, the indigenous pharmaceutical industry has grown rapidly after the passage of the 1970 Act. Not only this, the market share of Indian drug companies in the local drug market has grown from 30 per cent in 1970 to 61 per cent in 1993. Today, India is, infact, an exporter of drugs to other parts of Asia, Europe and even USA. But all this will change in the new order. The granting of product patents will effectively place the reins of the Indian pharmaceutical industry in the hands of MNCs who will exploit this advantage to the full by hiking the prices of drugs and medicines considerably. The range of price increase has been estimated to the extent of more than 240 per cent by different studies; (For eg: A study by Jayashree Watal in 2000 estimated the range of price increase as 242 per cent; and the study by Carsten Fink in 2000 estimated it between 182 to 225 per cent). This suggests that introduction of product patents would affect prices of medicines significantly leading, in turn, to a decline in the health levels of the population. The welfare loss to India consequent upon the introduction of product patents in pharmaceuticals would range between $ 1.4 billion and $ 4.2 billion a year.

Thirdly, the extension of IPRs to agriculture (via the patenting of plant varieties) has serious consequences for India. Plant breeding and seed production in India are largely in the public domain. Plant breeding is undertaken by agricultural universities and units of ICAR, whereas seed multiplication is entrusted to the National and State Seed Corporations; for the sole reason that India being a poor country where agriculture is the livelihood of the majority of the population, the government must bear the responsibility of ensuring the supply of adequate quantities of seeds at reasonable prices to the farmers. The aim is not to maximise profit as would be case in the private sector, but to sustain the livelihood of the majority of the population on the one hand, and to achieve self sufficiency in food grains on the other hand. But patenting of plant varieties will transfer all the gains to the MNCs; and almost all new varieties will belong to MNCs simply by virtue of their massive financial resources. Unfortunately, research is as much a matter of talent as of money. More money means more resources to invest in breeding and it means greater speed in putting varieties on the market. In terms of financial resources, there is absolutely no comparison between MNCs and Indian companies. In fact, the research budgets alone of some of these MNCs are more than the budget of the Indian Union. If Indian research institutions are unable to compete financially and are denied access to patented genetic material as per TRIPs Agreement, the Indian scientists will find it great difficult to breed new varieties; and gradually this will become the sole privilege of the large foreign companies. As a result, the control over our genetic resources will pass into the hands of MNCs who will easily control the seed production in our country. Since control of seed production implies control over food supply, the entire Indian food security system will be jeopardised and thrown out of gear.

Further, under TRIPs, patenting is also extended to the large areas of micro-organisms. Micro-organisms refer to very small forms of life i.e. such living creatures as bacteria, virus, fungus, algae, small plants and animals, and even genes. There are vital economic sectors that are linked to micro-organisms, the most important being agriculture, pharmaceuticals and industrial biotechnology. In the field of agriculture, efforts are on worldwide to develop bio-substitutes based on micro-organisms for chemical fertilizers and pesticides as the latter are not ecologically sustainable and will poison our land and water. In the field of pharmaceuticals, several kinds of drugs are derived from micro-organisms. The patenting of life forms will strike at the very roots of indigenous manufacturing of such drugs. In respect of industrial biotechnology, it is estimated that in the next coming few years, two-third of the global economy would rest on bio-technology since it is the most versatile technology now-a-days. Patents in all these areas linked to micro-organisms are either already with the MNCs of developed countries or are likely to be acquired at a much faster rate vis-à-vis the developing countries. As such, MNCs therefore are likely to dominate the 'global' economy that will emerge in the coming years.

(B) TRIMs: Under TRIMs Agreement, the developed countries achieved almost everything they wanted. In order to make the Agreement balanced from the print of view of the developing countries, it was necessary to formulate international rules for controlling restrictive business practices of foreign investors. However, the TRIMs Agreement is totally silent on this vital question and is concerned mainly with provisions for elimination of trade related investment measures which are designed to protect the interests of foreign investors in the developing countries. Of course, the developing countries are allowed to deviate from the provisions of TRIMs Agreement on B.O.P. grounds. But once there is an improvement in the B.O.P., the host country is required to eliminate the identified measures even if there is justification to maintain them on broader macro-economic and strategic considerations. The provisions of the TRIMs Agreement, when applied to the developing countries, will have adverse effects on any plan or strategy of their self-reliant growth, based on the technology and other resources available locally. They may also cause drain on the foreign exchange reserves of the developing countries, adversely affecting their B.O.Ps positions.

(C) SERVICES: In the development of services like banking, insurance, telecommunications and shipping, there is a great difference between the developed countries and the developing countries. Inclusion of trade in services is, therefore, bound to benefit developed countries much more than the developing countries like India. In fact, the very inclusion of trade in services in Uruguay Round negotiation was due to the persistent insistence of the developed countries who have all along been arguing that opening up of trade in services is an important requirement for globalisation and development of world trade. According to data, the size of the world market for services was $ 1000 billion in 1994 of which the share of the developed countries was as high as $ 950 billion or 95 per cent. All developing countries together had only a share of 5 per cent in world trade of services in 1994. The USA, France, Japan and Netherlands are the principal exporters of services and together accounting for about 60 per cent share of the world trade in services. Only these countries are going to get benefit most from the new agreement on services of Uruguay round and the share of the developing countries will decline further. The service industry is sitll in infant stage in many developing countries and its progress will now be throttled under the new Agreement (GATS). Similar is the case in respect of India; and it will be required to denationalise insurance and banking sectors as per new Agreement. Consequently these sectors may not be able to play a positive social role as they have been playing so far. Moreover, foreign firms will be free not only to expand their network in the Indian services sector but also to remit resources to their parent country in the form of profit, interest, royalties etc. All this will involve a foreign exchange burden on India and Indian firms will find it extremely difficult to compete with the firms supplying services in the developed countries and hence it will not be an easy task for them to penetrate the services sector in developed countries.

CONCLUDING OBSERVATIONS

From the above discussion, it is clear that under the guise of 'rule based multilateral order', 'global integration' and 'development of free international trade'; the developed countries have succeeded in building up of "New International Economic Order" that fully serves their interests and sacrifices the interests of the large, silent and deprived majority of the developing countries like India. The WTO Agreement, in contrast to GATT Agreement, annexes vast spaces of national decision making into its domain. The entire spectrum of IPRs has been lifted out of the national domain and subjected to a rigorous international discipline. The trade in services has been defined in an open-ended manner so as to bring within ambit of GATs, any and every possible activity except the essential law making, policing and judicial functions of the state. The national investment regimes will similarly be subject to the international disciplines as laid down under TRIMs. The developed countries are also trying to bring other issues like social clauses, labour services and issue of child labour, environmental protection etc. under the new international control regime. Of course, the WTO Ministerial Declaration signed by the 142 member trade body on November 14, 2001 at the fourth Ministerial Meeting held at Doha, capital of Qatar, has been widely debated in India with supporters claiming major victories for India and critics vehemently opposing all such claims. The important concentrated issues in the Declaration were: one on implementation of related issues and concerns, another on the TRIPs agreement and public health; and further a statement on subsidies. Under this Declaration, some concessions and gains are made available to developing countries like India in the field of TRIPs and public health. As a ray of hope, the specific concerns of the developing countries are also addressed by the Doha Declaration. A major gain has been including the issue of Special and Differential (S & D) treatment for developing countries with respect to market access, domestic support and export competition as an integral part of on going negotiations on agriculture. The declaration also recognizes the importance of non-trade concerns like food security and rural development for developing countries. All this implies that the WTO now recognizes the special needs of farmers in the developing world for greater domestic support and protection from a surge in imports for achieving food and livelihood security as also for overall development of rural areas. However, the discussions on TRIPs, TRIMs, Services, Agriculture, Labour standards and environment are likely to dominate WTO's agenda in future; and India will have to prepare a national and an international strategy to face challenges. The experience of the functioning of WTO so far and the Seattle meeting clearly show that "Might is Right" and 'It is power play' and the bargaining strength matters, and not abstract economic principles like comparative advantage or free trade or virtues of globalisation etc. To meet the challenges posed by the developed countries, the developing countries will have to join hands to protect their interests in WTO negotiations in future. The co-ordination and solidarity which they exhibited at Seattle and at Doha needs to be further cemented and strengthened.

REFERENCES

Jha Shishir Kumar, (2001), WTO: An Economic Right Perspective, Institute of Finance and International Management, Bangalore, pp. 3-8.

Goyal Arun, (2000), WTO in the New Millennium (ed), Academy of Business Studies, New Delhi.

Choudhary, Arundhuti Roy, (2000), "QR Removal and its Probable Implications", *Economic and Political Weekly*, April 15.

Ganguli Prabuddha, (1998), Gearing up for Patents: The Indian Scenario, University Press, Hyderabad.

Suman Sahai, (1999), "Agenda for Seattle", *Economic and Political Weekly*, November 20.

Dhavan Rajeev, (2000), "The Right to Seed", *The Hindu*, May, 05.

Vaidyanathan, A., (2000), "Indias' Agricultural Development Policy", *Economic and political Weekly*, May 13.

Bhadury, D., (1997), "New Vistas open up", *The Hindu Survey of Indian Industry*, p. 216.

Donal, G. McNeil Jr., (2000), "The Medicine Merchants: Drug Companies and the Third World", *The frontline*, June 23.

Dubey, Muchkund, (1996), An Unequal Treaty : World Trading Order after GATT, New Age International Ltd., New Delhi.

Joseph, Stiglitz, (2002), Globalization and its Discontents, Penguin Books.

Bimal Jalan, (2002), India's Economy in the New Millennium, UBSPD, New Delhi.

Suman Sahai, (1994), "GATT and Patenting of Micro-Organisms", *Economic and Political Weekly*, April 9.

Shukla, S.P., (1995), "WTO and Nation State: of Annexes and Annexation", The State of India's Economy 1994-95, Published by Public Interest Research Group, Delhi.

Nagesh Kumar, (2003), "Intellectual Property Rights, Technology and Economic Development", *Economic and Political Weekly*, January 18.

Suman Sahai, (1993), "Indian Patents Act and TRIPs", *Economic & Political Weekly*, July 17-24.

Dhar, Biswajit, (1999), "QR Phase Out: B.O.P. No Justification", *The Economic Times*, September 10.

Dasgupta, Biplab, (1998), Structural Adjustment, Global Trade and the New Political Economy of Development, New Delhi.

Lalitha, N., (2002), "Indian Pharmaceutical Industry in WTO Regime", *Economic and Political Weekly*, August 24.

Debroy, Bibek, (1996), Beyond the Uruguay Round: The Indian Perspective on GATT, New Delhi.

Nayar, Bolder Raj, (2001), Globalization and Nationalism, New Delhi.

Arun Kumar, (2000), "India at the Seattle Meeting", *Economic & Political Weekly*, January 15.

Chaudhari Sudip, (2002), "TRIPs Agreement and Amendment of Patents Act in India", *Economic & Political Weekly*, August 10.

Misra, S.K., and Puri, V.K., (2003), Indian Economy, 21st Edition, Himalaya Publishing House, Delhi.

WTO AND INDIA'S FOREIGN TRADE

*K.A. Rasure**

INTRODUCTION

World Trade Organisation (WTO) came into being on January 1st 1995 at Marakkesh for implementing its various provisions agreed upon by all the 148 member nations. The main objectives of WTO are pursuing functions of GATT such as Most Favoured Nation (MFN) clause treating all the countries equally and tariff to be the only method of protection. In addition, the scope of WTO was extended to perform some other functions not covered under GATT. It included the trade in agricultural and allied products with market predictability. All the NTBs were to be converted into tariffs not exceeding the Uruguay bound tariff rate, abolition of domestic support to agriculture and subsidies on export. Multifibre Agreement (MFA) allowing trade in textile products according to quota system on the part of developed countries was to be abolished within stipulated time.

New measures to meet the requirements of Trade Related Intellectual Property Rights (TRIPs), Trade Related Investment Measures (TRIMs) and General Agreement on Trade in services (GATS) were brought under WTO and provided legal sanctions. TRIPs were introduced for protecting the rights of inventors and allowing patent ability only in the final products. According to TRIMs, all the companies irrespective of their parent countries would enjoy equal treatment in foreign land. They are not compelled to use local raw-material and export obligations. Under GATS, the services will be open to the international competitiveness.

* Selection Grade Lecturer in Economics, Nrupatunga Arts & Commerce College, Sedam-585222. Dt : Gulbarga - Karnataka. E-mail : karasure@yahoo.co.in & k_rasure@indiatimes.com., karasure@yahoo.co.in

Foreign banks, insurance companies among others can freely operate, mobilize funds both for local use and investing abroad. Above all, WTO has been provided settlement mechanism acceptable by all members. Such a comprehensive coverage under WTO provides both challenges and opportunities to all the countries particularly the developing world looking for market access in the developed countries.

This paper attempts to analyse the impact of WTO on India's Foreign Trade. It also explains the destination of India's exports and suggestion. The paper is organized in three sections. The first section explains briefly the India's position in World Trade, section second, India's Export and Imports and lastly destination of India's Exports. The paper heavily depends upon the secondary data.

I

INDIA'S POSITION IN WORLD TRADE

Foreign Trade plays a vital role in economic development of our country. Exports earn substantial foreign exchange. Analysing and assessing demand in the world market and arranging production schedule according to demand are prerequisites for export transactions. The EXIM policy encourages export through subsidies, incentives, infrastructure development, etc. Export promotion and import liberalization are twin objectives of EXIM policy. Import is also given due importance to modernize Indian industries make them competitive in the world market. Export oriented imports are encouraged. Exports contribute to pay for imports. Export Promotion Schemes such as export-oriented units and special economic zones also aim at increasing exports in India.

India's share in world trade was 2.2. per cent when it became independent. Its share in world trade has shown a declining trend over the period of last 57 years. During 1952-53, Indian exports constituted 1.3 per cent of world exports. It was merely 0.5 per cent in the decade i.e., 1973-83. However, it had increased marginally to 0.6 in the year 1993 and 0.7 per cent in 2001. Really, its matter of deep concern that India has been much behind of its Asian counterparts as far as foreign trade is concerned. During 2001-02, Indian exports constituted only 0.70 per cent of world exports. In dollar terms, Indian exports amounted to $ 43.61 billion. India had the 30th ranking in world export trade. On the other hand the USA had top ranking having the highest share i.e., 11.9 per cent in the world trade during 2001-02. Its export amounted to $ 730.80 billion. China had the 6th ranking and 4.3 per cent in the world export trade. China's performance was remarkable during 2002-03 as its exports spurred by 23 per cent. India had 27th position and 0.80 per cent in world imports during 2001-02. Comparatively, China had better position (6th) and 3.8 per cent share in world imports during the same period.

Table 1
World Trade–Position of Selected Countries

($ billion)

Name of Country	*Export Trade*	*Percentage Share*	*Rank*	*Import Trade*	*Percentage Share*	*Rank*
USA	730.80	11.90	1	1180.20	18.30	1
Germany	570.79	9.30	2	492.80	7.70	2
Japan	403.50	6.60	3	349.10	5.40	3
France	321.84	5.20	4	331.80	5.20	4
UK	273.09	4.40	5	325.80	5.10	5
China	266.16	4.30	6	243.60	3.80	6
Canada	259.86	4.20	7	232.90	3.60	7
Italy	241.13	3.90	8	227.20	3.50	8
Netherland	229.46	3.70	9	207.30	3.20	9
Hongkong	191.07	3.10	10	202.00	3.10	10
India	43.61	0.70	30	49.60	0.80	27

Source: Economic Times, 2 September, 2003.

This clearly indicates that India has a long way to go as far as foreign trade is concerned. What India needs to do is to abolish quantitive restrictions, reduction in trade barriers and changing obsolute rules and regulations. One may find the reason of India's poor performance in foreign trade in its slow industrial and agricultire growth rate. It has been below 10 per cent during 1991-92 to 2002-03 except 1995-96 in which it was 12.10 per cent. India's industrial growth rate was 8 per cent. It was deteriorated substantially in the last year (2002-03). During the same period it was much higher in case of other developing countries viz. Korea (7.8 per cent), Thailand (11.2 per cent), Malaysia (16.2 per cent), China (16.9 per cent) and Indonesia (18.9 per cent). (Table 1).

II

INDIA'S EXPORTS AND IMPORTS

Table 2 shows that in the year 1999 Indian exports were valued at $ 33.2 billion, which increased to $ 44.2 billion in 2001 and $ 52.4 billion in 2003, showing the percentage increase of 58 per cent during the period 1999 to 2003. Similarly, the value of imports increased from $ 42.4 billion in 1999 to $ 61.5 billion in 2003, recording an increase of 45 per cent. The percentage increase in imports is more than the percentage increase by exports during the review period 1999 to 2003.

Trade deficit was $ 9.2 billion in 1999 and it remained more or less the same at $ 9.1 billion in 2003, though there is a change in value of exports and imports during the review period. Percentage of Trade deficit over exports is an important indicator to measure growth of exports. It was 28 per cent in 1999 and decreased to 17 per cent in 2003. In both years 1999 and 2003, trade deficit remained the same, whereas the percentage of trade deficit over exports decreased in 2003 compared to 1999. This shows that the volume of exports has increased during the review period.

Table 2
India's Exports and Imports

(in US $ billion)

Year	*Exports*	*Imports*	*Trade Deficit*	*Trade Deficit As per cent of exports*
1999	33.2	42.4	-9.2	28
2000	36.8	49.8	-13.0	35
2001	44.2	50.1	-5.9	13
2002	44.0	51.6	-7.6	17
2003	52.4	61.5	-9.1	17

Source: CMIE.

The total exports are analysed for important products in terms of value. This assessment reveals demand of products in the overseas market. (Table 3).

Table 3
Composition of India's Exports.

(in US $ billion)

Items	*1999*	*2000*	*2001*	*2002*	*2003*
1. Agricultural & Allied products	6.03 (18.2)	5.61 (15.3)	5.98 (14.0)	5.92 (13.5)	6.43 (12.4)
1. Ores and Minerals	0.89 (2.7)	0.92 (2.5)	1.15 (2.6)	1.27 (2.9)	1.9 (3.6)
2. Leather & Leather products	1.66 (5)	1.59 (4.3)	1.95 (4.4)	1.92 (4.4)	1.79 (3.4)
3. Chemical & related products	3.06 (9.2)	3.57 (9.7)	4.26 (9.3)	4.32 (9.8)	4.99 (9.5)
4. Engineering Goods	4.38 (13.2)	5.11 (13.9)	6.76 (15.3)	6.96 (15.8)	8.38 (16)
5. Textiles	4.5 (13.6)	5.06 (13.8)	5.73 (13)	5.22 (11.9)	5.75 (11)
6. Readymade Garments	4.36 (13.1)	4.77 (13)	5.58 (12.6)	5.02 (11.4)	5.39 (10.3)
7. Other manufactured goods	7.83 (23.6)	9.64 (26.2)	10.12 (22.9)	10.05 (22.8)	12.34 (23.2)
Sub-Total	26.68 (80.4)	30.66 (83.4)	35.55 (80.1)	34.76 (79.0)	40.45 (77.0)
1. Petroleum & Crude oil products	0.09 (0.3)	0.03 (0.1)	1.9 (4.3)	2.13 (4.08)	2.43 (4.6)
2. Other commodities	0.41 (1.2)	0.45 (1.2)	0.72 (1.6)	1.18 (2.7)	3.16 (6)
Total Exports	33.22 100	36.75 100	44.15 100	43.99 100	52.47 100

Source: CMIE.
Note: Figures shown in brackets indicate percentage to total.

Table 3 reveals composition of India's exports during the period 1999 to 2003. Marine products, rice, tea, cashew, oil meals, coffee, fruits and vegetables, spices, meat and meat preparations and sugar are important agricultural and allied products exported from India. The share of agricultural and allied products exported from India. The share agricultural and allied products in total exports was 18.2 per cent in 1999 and it declined to 13.6 per cent in 2001 and 12.3 per cent in 2003. There was no increase in the value of agricultural product exports during the period 1999 to 2003. The export potential of agricultural products is not encouraging, though a majority of Indian population is employed in agriculture.

The share of manufactured goods in total exports remained at 76 to 80 per cent during the review period. Gems and Jewellary were an important item in the export of manufactured goods. The share of gems and jewellary exports in total exports was 16.7 per cent in the year 2003, followed by engineering goods at 16 per cent, chemicals and related products at 9.5 per cent, readymade garments at 10.3 per cent and textiles at 11 per cent. The export of manufactured goods was worth $ 25.79 billion in 1999 and it increased to $ 34.39 billion in 2001 and $ 38.45 billion in 2003, showing a growth of 49 per cent. Core competency and cost advantage are essential to make the Indian manufacturing sector competitive in the overseas market.

The export of petroleum and crude oil products is increasing. It was $2.13 billion in the year 2002 and increased to $ 2.43 billion in 2003. Until 1999, India used to be a net importer of crude oil as well as various petroleum products. Imports of crude oil were inevitable since domestic reserves are limited. Oil products were imported because of insufficient domestic refining capacity. However, with the commissioning of Reliance refinery at Jamnagar, having a capacity of 27 million tones per year, we now have excess refining capacity. As a result, crude imports have replaced product imports of earlier days. Crude imports are large enough to meet the domestic requirements. The excess is processed and exported as products.

Table 4 shows composition of India's imports during the period 1999 to 2003. The value of imports of petroleum crude and products was $ 6.4 billion in 1999 and it increased to $ 15.7 billion in 2001 and $ 17.69 billion in 2003. Gradual increase in international oil prices over the years and the commissioning of mega refining capacities in India over the last two to three years have increased the overall demand for crude.

Table 4
Composition of India's Imports

(in US $ billion)

Items	*1999*	*2000*	*2001*	*2002*	*2003*
1. Petroleum Crude & Products	6.4	12.63	15.7	14.05	17.69
	(15.1)	(25.4)	(31.3)	(27.2)	(28.8)
1. Food and related items	2.76	2.66	1.7	2.33	2.65
	(6.5)	(5.3)	(3.4)	(4.5)	(4.3)
2. Textiles (including Readymade)	0.45	0.54	0.6	0.75	0.96
	(1.1)	(1.1)	(1.2)	(1.5)	(1.6)
3. Chemical & related products	4.49	4.94	3.9	4.47	4.69
	(10.6)	(9.9)	(7.7)	(8.7)	(7.6)
4. Capital Goods	8.12	6.42	5.7	6.54	7.72
	(19.2)	(12.9)	(11.5)	(12.7)	(12.6)
5. Other Non-POL items	18.3	20.72	20.4	21.46	24.26
	(43.2)	(41.6)	(40.8)	(41.6)	(38.5)
6. Other Commodities	1.85	1.9	2.1	1.99	3.49
	(4.4)	(3.8)	(4.2)	(3.9)	(5.7)
Sub-Total	35.97	31.17	34.4	37.54	43.76
	(84.9)	(74.6)	(68.7)	(72.8)	(71.2)
Total Imports	42.37	49.8	50.06	51.59	61.45
	(100)	(100)	(100)	(100)	(100)

Source: CMIE.
Note: Figures shown in brackets indicate percentage to total.

The share of import of petroleum crude and products in total imports was 15.1 per cent in 1999. It slowly increased to 31.3 per cent in 2001, 27.2 per cent in 2002 and 28.8 per cent in 2003. There is a reverse trend in import of other non-POL items. The share of import of other non-POL items in total imports was 43.2 per cent in 1999 and it decreased to 41.6 per cent in 2000, 40.8 per cent in 2001, 41.6 per cent in 2002 and 39.5 per cent in 2003.

In total imports, the share of petroleum crude and products is 28.8 per cent and the share of non-petroleum and oil items is 71.2 per cent. In non-petroleum and oil items, the share of food and related items is 4.3 per cent, textiles 1.6 per cent, chemicals 7.6 per cent, capital goods 12.6 per cent, other non-POL items 39.5 per cent and other commodities 5.7 per cent. It is concluded that petroleum crude and products occupy one-third of the total imports.

III

DESTINATION OF INDIA'S EXPORTS

The USA, the UAE, the UK, Hong-Kong, Germany, China, Japan, Belgium, Singapore and Italy are important export markets for India. Thus USA continues to be India's largest destination for export goods, accounting for a little over one-fifth of India's total exports.

Table 5
Destination of India's Exports

(in US $ billion)

Country	*1999*	*2000*	*2001*	*2002*	*2003*
USA	7.2 (21.7)	8.4 (22.8)	9.3 (21)	8.5 (19.4)	10.9 (20.8)
UAE	1.9 (5.6)	2.1 (5.7)	2.6 (5.9)	2.5 (5.7)	3.3 (6.3)
UK	1.9 (5.6)	2 (5.5)	2.3 (5.2)	2.2 (4.9)	2.5 (4.7)
Hong-Kong	1.9 (5.7)	2.5 (6.8)	2.6 (6)	2.4 (5.4)	2.5 (4.7)
Germany	1.9 (5.6)	1.7 (4.7)	1.9 (4.3)	1.8 (4.1)	2.1 (3.9)
China	0.4 (1.3)	0.5 (1.5)	0.8 (1.9)	1 (2.2)	2 (3.8)
Japan	1.7 (5)	1.7 (4.6)	1.8 (4)	1.5 (3.4)	1.9 (3.6)
Belgium	1.3 (3.9)	1.3 (3.6)	1.5 (3.3)	1.4 (3.2)	1.7 (3.2)
Singapore	0.5 (1.6)	0.7 (1.8)	0.9 (2)	1 (2.2)	1.4 (2.7)
Italy	1.1 (3.2)	1.1 (3)	1.3 (2.9)	1.2 (2.8)	1.3 (2.6)
Others	13.6 (41)	14.7 (38.9)	19.3 (43.7)	20.5 (46.7)	22.9 (43.8)
World	33.2 (100)	36.8 (100)	44.2 (100)	44 (100)	52.4 (100)

Source: CMIE.
Note: Figures shown in brackets indicate percentage to total.

Table 5 shows destinations of India's exports during the period 1999 to 2003. It reveals that value of exports to the USA is on increasing trend. It was $ 7.2 billion in 1999 and increased to $ 9.3 billion in 2001 and $ 10.9 billion in 2003. The increase is 51 per cent during the period 1999 to 2003. Similarly, the percentage increase in exports to the UAE, the UK, Hong-Kong, Germany, China and Singapore are 74 per cent, 32 per cent, 32 per cent, 11 per cent, 400 per cent and 180 per cent respectively.

SUGGESTIONS

1. There is urgent need of removing infrastractural deficiencies. For this purpose, private or foreign investment must be invited on priority basis in power generation,

transportation, communication, warehousing, cold storages, ports and other infrastracture.

2. Indian entrepreneurs should come out their shell so far provided by the government and get globalised through joint ventures, product based technology transfer agreements, R & D agreements to achieve technological superiority for increasing productivity and quality of their products.
3. Free Trade Zones and Special Economic Zones should be made realistic to promote foreign trade.
4. Agriculture sector needs technological upgradation, adequate finance, improved seeds, manurs, fertilizers, power, irrigation, better prices and good marketing facilities which should be provided on priority basis to promote agro-exports.
5. There is also urgent need of a common forum of all developing and under developed countries to discuss the issues regarding global trade and oppose unitedly unjustifiable trade and non-trade barriers.
6. The government should set up an institution for imparting knowledge and information regarding international trade, WTO commitments, import-export procedures, standards of different commodities set by different countries, customs and traditions etc., so that manufacturer, traders, become well aware to the global economy and trade.
7. Information technology and bio-technology are termed as sunrise industries as they have tremendous potential in India. It may be suggested that these industries should be assisted with soft credit and required infrasture.
8. To check the ever-increasing trade deficit, we need to explore new avenues for exports on one hand and import substitutes on the other hand.

CONCLUSIONS

India became member of WTO in 1995 and since then has been following the trade rules set by WTO well known as liberalization of trade. It is to be noted that India, inspite of continuous efforts, could not achieve the target of 1 per cent share in the global trade. Impediments being slow growth rates in agricultural and manufacturing sector, slowdown in world economy, wars and terrorist activities and the most dangerous trade and non-trade raised by the developed countries. India, being an agrarian country having more than 70 per cent of its population dependent on agriculture, cannot liberalize this sector fully. There is a sizeable number of the developed countries who have not fulfilled WTO commitments and have continued providing high subsidies which poor developing countries cannot afford. To add to the fuel, a number of trade and non-trade barriers are in practice in developed countries for protection of domestic commodities. It is heartening fact that the performance of India's service sector, particularly software sector is appreciable and it proved that India can be a global player. Another factor in favour of India is that its agriculture and industrial sectors have shown improvement in their performance and this may help India to achieve the target of one per cent share in global trade in coming years.

REFERENCES

Banik, N., (2001), "Analysis of Indian Exports during 1990's EPW, Vol. XXXVI 44, November, 3-9.

Bhattacharya, Band Mogo L.D., (1998), "Trade and Environment issue in the WTO-Indian Experience", Foreign Trade review, ILFT, New•Delhi.

Datt, Ruddar/Sundaram K.P.M., (2002), "Indian Economy, 6th Edition, S.Chand & Co, New Delhi.

Dhingra, I.C., (1994), " Indian Economy, 9th Edition, S. Chand & Co., New Delhi.

GOI, (2000-02), Economic Survey.

GOI, (1991) "Indias New Economic Policies".

Gulati, Ashok, (1999), "From Marakkesh to Seattle-Indian Agriculture in Globalisaing World", EPW, Vol. 34, Oct., 9-15.

Gulati, Ashok, (2000); Indian Agriculture and the WTO: Preparing for the New Millennium; IEA Conference (83rd) Volume.

Gupta, C.S., (2001), " Conceptualising Globalisation and its Implications", EPW. Vol, XXXVI, 36 August 18-21.

Mukhopadhya,s (2000) "The Uruguay Round and India Export Response; IEA Conference (83rd) Volume.

The Economic Times, 29th April, 2003.

HEALTH INSURANCE IN INDIA: ISSUES AND CHALLENGES

Vishwanatha[*], *Jayasheela*[**], *Shoukat Ali M.*[***] *& Sudhakar S.*[****]

INTRODUCTION

India has made considerable progress in improving the health status of its population. Crude death rate has fallen from about 40 per 1,000 at the time of independence to 9 per 1,000 in 1998 which can be attributed to the mortality reduction of under five age group from around 161 per 1,000 live births to 71 over the same period. Consequently, life expectancy has increased from about 31 years to 63 years. Yet challenges remain; life expectancy is still four years below the world average and under-five mortality (12 per 1,000 per year) is higher than the world average.

Through its budgetary allocations the government has set up remarkably impressive health infrastructure. The system envisages availability and accessibility of publicly funded healthcare to all, regardless of their ability to pay. However, it faces serious challenges in meeting its objectives.

In India, while five per cent of GDP is spent on health, the government contributes only 0.9% of it or less than Rs. 100 per capita per year. Internationally this is one of the lowest health expenditures by any government. More than 80% of most government budgets are earmarked for salaries. This means that there are very little funds for drugs, programmes and other

* Professor and Chairman, Department of Economics, Mangalore University, Mangalagangothri - 574199.

** Reader, Department of Economics, Mangalore University, Mangalagangothri.

*** Department of Economics, Mangalore University, Mangalagangothri.

**** Department of Economics, Mangalore University, Mangalagangothri.

activities. And finally there is an inequitable allocation of health resources, about 30% of the government health budget is used by the richest quintile while the poorest quintile gets only 10%. This under funded government health services thus provides poor quality of care. Common complaints include poor utilisation of the primary health care facilities, overcrowding at the secondary and tertiary health care facilities, lack of adequate manpower, drugs and equipment. This causes most patients to shift over to private sector for health care. About 85% of the patients use the private sector for health care. About 85% of patients use the private sector for ambulatory care, while 40-60% use the private sector for inpatient care. (Devadsan et. all, 2004).

HEALTH INSURANCE

Insurance provides protection against risk or uncertain events and is based on the principle that what is highly unpredictable to an individual is predictable to a group of individuals. Health insurance protects against the cost of illness, mobilises funds for health services and achieves certain equity objectives (Mills 2000). Various forms of health insurance can be broadly categorized (based on ownership of scheme) as follows; state-based systems, market-based systems, member organization (NGO or Co-operative) based systems, and private household-based systems. (Jatting 1999).

Social Health Insurance: Organised by the state or a public body, funding comes from payroll tax levied on workers and employers, and often supplemented by user fees and government contribution from tax revenues. A wide range of benefits is offered but access is based on healthcare need. Social insurance schemes are managed by autonomous bodies under government regulations and the providers of care have to meet certain standards in terms of capacity, staff, equipment and other parameters.

Private Insurance: Both individuals and groups can avail of this voluntary coverage, which could be profit or non-profit oriented. Contributions are based on risk and coverage; benefits are specifically defined in this type of insurance.

Community-based Insurance: Expenditure is shared among the community and generally community organizations or NGOs handle the business. Contributions can be mandatory or voluntary, usually a flat rate per individual or household.

Health care financing in India can be considered almost unique in several respects. One, the share of public financing in total health care financing in the country is considerably low-just around 1% of the GDP compared to the average share of 2.8% in low and middle income countries and relative to India's share in disease burden. Two, the beneficiaries of this limited public health financing are not only the poor as one would expect in the case of limited public spending, but also the well-off section of society, Third, over 80% of the total health financing is private financing much of which takes the form of out-of-pocket payments (i.e. user charges) and not pre-payment schemes. Peters et al (2002) estimate that one-quarter of all Indians fall into poverty as a direct result of medical expenses in the event of hospitalisation.

One of the important challenges facing the Indian Health policy experts is: how to convert predominantly private out-of-pocket spending into health insurance premium where this amount is collected from a much larger group of insured individuals rather than from the limited number of households affected by illness. Another important challenge is how to provide health insurance to the people who cannot afford to pay (full) premium.

RE IMBURSEMENT SCHEME

This system refers to the manner in which providers are paid. The characteristics of health insurance programme can be described as follows (Kutzin and Barnum 1992).

1. In the traditional indemnity systems, customers first incur expenditure on services and later submit claim to insurance company for reimbursement (such as mediclaim insurance scheme).
2. Managed indemnity in which a Third Party Administrator (TPA) takes care of claim settlement of enrolees and directly reimburses service provider.

3. Insurer pays service provider a fixed amount, out of which provider will serve health needs of the enrolees for a specific period.
4. Reimbursement can be fee – for – service, which would involve charging for each individual service, such as inpatient bed-days, drugs, investigations.
5. Case- specific reimbursement based on category of patient admitted. Under this system admissions are grouped into categories called diagnostic-related groups (DRGs), based on their clinical characteristics.

INDIAN SCENARIO

The promulgation of the Employee State Insurance (ESI) Act in 1948 ushered in health insurance in India. The legislation introduced a mandatory social insurance scheme with managed care concepts for employees in the formal sector.

The Employee State Insurance Scheme (ESIS), introduced in 1952, is managed by the Employees State Insurance Corporation (ESIC), a wholly government owned enterprise. It provides cash benefits, medical benefits, preventive and primitive care and health education. It is a compulsory social security benefit for workers having an income less than Rs. 6,500 a month in the formal sector, covers employees and their dependents and is mainly financed by contributions from employers, employees and the government. Employers and employees contribute 4.75% and 1.75% of their wages respectively. The state government's share is 12.5 per cent of the total expenditure. In 2000, about 33.4 million beneficiaries were covered under this scheme. ESIC has set up 136 hospitals with 43 annexes having 23,720 beds. There are 1,443 ESI dispensaries, 6,542 medical officers and 2,988 medical practitioners.

The second initiative was the Central Government Health Scheme (CGHS) in 1954 for employees of the Central government, members of parliament, judges, freedom fighters and their families. Mainly financed by the central government, this contributory health scheme-contribution varies from Rs.

15 to Rs. 150 per person based on the salary of the employee, provides comprehensive medical care to about 4.4 million beneficiaries (1996 figure). Separate dispensaries are maintained and inpatient facilities are available in government hospitals and approved private hospitals on referral.

For persons not covered by these schemes, government-run insurance companies have introduced market-based schemes, such as the Mediclaim scheme of General Insurance Corporation, introduced in 1986. An indemnity-based health system, covering only inpatient treatment, the premium is based on age and sum insured, clients can avail of medical services from any public or registered private hospital. In 1991, however, the internal limits for doctor's fees, medicines, diagnostics and room charges were removed, making it a single benefit policy.

There are health benefit packages that are directly managed by employers in both the public and private sector; either special healthcare facilities are set up or reimbursement of medical expenses and mediclaim insurance premium amounts (Often a group Mediclaim Scheme) can be claimed.

Many charitable and voluntary organisations have also designed social security schemes for specific groups of the population and NGOs often provide some kind of social security to the poor and those working in the unorganised sector, especially in rural areas. The Self Employed Women's Association (SEWA) has been in the forefront and other important organisations such as Child in Need Institute, Streehitkarini, Tribhuvandas Foundation and Accord have also taken the initiative.

The government has now allowed private companies to enter into health insurance and has established the Insurance Regulatory and Development Authority (IRDA) to regulate this sector. It is estimated that the present health insurance market is Rs. 2.5 billion to 3 billion and it has a potential to grow to Rs. 50 billion in the next five to seven years. The potential insurance lives in the country are estimated to be around 300million and only 10% of the health insurance market has been tapped so for.

PRIVATE HEALTH INSURANCE IN INDIA

Unlike most OECD countries where private/social health insurance is the main source of health care financing, in India, and more generally in developing countries, most private insurance is a supplementary service. Health insurance, whether social or private, whether formal or informal, is extremely limited in India. Existing health insurance schemes in India are mandatory schemes, private (voluntary) schemes, employer based insurance, and schemes in the NGO/voluntary sector. All these schemes put together cover about 110 million people or about 11% of the population (Garg 2000). This number falls far short of the private health insurance potential that is estimated anywhere between 400 and 500 million people.

Table 1
Mediclaim Policy

	1997-98	*1998-99*	*1999-00*	*2000-01*	*2001-02*
No of persons insured	2783862.0	3534417.0	4894129.0	5623864.0	7784491.0
Premium (Rs. in lakhs)	21569.0	27173.5	38040.7	51898.2	74204.5.
Claims (Rs. in lakhs)	18612.4	21810.3	33226.1	47152.8	62038.6
Claim ration (per cent)	86.3	80.3	87.3	90.9	83.6

Table 2
Jan Arogya Bima Policy

	1997-98	*1998-99*	*1999-00*	*2000-01*	*2001-02*
No.of persons inco insured	139354.0	313643.0	686685.0	348413.0	348912.0
Premium (Rs.in lakhs)	115.3	2880.0	6569.0	6800.3	9079.3
Claims (Rs. in lakhs)	97.1	2882.4	7978.0	6689.0	8818.2
Claims ration (per cent)	84.3	100.1	121.4	98.4	97.1

Source: Annual Reports of (non-life) public insurance companies.

Although a number of private insurance companies have entered after the liberalisation of the insurance market in 2000, no significant change in health insurance has been observed either in forms of new health insurance products or in terms of the volume of business. Mediclaim for the general public and Jan Arogya for the poor, launched prior to the liberalisation, have not shown any significant growth either in terms of volume of business or in the number of policies sold (Table 1 and 2).

COMMUNITY BASED UNIVERSAL HEALTH INSURANCE SCHEME

In the budget of 2003-04, the Govt. of India launched community based universal health insurance scheme for the low-income population. Some of the important features of this scheme are as follows:

The scheme comes in three different types:

(i) Rs. 1 per day per year for an individual

(ii) Rs. 1.5 per day per year for a family of up to five members.

(iii) Rs. 2 per day per year for a family of up to seven members.

In case of hospitalisation the scheme provides medical expenses up to Rs. 30,000 per family, if an earning member falls sick the scheme also provides for the loss of livelihood at the rate of Rs. 50 per day up to a maximum of 15 days, and in case of death of the earning head of the family due to personal accident, Rs. 25,000 is given to the nominee.

In all these options while the government provides a subsidy of Rs.100 which, remains fixed whether it is an individual who buys insurance or a family of five or of seven. While the scheme is open to anybody who wants to participate in it, the subsidy is given only to BPL families. The proposed scheme is a group insurance scheme with a membership of at least 100 families which consists of cooperative societies, beedi workers, handloom weavers etc.

Some other salient features of the scheme are:

1. Individuals between the age of 3 months and 65 years can join the scheme.
2. Total hospital expense that can be reimbursed under the scheme for any one illness is up to Rs. 15,000 with a cap on the amount payable for different types of hospital expenses.

3. A number of illnesses/situations are excluded, for example, maternity insurance is not included.
4 Claims are to be settled either by an intermediary called third party administrat (TPAs) or by the insurance companies themselves.

The scheme is expected to cover 10 million families that are below the poverty line in the first year. The scheme was envisaged to implement as a community-based insurance scheme by the NGO's through the four Public Sector National Insurance Companies.

In the 2004 budget this policy was revised in three ways:

1. Restricted to BPL families.
2. Increased the subsidy element to Rs. 200 against the Rs. 365 premium paid for individual coverage; Rs. 300 for the Rs. 547.5 premium for a family of five and Rs. 400 for those paying premium of Rs. 730 for covering a family of seven persons.
3. A new scheme for covering the member of a self-help group (SHG) under a scheme providing health cover of Rs. 10,000 for a premium of Rs. 120 per annum or Rs.10 per month.

ROLE OF THIRD PARTY ADMINISTRATORS (TPA)

Insurance Regulatory and Development Authority (IRDA) defines Third Party Administrator (TPA) as "an insurance intermediary licensed by the Authority who, either directly or indirectly, solicits or effects coverage of, underwrite, collect, charge premium from an insured, or adjust or settle claims in connection with health insurance, except as an agent or broker or an insurer". IRDA has approved services of TPAs as insurance intermediaries and would be regulating their practices. The final draft of these regulations has strictly barred TPAs from marketing health insurance products and charging the insured.

IRDA regulations place stringent conditions for licensing TPAs. Current regulation requires TPAs to meet a minimum equity capital of Rs. 10 million. The capital requirements for entering into this sector are not stringent. As a result, there may be a proliferation of players, not all of the best quality. A large number of players will mean pressure on margins. Besides this, TPAs, need to set up infrastructure which would involve large investments, the payback period of which is likely to be long. TPAs face high operating risk of obtaining economies of scale necessary to break even. Volumes are critical because the revenue generation of TPAs is linked to the number of policies they undertake to administer. According to current regulations, TPAs will get 6% of the premium collected as their share of revenue.

The effectiveness of TPAs in managing claims and reimbursements depends on their bargaining power vis-à-vis healthcare service providers. It is envisaged that TPAs can get better negotiated agreements with hospitals and medical practitioners and will introduce better monitoring system leading to lower claim ratios. However, in practice, there are many challenges which TPAs face in achieving these goals. The management of claims and reimbursements in highly fragmented, un regulated markets and dealing with a large number of small-sized services is bound to affect the revenue generation of TPAs.

It is expected that with the introduction of TPA services, the claim settlement process would be simplified. IRDA has suggested that all claims should be settled in seven days. TPAs will face major challenges in binging down the settlement period to seven days. It has been observed that lack of proper documents related to treatment often results in deferred or non-payment of claims. Of course, examination of exclusion clauses in the policy is imperative before authorising admissibility and further treatment. TPAs will have to sort out these issues when the policyholder is seeking health care services. Winning the confidence of policyholders and maintaining the client base will be challenging. All attempts by insurance companies to tie-up with private hospitals through the TPA system in the past have had little success, as there is generally a mutual feeling of distrust. This will pose a major challenge.

LIMITATIONS OF HEALTH INSURANCE SCHEMES IN INDIA

The scope of the existing health insurance schemes in India has remained limited. Two important reasons cited are:

1. Poor product design, and
2. Lack of vigorous marketing of the products in order to sensitise the public to the need for health insurance.

The existing health insurance schemes are indemnity-based products where in the payment to the health provider is first made by the sick individual and this amount is later reimbursed (partly or fully) by the insurance company to the insured individual. A large section of the population that cannot afford such large payments at the time of illness, even if the payments are reimbursed later, does not feel attracted to this type of insurance. Further more, the scheme provides for reimbursement only in the case of hospitalisation and not for outpatient care and for allopathic treatment and not for treatment under alternate systems of medicine. Reimbursement of hospital expenses exposes the policyholders to the "service" of insurers which is far from satisfactory. Coming to the second reason, when the public is not always aware of the need for health insurance, vigorous marketing of schemes becomes essential for popularising the scheme. Finally, health insurance is not demanded for its own sake but for reducing the financial barrier to health services. In rural and remote areas where the supply of health services particularly in patient facilities is weak the demand for insurance naturally becomes constrained.

More generally, why has the health insurance business remained underdeveloped in India? Why has no reputed global health insurance company entered the market? Impediments to the establishment and development of private health insurance stem directly or indirectly from government policies regarding insurance and the health care sector (GOI 2002). The most important impediments arise from the supply side i.e. from the health care providers. Lack of standards for diseases and treatment procedures (where these standards and procedures exist, their adoption is lacking); absence of rating and credentialing of providers; non-existence of a centralised database, lack of standardised billing, claims and proposals forms are some of the problems facing the health care industry.

On the insurance regulation side too there are some issues affecting the development of the market.

CONCLUSION

Health insurance is made out to be a panacea for all the ills facing the poor. Health insurance, no doubt, has emerged as an important financing to as it promises to mobilise some resources from the people them selves i.e. those who buy insurance. But health insurance which strengthens the demand side, makes sense only when the supply of health care is reasonably well developed. Where this is not so, health insurance is meaningless. The supply of health cares in the rural and remote areas of the country far from satisfactory. Although public health care centres are pervasive, they have degraded over time in most states due to lack of funds, accountability and so forth. Any attempt at introducing health insurance for the poor must also be accompanied by the revival of health care facilities at these centres.

THE ECONOMICS OF ENVIRONMENTAL POLLUTION AND HUMAN RIGHTS WITH SPECIAL REFERENCE TO WATER POLLUTION IN KANYAKUMARI DISTRICT

*J. Cyril Kanmony**

INTRODUCTION

The right to life is the most fundamental of all human rights. Human beings can survive only in good environment and any imbalance causes a severe threat to human health and survival. Moreover, with the rapid population growth and thereby an increasing demand for food and other consumer goods, the economic activities of mankind expand, which are the reasons for environmental imbalance in the world. In the industrial sector, the mushrooming of industries specially after the industrial revolution leads to high competition and maximum production at the lowest cost with almost negligible means and funds for pollution control measures. All these result in uncontrolled emission and discharge of toxic and hazardous gases, liquid and solid emissions and effluents being thrown into atmosphere and in water outlets and finally in both surface and underground water sources (Raja Singh, 2005). Agricultural production has increased considerably by applying fertilizers and pesticides. But, the unscientific and untimely utilization of fertilizers and pesticides and insecticides in agriculture pollutes environment especially water and air. Power plants especially thermal power plants, automobiles and domestic wastes including hospital wastes contribute a lot to environmental pollution. Because of all these,

* Post-Graduate and Research Centre, Department of Economics Scott Christian College Nagercoil.

pollution has grown up by leaps and bounds and pollution levels have outstripped nature's capacity to digest these pollutants.

Environmental problems threaten the whole mankind. It is said that mankind has reached a point of historic crisis. The forces generated by the techno-scientific economy are now great enough to destroy the environment, which is the material foundation of human life. Pollution is the cause for many diseases, which affect not only children and the old but also the young and the energetic and all animals and plants. A recent WHO report points out that over 20,00,000 children worldwide suffer from environmental hazards. Hence, there is a worldwide consensus today to control the degradation of the environment for the sustainable development and a pollution free universe. In the Indian Constitution article 21 of Part III, "Right to the enjoyment of pollution free water and air" is a recent addition to fundamental rights (Hajela & Hajela, 2005). Internationally, the links between human rights, health and environmental protection were apparent in the first International Conferences on the Human Environment held in Stockholm in 1972. It is declared in the conference that both aspects of man's environment, the natural and man-made are essential to his well-being and to the enjoyment of basic human rights - even the rights to life itself. Principle 1 of the Conference declares that man has the fundamental right to freedom, equality and adequate condition of life in an environment of a quality that permits a life of dignity and well-being. By recalling the language of Stockholm Conference the UN general assembly recognised and asserted that those who pollute or destroy the natural environment are not just committing a crime against nature but are violating human rights as well (Pandey & Pandey, 2005). In short, environmental pollution especially pollution of water and air is violation of human rights.

This paper tries to analyse the causes, volume and impact of water and air pollution with special emphasis on water pollution in Kanyakumari District. Both primary and secondary data are made use of to substantiate each and every important point. Growth rate and R^2 values are also calculated and used to make the analysis scientific and fruitful. First part of this paper highlights air pollution. Second part concentrates on water pollution and water pollution in Kanyakumari district is discussed in third part. Policy implications are pointed out in the last part.

I

AIR POLLUTION

Air pollution occurs when Suspended Particulate Matter (SPM) and noxious gases occur in the air. Air pollution may be either outdoor or indoor. Impact of indoor pollution, which is caused by burning of dung, firewood and crop residues for cooking especially in rural areas is more serious than outdoor pollution. Nearly 50 per cent of the world population continues to cook food with solid fuels. This includes more than 75 per cent of people in India, China and nearby countries. The indoor use of solid fuel causes about 35.7 per cent of lower respiratory infections, 22 per cent of chronic obstructive pulmonary diseases and 1.5 per cent of trachea, bronchitis and lung cancer. It is also associated with tuberculosis, cataracts and asthma (The World Health Report–2002). A UN report says that of the 3 million people who die every year because of illness caused by air pollution, the majority are women and children who contract respiratory illness (D. Aravazhi 2003) The Tata Energy Institute estimates that of the 3 million premature deaths due to air pollution, 2.8 million are due to indoor pollution (The Hindu 21.6.2003). But, the World Bank report says that an estimated 5,00,000 women and children die due to indoor pollution in India each year (Aruna Chandaraju, 2004).

Outdoor air pollution is generally an urban and industrial phenomenon. In urban areas the main source of air pollution is vehicular pollution or emission from automobiles. The number of automobiles is ever increasing, at an estimated number of 5 lakhs per year and emitting burnt and unburnt organic chemicals (Raja Singh, 2005). This contributes to nearly 60 per cent of the total air pollution (R.N. Bhatacharya 2001).

The Centre for Science and Environment has found that between 1975 and 1995 the country's GDP grew about 2.5 times against the total amount of pollutants emitted by vehicles which grew by 8 times (Anil Agarwal-2000). In the industrial sector thermal power plants top the list of industries contributing to air pollution due to very high emission of discharge of smoke and ash. A thermal power plant designed to generate 500 mw of electricity per day typically discharges about 2000 tonnes of fly ash per day. There are 66 thermal power stations in India and together they generate one-lakh tonnes of fly ash per day apart from the smoke coming from them. The WHO estimates that the maximum quantum of SPM in the air that does not affect human health is 90 micrograms per cubic meter. In Kolkotta, it is observed that 5.5 tonnes of dust, 122 tonnes of sulphar-dioxide, 440 tonnes of carbon-mono-oxide, 70 tonnes of nitrogen oxide and 102 tonnes of hydrocarbons are carried per day with the wind. (Raja Singh, 2005). Hence, Kolkatta the SPM in the air is at least 410 micro grams per cubic meter, which is the highest in the country. It is also estimated that a non-smoker in Kolkatta suffers the same consequences as those of smoking 20 cigarettes a day simply by breathing the air (R.N. Bhattacharya 2001).

In India the Central Pollution Control Board estimated the air quality for 70 cities in 1997. Of the 70 cities, Shillong is the only city where the air quality in terms of SPM is clean round the year. Of the remaining 69 cities 29 cities (42 per cent) are critically polluted (more than 1.5 times the standard) 22 cities (32 per cent) have high pollution levels (between 1-15 times) and 18 cities, including Chennai (26 per cent) have moderate pollution levels (between 0.5 and 1 times) (Anil Agarwal, 2000). In Chennai, the Asthma Foundation found that the prevalence of asthma in children is approximately 20 per cent (Raj B. Singh 2003).

Air pollution causes bronchitis and lung cancer, in about 5 per cent of the total population and cardio respiratory mortality due to its hazards is 3 per cent globally. In absolute terms it causes 0.8 million deaths and 7.9 million DALYS. (Disability Adjusted Life Years) (The Health Report-2002).

The effects of air pollution on domestic animals are similar to those observed in man. Plants are also damaged by pollutants such as sulphurdioxide, fluorine compounds and smog. When the absorption of these exceeds a particular level, plant cells are damaged or made inactive and it results in low productivity in agriculture (N. Manivasakam 1999). Of the total cost of environmental degradation which is estimated at 5 per cent of our GDP, 15 per cent is due to air pollution (Sanjay Sangole, 2003).

II

WATER POLLUTION

Water is not fit for consumption if it has biological organisms like guinea worms, tape worms and cholera and typhoid creating bacteria and excess chemicals such as fluoride, iron, arsenic and nitrate (Joseph J Seneca & Michael K. Tausig 1984). Pollutants may be either bio-degradable or non-degradable or persistent. Degradable pollutants decompose into harmless substances or are removed from water sources by natural, biological or physical processes. They affect the quality of water only if the quantum of pollutants exceeds the rejuvenative powers of water. But non-degradable wastes cannot be altered by the above mentioned processes and so they affect the quality of water irrespective of the quantum. Persistent pollutants are neither strictly degradable nor non-degradable. They degrade or deteriorate very slowly.

Though both natural forces and human activities cause pollution, human activities, agricultural, industrial and domestic, cause more pollution in water than natural forces. In agriculture, pesticides and insecticides and fertilizers are used unscientifically and untimely. All these together with the wastes that come from domestic animals cause pollution. A lot of poisonous effluents from various types of industries also cause pollution. The sewer system, synthetic detergents, household refuse, hospital wastes, butcher wastes and garbage constitute domestic pollution (Raymon Furon, 1967). It is estimated that a global annual discharge of 440 cubic kilometers of sewage and a considerable amount of the 510^8 tonnes of diverse agricultural, industrial and other wastes get into the biosphere (John Kurian 1983). Apart from these, according to a data compiled by Greenpeace, until September 2000, more than 100,800 tonnes of hazardous wastes have entered India illegally from countries including OECD nations such as, Germany, the USA, Australia, Denmarks, the Netherlands, U.K., Belgium and Norway (D.R. Karthikkeyan, 2005). The Ministry of Environment and Forests points out that in India alone the municipal sewage accounts for 22900 million litres a day (mld). It is almost twice as much as the 13,000 million litres a day of industrial wastewater. But the treatment capacity available in domestic wastewater is only for 6000 mld and for industrial wastewater 8000 mld. (N. Gopal Raj, 2003).

W. Carty (1991) points out that 90 to 95 per cent of all domestic sewage and 75 per cent of industrial wastes are discharged into surface water without any treatment. Hospital waste, which contain germs of all types of possible diseases, in modern hospital ranges from 1.5 to 2.5 kg per day per bed (Raja Singh, 2005). The solid waste generated has increased from 6 million tonnes in 1947 to 60 million tonnes in 2002 (Aarti Dhar, 2003). The quantum of hazardous wastes generated by 13,011 industrial units spreading over 373 districts of the country was estimated at 4.4 million tonnes and the three states, namely Maharashtra, Gujarat and Tamil Nadu account for over 63 per cent of the total hazardous wastes generated in the country (N. Gopal Raj 2003). The National Environmental Engineering and Research Institute reveals that almost 70 per cent of our surface water is polluted (Helen Matzgar and Marcus Moench, 1994). In Delhi itself nearly 50 per cent of the ground water is unfit for human consumption. It is the reason that in bottled water of 7 big companies, there are residues of pesticides and the 12 soft drink brands collected for testing from in and around Delhi contained residues of four extremely toxic pesticides and insecticides, namely lindane, DDT, malathion and chlorpyrifos (Sunita Narain, 2003). The use of pesticides has doubled in the past three decades. Pesticides can persist in the water long after the chemical has been used.

In the U.S.A. DDT is still found in ground water three decades after the chemical has been banned. Excessive application of nitrogenous fertilizers has resulted in nitrate pollution of ground water. In 1991, India's fertilizer use per hectare was 60 per cent higher than in the U.S.A. India uses over 11 million tonnes of nitrogenous fertilizers annually. All these affects over 100 million households which depend on ground water for their daily needs (N. Gopal Raj 2003).

Further, the coastal areas are affected by seawater intrusion, which increases the salt content in ground water. For example in Chennai, Seawater intrusion has increased from 3 km in 1983 to 9 km in 1987 (V. Padmanand, 1993). In some other parts seawater has intruded to more than 15 kms (R.K. Sivanappan 2003). It is mainly due to over exploitation of ground water. The use of diesel and electric pump sets has increased from 87000 in 1950 to 15 million in 2000 (Marcus Moench 1997 and Sivanappan, 2003).

Some other areas have been affected by the presence of excess chemicals, such as nitrate, arsenic, nickel, chromium and chrome based dyes. In India 37,000 villages are facing the problem of excessive fluoride in water and 26300 villages are having water with excessive salinity (Vasavada, 1996). About a million people are drinking arsenic contaminated water and approximately 2 lakh people have arsenical skin manifestation (Dipankar Chakraborthi 1996).

Table I shows the water quality across India in 1993 and now it has further worsened. It is very clear from the table that the quality of water in India is very bad. It has almost all unwanted elements, which are harmful to human health and development.

Polluted water is one of the reasons for many diseases and deaths in the world. The majority of infectious and parasitic diseases in developing countries are related to water. In India it is estimated that nearly 80 per cent of diseases are in one way or the other related to polluted water (S. Anand, 1996). Diseases spread when people drink dirty water or take bath in contaminated water, or through the insects which thrive in or around water or when water is not sufficient to meet

Table – 1
Water Quality In India

Quality Issue	*Quality*
Pathogenic agents	1 – 3
Organic matter	1 – 3
Salinization	0 – 1
Nitrate	0 – 1
Fluoride	0 – 1
Eutrophication	0 – 1
Heavy metal	0 – 1
Pesticides	0 – 1
Sediment load	0 – 2
Acidification	0

Note: 0 = No pollution 1 = Some pollution and water can be used if appropriate measures taken 2 = Major problem 3 = Severe problem.

Source: Urban Water Resource Management, ESCAP United Nations, New York, 1993.

personal demands. Thus, there are four types of water related diseases, namely water-borne diseases, water-based diseases, water-related vector diseases and water scarce diseases. Diseases like cholera, typhoid, polio and hepatitis A and E are some of the water-borne diseases or dirty water diseases. Diseases caused by aquatic organisms like guinea worms, round worms and tape worms are called parasitic diseases or water based diseases. Water-related vector diseases are caused by insects such as mosquitoes and tsetse flies and these vectors spread diseases like malaria, yellow fever, dengue fever, sleeping sickness and filariasis. Water-scarce diseases or filth borne diseases are caused by water scarcity and diseases like trachoma, leprosy, conjunctivitis, tuberculosis, dysentery, scabies and skin sepsis are of this type (Don-Hinrichsen, et al, 1999). Water related diseases like any other disease reduce the efficiency of labour and cause deaths which reduce the number of working population and increase expenditure on health. It is estimated that water-borne diseases alone are responsible for 41.5 per cent of deaths below the age of six. But A. Lopez (1983) points out that 45 per cent of all deaths in developing countries are due to infectious and parasitic diseases such as diarrhoea and malaria. According to an estimate made by James Winpenny (1994) each year nearly 3 million deaths occur among children under the age of five due to diarrhoea, about 200 million are affected with diarrhoeal diseases, nearly 300 million people with round worm infections, about 150 million with schistosomiasis, and about 300 million with trachoma which makes nearly 5 million people blind. In India water-borne diseases alone cause deaths of nearly 1.5 million children annually. (S.K. Pant, 1996), while K. Balachandra Kurup (1994) explains that 100 million children below 5 years of age may have 300 million incidence of diarrhea per annum, of which 30 million may develop into dehydration 3 million require hospitalisation and many face death. Nearly 2500 children die every day for want of adequate safe drinking water. Guinea worm disease which is a debilitating illness affects 40 to 50 lakhs people each year in African and Asian countries. A.S. Anand, the NHRC Chairman (2004) says that 66 million people in 19 states and 196 districts were affected by fluorisis.

Out of a total of 5,83,000 villages in India nearly 1,64,000 villages are reeling under problems of acute water shortage and water pollution and water related diseases. Due to non-availability of medical facilities and nutritious food and lack of proper treatment of drinking water in rural areas, rural people are prone more to water-related diseases than urban people. V. Hara Prasad (1980) says that the death rate due to dysentery is 9.6 and 16.5 per thousand in the urban and rural areas respectively. Recently in Tamil Nadu hundreds of persons were affected by diarrhoea and admitted in hospital in Kancheepuram area (The Hindu, 1.8.2003), thousands of persons were affected by cholera and of the affected persons 12 persons faced deaths in Dharmapuri district (The Hindu, 29.6.2003) and 6 persons were killed by dengue fever in Kanyakumari district. In Kerala also more than 100 persons died due to dengue fever (The Hindu 4.7.2003 & 27.8.2003). In Andhra Pradesh the number of persons died due to encephalitis (viral fever caused by mosquito) was 148 (The Hindu 24.7.2003).

According to A.L. D'Souza (1995) in India the cost in terms of medical treatment and decline in production because of pollution is around Rs 4500 million annually. S.K. Pant (1996) says that India loses 1800 million man hours or over 200 million man days annually. In Uttar Pradesh, the polluted river Ganga contributes 9 to 12 per cent of the total disease burden. The monetary loss suffered has been put at Rs.960 crore a year (Y. Mallikarjun, 2003).

The ingestion of fluorosis by cattle causes abnormal calcification of bones and teeth resulting in loss of weight and lameness. When water with excess arsenic is consumed by animals, the animals are affected by various ills. Water pollution also affects aquatic life and every year millions of fish perish because of contamination due to municipal sewages and industrial effluents. In short, there is no gainsaying that water pollution accounts for almost 60 per cent of the total loss caused by environmental degradation per annum.

III

WATER POLLUTION IN KANYAKUMARI DISTRICT*

Kanyakumari district is noted for its industrial backwardness. Hence, it could be logically contended that the problem of water pollution in the district cannot be attributed to industrial effluents. However, it could be claimed that water here is defiled mostly by an unscientific disposal of agricultural, domestic, hospital, animal and human wastes into water sources. Further, the percolation of seawater and the accumulation of coir pith in an around water sources make matters worse.

QUALITY OF SURFACE WATER

Surface water refers to water available in ponds and tanks, channels and rivers. Surface water gets polluted due to dumping of various wastes or flowing of sewage and other effluents into water bodies. To know the quality of surface water a sample of pond water and two samples of river water from two different points, one at the origin and the other from the end were taken and tested. The test report is given in the following table:

---

* It is based on a project financed by the UGC.

Table - 2
Quality of Surface Water Available In Kanyakumari District

	Parometers	*Pond water*	*River Water*	
			Station I	*Station II*
1.	E. Coli cell/ 100 ml	300	200	2425
2.	Turbidity (NTU)	3.83	2.75	15.42
3.	Conductivity (μmhos/cm)	110.35	102.5	159.5
4.	pH	6.9	6.7	7.1
5.	Co_2(ppm)	3.6	3.2	4.8
6.	O_2 (ml/l)	4.13	4.75	3.34
7.	Total hardness (mg/l as $CaCo_3$)	3.19	2.89	4.5
8.	BOD (mg/l)	0.028	0.02	0.04

Note: BOD = Bio-chemical Oxygen Demand.
E.coli = Escherisia coli.
Source: Test Reports.

As it could be seen from the above table, 100 ml of pond water in Kanyakumari district generally contains 300 E.coli cells. It also contains Klbesiella species. It means that the pond water carries a heavy load of bacteria and this is due to the use of ponds as garbage dumps. The laboratory tests, to which river water was subjected, have made it clear that it contains certain physico-chemical and microbial characteristics as well. Further, water in the first station of river or places close to their origin is not too turbid and pollution ridden. However, it becomes quite dirty as it courses its way to its destination. There is an increase in BOD indicating an increase in the number of microbes and organic load. The organic load is due to domestic and agricultural wastes. Concentration of Chloride, Calcium and Potassium ions increases in Station II, perhaps due to the addition of ash from nearby crematoria. This is clear from the abnormal increase in turbidity noted in Station II. Such polluted water from pond and river is used by the local people for bathing and washing purposes.

QUALITY OF DRINKING WATER IN TWO SAMPLE REGIONS

As a prelude to a closer and personal study of the problem the investigator picked up two samples at random: one an urban sample and the other a rural sample. The urban sample is the Nagercoil Municipality and the rural sample is South Thamaraikuzham Panchayat. The pollutants contained in the water obtained from the rural and urban samples are given in the following table.

Table – 3
Quality of Drinking Water Supplied in Kanyakumari District

Area	No. of E.coli cells per 100 ml
Rural	50
Urban	0

Source: Test Reports, Rural Primary and Urban Secondary.

The sample water tested clearly indicated that the potable water supplied in the rural area was highly questionable, as the E.coli count was beyond the acceptable level. If this water is continuously used for drinking purposes, the chances of contracting contagious diseases are very high. The presence of E.coli indicates that the water was affected by faecal contamination. Presence of E. coli suggested the occurrence of other pathogenic organisms of faecal origin in the sample water. The most probable reason for the contamination is the unavoidable seepage of pond water in to wells sunk for drinking water. This kind of seepage takes place through under water tunnelling caused by masonry breakdown along the lower rim of the well. Hence, the investigator feels that people should be advised to keep away from untreated well water. The treated water samples obtained fromNagercoil Municipality were not infested by vermins. Their qualities conformed to normal health standards. Further, it is also reported that the water in Mukkudal dam, from where water is taken for the urban water supply, recorded a total colony count of 1200 with a MPN of about 1100-coliforms/100 ml of water. Filtration and chlorination resulted in the reduction of bacteria to more acceptable levels. But it is observed that the chlorine level was very high 3.54 mg/l to 8.86 mg/l in comparison with the maximum accepted level of 3.5 mg/l. The higher chlorine level was due to abnormally large doses of bleaching powder added to water to kill the pathogenic microbes. The absence of solids, ammoniacal, albuminoid and nitrate nitrogen, sulphates and phosphates endorsed the absence of organic pollutants. Absence of fluorides and minimum content of iron were also indicators of good quality water. The electrical conductivity was between 100 m and 120 m and this was due to the ions present in the sample. There was no obnoxious odour also. Thus, if the water samples are of potable quality, health hazards will not be expected among the consumers except in areas where purified dam water mixes with water from tubers in sumps meant for storage. For example in the Soorangudi sump, E.coli count was positive which is about a MPN of 75 coli forms/100 ml even though other parameters were mostly similar. The presence of E.coli indicated leaking of contaminated water into the storage area. However, the overall picture in Nagercoil municipal area is not dismal, since in most water outlets in the town, properly treated healthy drinking water is supplied.

QUALITY OF GROUND WATER

The ground water is contaminated by the chemicals or materials, which are in or around the water sources. In Kanyakumari district, the ground water defilement is in general within the permissible limit. The following table gives the important parameters used to measure the quality of surface water in Kanyakumari district.

Table - 4
Quality of Ground Water in Kanyakumari District

Quality indicators Location	*Total hardness*							
	pH	*ECM mm hrs/cm at 25°c*	*$CaCo_3$*	*CA ppm*	*Mg ppm*	*NA ppm*	*HC_3 ppm*	*CL ppm*
Kanyakumari	8.20	1449	245	52.1	28.0	220.8	329.5	248.22
Kundal	7.80	1331	200	44.1	21.9	213.9	323.30	237.58
Nagercoil	7.00	300	65	16.0	6.1	33.60	62.01	49.64
Thuckalai	7.60	1113	275	61.2	29.2	103.5	49.61	269.50

Source: Ground Water News, September, 1995, p.18.

The ground water quality in Kanyakumari district shows very wide variations. The quality of water in Nagercoil is found to be better compared to other areas. The pH of water is high in Kanyakumari with an increase in electrical conductivity and ionic concentration. Prominent changes in water quality parameters observed in Kanyakumari and Kundal are mainly due to the contiguity of these locations to the sea. There is probably leaching of salt from seawater, leading to an increase in the concentration of ions. Water from Thuckalay area seems to be very hard. This is a rocky terrain, where different types of salts are found mixed with water. The ground water resources from Nagercoil area could be properly exploited for domestic use, since it is comparatively of a more potable quality.

STEPS TAKEN BY CIVIC BODIES FOR TREATING WATER

The investigator could see in the area of his investigation, diseases like dysentery, gastroenteritis, typhoid, skin diseases, diarrhoea, filarisis, hepatitis, trachoma and malaria among the people settled in both urban and rural areas. He could see in the course of his investigation a fast growing awareness about the need for using disinfectants to keep drinking water free from certain highly toxic bacteria. To assuage the feelings of the people, both at the panchayat and municipality levels, efforts are made to chlorinate water as frequently as possible. The processes involved in chlorinating water are quite simple indeed. However, it cannot be denied that the expenses incurred on them constitute a very huge amount as it could be seen from the following table.

Table - 5
Average Annual Expenditure Involved in Chlorination (In 2000)

	Area		
	Municipality	*Town Panchayat*	*Village Panchayat*
Average expenditure (in Rs.)	40,500	11340.33	822.92

Source: Primary Data.

The expenditure, as given in the above table, involved in chlorination is the maximum in urban areas, followed by town panchayats. The average annual expenditure on chlorination in village panchayat has been estimated at Rs. 822.92. It is also reported that in most of the village panchayats, chlorination of drinking water is done only during the rainy seasons. It means that the water supplied in the rural area is not treated regularly. However, there is no complaint from the rural people regarding the quality of the water supplied.

WATER RELATED DISEASES AND THEIR TREND IN RURAL AREAS

The diseases of mankind could be attributed to numerous factors. Among the major diseases to which man is a helpless victim, water related diseases constitute the maximum number. The investigator has collected statistics about water related diseases such as diarrhoea, typhoid, dysentery, scabies, hepatitis, malaria and dengue fever for eight years from 1996 to 2003 from the office of the Deputy Director of Health Services, mainly with a view to study their growth over the years. They are contained in the following table:

Table – 6

Number of Rural People Affected by Seven Important Water Related Diseases in Kanyakumari District During 1996-2003

Year	*Diseases*						
	Typhoid	*Diarr-hoea*	*Dysen-tery*	*Scabies*	*Hepatitis*	*Malaria*	*Dengue fever*
1996	256	396	2834	18637	195	1243	0
1997	218	223	3431	15568	176	1186	0
1998	213	261	2487	10561	161	1066	0
1999	107	218	3784	16663	58	1148	0
2000	182	150	2982	14632	138	957	0
2001	72	61	1061	15645	0	587	0
2002	56	42	912	16712	0	630	0
2003	40	3	816	15901	0	711	201
Growth Rate*	-0.058**	-0.175**	-0.030**	0.0004N.S	-0.918**	-0.016**	

Note: * Calculated figures. NS – Not Significant.
** Significant at 1 per cent level.

Source: Office of Deputy Director of Health Services, Nagercoil.

TREND LINE (*ln*) OF SIX IMPORTANT WATER-RELATED DISEASES

TYPHOID

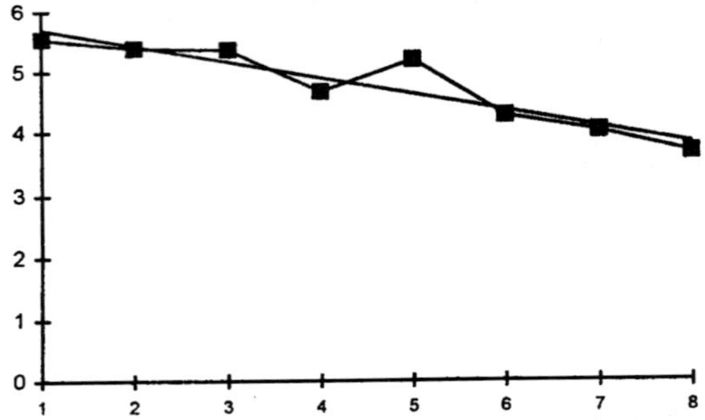

DYSENTRY

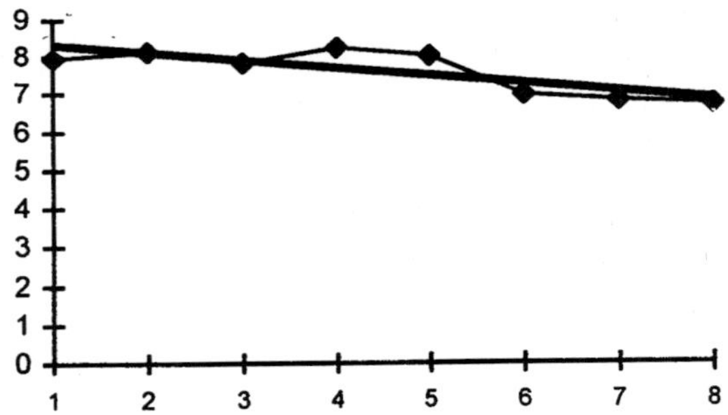

HEPATITIS

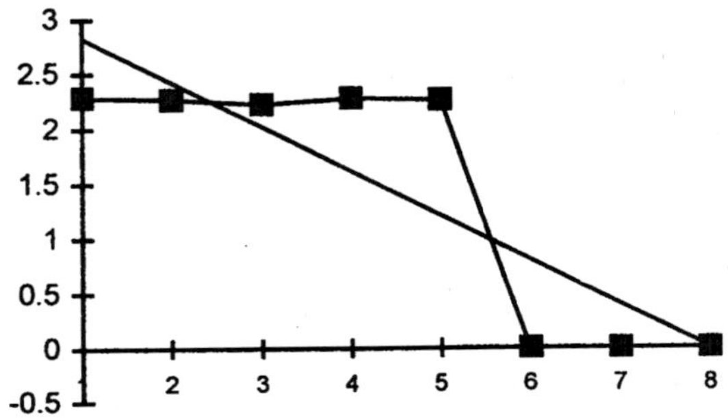

DIARRHOEA

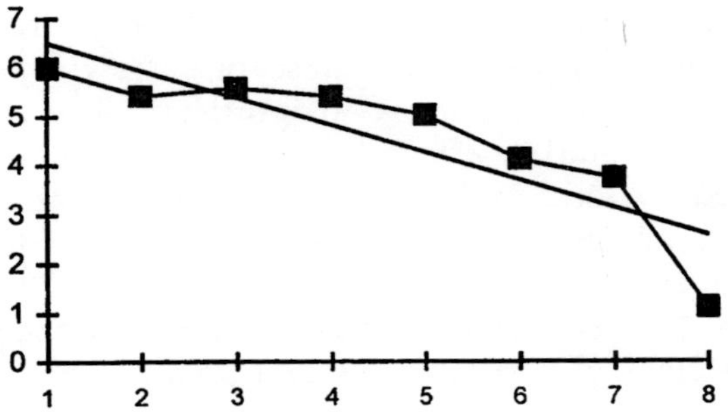

SCABIES

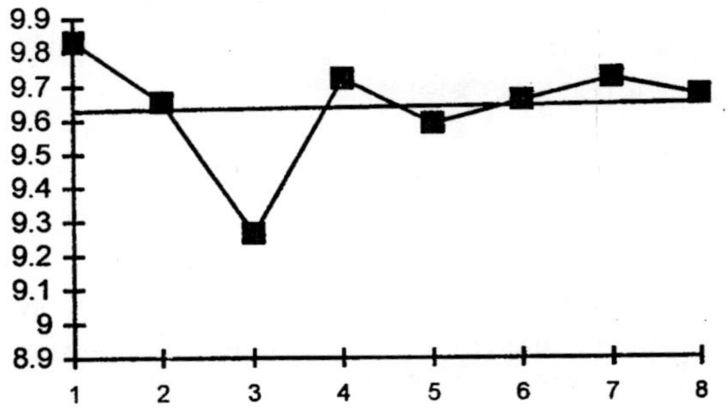

MALARIA

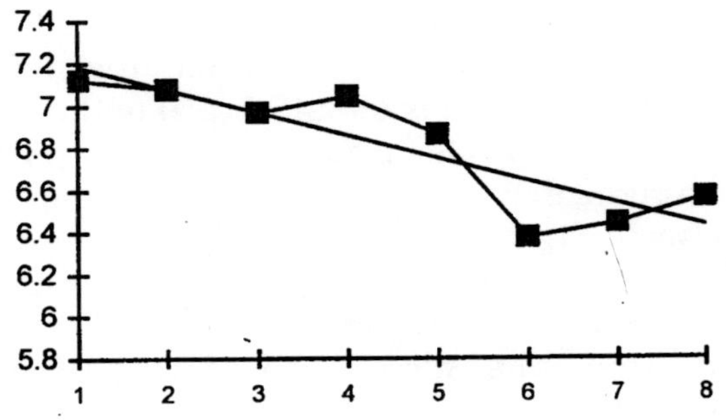

The growth rate calculated for the above six types of diseases (Table-6) clearly shows that out of 6 diseases, five show a significant negative growth rate. But scabies shows a positive growth rate and it is statistically insignificant. The positive growth of scabies could be attributed to the lower quantity of water supplied by local bodies due to very poor rainfall for the last three years in the district. It is further noted that the growth rate for the period from 1996 to 2000 was –0.028, which is significant at 1 per cent level of probability, but for the period from 1996 to 2003, it turned out to be positive due to the increase in the occurrence of scabies in the last three years. Another interesting factor to be noted is that there was a sudden spurt of dengue fever in 2003 in the district.

Water pollution and water-related diseases are not only prevalent in industrially developed districts but also in industrially backward district like Kanyakumari and contribute to human rights violations.

IV

POLICY IMPLICATION

It is very obvious from the above analysis that environmental pollution is a major cause for various types of diseases and a significant number of deaths daily and thereby violation of the basic right of human beings. So steps should be taken to control all types of pollution especially air and water pollution. The following suggestion may improve the quality of air and water.

First of all air pollution must be controlled by effectively enforcing the existing Environment Pollution Prevention and Control Acts. Drastic measures should be taken to regulate vehicular pollution which is the major cause for air pollution. Thanks to the introduction of unleaded petrol the lead content in the air has been reduced. Now nearly 85 per cent petrol sold worldwide is lead-free. Vehicles which emit fumes excessively must be taken off the road.

Water pollution must also be controlled by proper application of Pollution Control Acts. Dumping of agricultural, industrial and domestic wastes into water sources must be immediately stopped by suitable fiscal and legislative measures. The "polluter pays" principle should also be introduced strictly to control all types of pollution.

Environmental education is another method to create environmental awareness enmasse. Student agencies such as NSS, NCC, social service and various other voluntary agencies and people movements including Self Help Group should be used to make people aware of the various types of pollution and their consequences and all of their rights. Then only, the life threatening pollution can be controlled and thereby we can attain a sustainable development and a pollution free universe.

BIBLIOGRAPHY

Furon, Raymon, *The Problem of Water: A World Study,* Faber & Faber, London, 1967.

Seneca, Joseph, J. & Tausig Michael, K., *Environmental Economics,* Prentice Hall, New Jeroy, 1984.

Winpenny James, *Managing Water as an Economic Resource,* Routledge, New York, 1994.

Bhattacharya Robindra, N., *Environmental Economics: An Indian Perspective,* Oxford, New Delhi, 2001.

Manivasakam, N., *Environmental Pollution,* National Book Trust India, New Delhi, 1999.

Kurien, John Water, Fisheries and the Depletion of Marine Resources, Protected Water, Protected Life - The KK.

The World Health Report-2002, AITBS Publishers, New Delhi, 2003.

Hinrichson, Don, Rubey, Bryant., and Upadhayay Ushma, D., Population Reports 1999 Series M. No. 14.

Proceedings, National Seminar on Rural Water Supply and Sanitation, CDS Thiruvananthapuram.

Economic and Social Commission for Asia and the Pacific, Urban Water Resource Management, United Nations, New York, 1993.

Moench, Marcus, "Drawing Down the Buffer: Science, Politics of Groundwater Management in India", *Economic and Political Weekly,* Vol. XXVII, No. 13, March 28, 1997.

Karthikkeyan, D.R., *Human Rights, Problems and Solutions,* Gyan Publishing House.

Aravazhi, D., "Environment, Education and Its Importance in Rural Areas", *Kisan World,* Vol. 30, No. 7, July 2003.

D'Souza, A.L., "The International Drinking Water Supply and Sanitation Decade", *Yojana,* Vol.29, No.10, July 1-15, 1995.

Gopalraj, N., "How Safe is our Water", *The Hindu,* 24.8.2003, p.14.

Dhar Aarti, "India Moving Toward Water Stress Level", *The Hindu,* 7.9.2003, p. 16.

Mallikarjun, "Pollution Levels in Ganga Alarming", *The Hindu,* 7.9.2003, p. 13.

Agarwal, Anil, "Pollution is Snuffing us out", *The Hindu Magazine,* 23.1.2000, p. I.

Helen Mitzgar and Marcus Moench, "Ground Water Availability for Drinking in Gujarat, Quantity, Quality and Health", *Economic and Political Weekly,* Vol. XXIX, No. 13, January 26, 1994.

Padmanand, V., "Resources Friendly Management", *The Hindu,* 2.5.1993, p. 3.

The Hindu, 20.6.2003, 21.6.2003, 29.6.2003, 4.7.2003, 16.7.2003, 22.7.2003, 6.8.2003, 7.8.2003, 27.8.2003, 03.11.2004.

Bhat, Mohd. Yousuf, *Environment and Human Rights,* Reference Press, New Delhi, 2005.

Malhotra Suresh, Upadhayay Pratibha, Gupta Meena, Srivastava Ranjana, Pandey Saroj, *Human Rights, Emerging Issues* (Ed) Kilaso Books, New Delhi, 2005.

WTO AND TRADE IN SERVICES

*D.N. Patil**

In the process of economic development, services sector plays an important role. It provides maximum contribution to the gross domestic product and there is also enough scope for labour absorption. Therefore services sector is considerd high potentiality in both employment and growth.

The service sector contributes about half of the world GDP and trade in service is growing and currently account for more than 20 per cent of all international trade. The advanced economies are predominantly service economies in the sense that services produce, on an average 60 per cent of the GDP and generate about 60 per cent of the total employment. In the low income economies, services contribute more than one-third of the GDP. The services sector in India has grown over the years. Recently some technology or knowledge based service such as software services have also contributed significantly to the growth of this sector. There is a vast level of differences in the development of services, as between the developed countries and developing countries. Therefore inclusion of trade in services is bound to benefit developed countries much more than developing countries like India.

An attempt has been made in this paper to analyse contribution of service sector to GDP and trade in services. Section I deals with the WTO and service sector. Section II compares the share of service sector in GDP and share of selected countries world trade in services. Challenges and opportunities are brought out in section III. The last concluding section presents a brief summary of the paper.

* Faculty, Department of Economics, Karnatak University, Kittur Rani Channamma P.G. Centre, Belgaum (Bhootramhatti) 591156.

SECTION - I

WTO AND SERVICES SECTOR

Service for the first time were brought under the ambit of World Trade Organisation (WTO) agreements in 1995. The General Agreement on Trade in Services (GATS), negotiated in the Uruguay Round, applies the basic rules to trade in goods and services after suitably modified. The GATS provide successive round for services negotiation not later than five years once it comes into force. Negotiations under the GATS of World Trade Organisation (WTO) have officially begun in early 2000.

According to WTO secretariat, the term "Services" covers a wide range of economic activities, viz., (i) business services (including professional and computer), (ii) communication services, (iii) construction and engineering services, (iv) environmental service, (vii) financial services (insurance and banking), (viii) health services, (ix) tourism and travel service, (x) recreational, cultural and sporting services, (xi) transport services, and (xii) other services not included elsewhere.

The WTO recognizes four modes of supply through which trade in services can occur. They are:

- Model 1: Cross-border trade, where the trade takes place from one country into other. Only the service itself crosses the border (e.g. international telephone call).
- Mode 2: Consumption abroad, where the customer travels to the country the service is supplied (e.g. tourism).
- Mode 3: Commercial presence, where the supplier establishes a commercial presence abroad (e.g. foreign banks); and
- Mode 4: Movement of natural persons, where the provider of the service crosses the border (e.g. consultant).

BASIC PRINCIPLES OF GATS:

- Most favoured national treatment: No discrimination amongst other members of the agreements in terms of treatment accorded to their service suppliers.

- National treatment: Foreign services and service suppliers to be treated no less favourably than nationals.
- Progressive liberalisation: The process of liberalisation is irreversible, because of binding commitments on negotiated levels of market access; and
- Transparency: All policies related to barriers to market access and discriminatory restrictions by members are to be notified.

SECTION - II

COMPARISON OF INTERNATIONAL SHARE OF SERVICES SECTOR IN GDP

One of the most encompassing and growing areas of activity is the service sector today. Traditionally we have been thinking only of finance, insurance, transport, communication and tourism in the service sector. But the present development has crossed these boundaries. Nascent and emerging areas such as environmental, educational and counselling services are also part of this emerging sector today. The sheer heterogeneity of activities within this sector is going beyond the hitherto static features of non-storability, non-tradability and intangibility. This has led to a world boom in respect of services, which can be seen from table 1.

In the last two decades, it is evident, the services sector has expanded rapidly all over the world, through by comparison in India the growth has not been so pronounced. In fact, India has lagged behind even compared to some countries in South Asia. Interestingly some of the developing countries like, those of Latin America have services accounting for a higher per centage of GDP than the world average and even Japan. Generally speaking, the developed countries have dominated this expansion of services accounting for three-quarters of world services output. In 1999, services sector accounted more than 70 per cent of GDP in developed countries like, U.S.A., Japan and France. In South Asia, service sector accounted less than 50 per cent of GDP. Correspondingly services today constitute over 50 per cent of economic activity in developing countries which is significantly more than the traditional sectors such as agriculture.

Table 1
Share of Services in Gross Domestic Product

(Per cent)

	Share of Services in GDP	
	1980	*1999*
South Asia		
India	36	46
Pakistan	46	49
Bangladesh	34	50
Sri Lanka	43	52
Nepal	26	37
Regional Average	37	47
East Asia		
Hong Kong	49	85
Singapore	61	64
Korea	45	51
China	21	33
Regional Average	28	41
Latin America		
Argentina	52	67
Brazil	45	61
Mexico	59	67
Regional Average	50	62
Africa		
South Africa	43	64
Kenya	47	51
Zimbabwe	50	55
Regional Average	43	56
High Income		
USA	64	74
Japan	54	62
France	62	74
Regional Average	61	71
World	55	63

Source: World Development Indicators, 1998, 2001.

TRADE IN SERVICES

The growing importance of services is reflected in the international trade too. Trade in services is growing and currently account for more than 20 per cent of all international trade. Service for the first time was brought under the ambit of World Trade Organisation (WTO) agreements in 1995. It may be noted that the growth of international trade in services in the last two decades has been much faster than that of the trade in goods. The value of international trade in services comes about one-fourth of the value of the trade in goods. Services make up a major share of the invisible accounts in the balance of payments. The most important services in international trade include transportation, travel, communications, media, business services, engineering and construction, and banking and financial services.

There is a common belief that developed countries have tremendous potentialy in the services sector and the developing countries have limited options to improve their position.

There is a vast level of difference in the development of services, as between the developed countries and the developing countries. Therefore inclusion of trade in services is bound to benefit developed countries much more than the developing counties like India. The share of selected countries world trade in services is presented in Table 2. Data indicate that the share of developed countries in services trade was higher than developing countries during 1997 and 2001. The principal exporters of services are the USA, UK, Germany, France, Japan, Italy, Hongkong and Canada. They account for about more than 50 per cent share of the world trade in services. It is these countries that will benefit most from the new agreement on services as arrived at in the Urugay Round and the share of developing countries declined like Malaysia, Thailand, Mexico etc. The share of the Indian world trade in services has increased marginally. But export of services is less than import of services during the period of 1997 and 2001.

The service industry is in an incipient stage in many developing countries and its progress will now be throttled under the new agreement. As far as India is concerned, services sector is not as underdeveloped as in many other developing countries. Yet, in terms of the new agreement, it will be required to denationalise insurance and banking. Thus the banking sector may not be able to play a positive social role as it has been playing since 1969 when the major banks were nationalized. Foreign firms will now be free to expand their network in the Indian services sector. They will also be free to remit resources to their parent country in the form of profits, interest, royalties etc. All this will involve a foreign exchange burden on India. As far as Indian firms are concerned, they will find it difficult to compete with the firms supplying services in the developed countries. Thus it will not be an easy task for them to penetrate the services sector in developed countries.

Table 2
Share of Selected Countries' World Trade in Services

(Percentage)

Sl. No.	*Country*	*1997*		*2001*	
		Export	*Import*	*Export*	*Import*
1	2	3	4	5	6
1.	India	0.65	0.94	1.4	1.7
2.	U.S.A.	17.48	11.65	18.3	13.1
3.	U.K.	6.92	5.45	7.5	6.2
4.	Germany	5.63	9.03	5.5	9.0
5.	France	6.05	4.74	5.5	4.2
6.	Japan	5.13	9.33	4.4	7.5
7.	Italy	5.40	5.36	4.1	4.1
8.	Hong Kong	2.88	1.77	3.0	1.6
9.	Canada	2.20	2.74	2.4	2.8
10.	China	1.84	2.30	2.2	2.5
11.	Korea	1.91	2.21	2.0	2.3
12.	Singapore	2.29	1.48	1.8	1.4
13.	Malaysia	1.12	1.33	0.9	1.1
14.	Thailand	1.17	1.30	0.9	1.1
15.	Mexico	0.84	0.90	0.9	1.2
16.	World	100	100	100	100

Source: Statistical Outline of India, Tata Services Ltd., 1999-2000, 2002-2003.

SECTION - III

CHALLENGES AND OPPORTUNITIES

WTO offers both challenges and opportunities for the Indian services sector. Obviously, challenges are far more serious and striking given the lack of competitive strength of Indian services sector. Already, India has experienced almost a decade of market oriented reforms and many serious problems are coming to the surface.

1. The economy in general and services in particular are victims of high cost.
2. The technology gaps of several years are too glaring. Even more worrisome are the difficulties in securing technology transfers from developed countries.
3. Hard core reforms (e.g. exist policy, privatisation, etc) are still politically difficult for implementation and hence, there is a virtual lack of flexibility in operations.
4. As a consequence, Indian services are not competitive in terms of price, quality and delivery schedule.
5. Most developed countries are unreceptive to Indian's problems and are always demanding larger market access into India, including her to fulfill WTO compliance on many issues earlier than required.
6. India's share of world exports is a meagre 0.5 per cent and her share of trade in world services is 1.4 per cent (export) during 2001; hence, it does not command any bargaining strength in WTO level negotiations.
7. India's political economy is not very stable. The prevailing system of coalition governance is not conducive for prompt and effective policy changes and their implementation.

Obviously, most of these problems are of our own making and will have to be resolved by our own internal efforts. At the WTO negotiating table, we can only raise, issues applicable to global trade, which do not comply with its given provisions and conditionalities. While effective negotiations are a must, we can neither procrastinate the day of reckoning nor reverse the imperatives of WTO driven globalisation of the Indian services industry.

CONCLUSION

In the last two decades, the services sector has expanded rapidly all over the world. Services sector accounted more than 70 per cent of GDP in developed countries. Inclusion of trade in services is bound to benefit developed countries more than developing countries like India. The principal exporters of services are the USA, Germany, UK, France, Japan, Italy, Hong Kong and Canada. They account for about more than 50 per cent share of the world trade in services. But India account for 1.4 per cent share of the world trade in services in 2001. India will find it difficult to compete with the firms supplying services in the developed countries. Thus it will not be an easy task for India to penetrate the services sector in developed countries.

REFERENCES

Bhandare S.S., (2001), WTO and Indian Industry, Forum of Free Enterprise, Mumbai.

Central Statistical Organisation (Various issues): National Accounts Statistics, Ministry of Statistics, Government of India.

Mathew Joseph, Rupa Rege Nitsure, (2002), WTO and Indian Banking Sector: The Road Ahead, *Economic and Political Weekly*, Vol. XXXVII, No. 24, June 15-21.

Mattoo, A.R. Rathindvan, and A. Subramanian (2001), Measuring Service Trade Liberalisation and Its Impact on Economic Growth: An Illustration; Policy Research Working Paper, 2655, World Bank, August.

Prithwis K. De, (2000), Trade in Services: Opportunities and Constraints, Yojana, Vol. 44, No. 9, September.

Statistical Outlie of India, Tata Services Ltd., 1999-2000 and 2002-2003.

World Development Indicators, 1998, 2001.

World Development Report, 1999-2000.

GLOBALISATION, INTELLECTUAL PROPERTY RIGHTS AND PROSPECTS OF INDIAN AGRICULTURE

*Geetanjali Sharma**

GLOBALISATION

Globalisation means increasing integration of developing countries into the global economy.[1] It is achieved through Liberalisation of Trade and Capital Markets, increasing Internationalisation of Agricultural Production, Corporate Production and Technological Change that is rapidly dismantling barriers to the international trade ability of goods and services and the mobility of capital.

Indian economy was at the height of economic crisis in 1991 that let India to adopt certain reforms which could be termed as 'New Deal' or 'New Economic Policy'.[2] A major component of this New Economic Policy is Globlisation i.e. linking the Indian Economy with the World Economy. Globlisation is associated not only with an increasing cross-border movements of goods, services, capital, technology, information and people but also with an organisation of economic activities which straddles national boundaries.'[3]

Globalisation implies the degree to which a particular economy is integrated with the rest of the world. There are 3 aspects of the globalisation process namely ; (i) Trade in Goods, (ii) Trade in Services and (iii) Trade in Finance[4]. While the above exchanges between nations are important, I shall only concentrate on 'Trade in Goods' only. The present study fills the void in the existing literature by considering Trade in

* Institute of Management, Jiwaji University, Gwalior.

Goods explicitly and focuses upon the relationship between economic growth and Trade in Goods. Trade in Goods of all descriptions (agricultural, industrial or others) is to be governed under GATT re-formulations.

WORLD TRADE ORGANISATION

On January 1, 1995, just after the most comprehensive but the most contentious GATT trade round was concluded, the first and the most powerful world trade regulating agency, named, World Trade Organization (WTO) came into existence[5]. India is one of its 132 founding members. Many more countries, notably China, Russian Federation, Saudi Arabia, etc. are waiting to join it. The WTO is the umbrella organization responsible for overseeing the implementation of all agreements that have been negotiated just before it came into existence or those that will be negotiated in future. The WTO is expected to provide a forum for further negotiations on matters already covered by the agreements as well as new issues. It is also responsible for settlement of disputes among its members. Finally, periodic review of the trade policies would also be initiated under the auspices of WTO.

Before the WTO came into existence, until 1994, international trade in merchandise was guided by the rules and provisions of the General Agreement on Tariffs and Trade (GATT). The GATT rules, however, did not work effectively to absorb the complexities of world trade which had been growing steadily since the Bretton Woods days, both, in terms of commodity coverage and the nature of regulators applied by the regional trade blocks and "big players of the trade game"[6]. Moreover, the GATT umbrella did not cover trade in services which was assuming extreme significance to a number of countries, partly because transnationalization of finance and capital was increasing under global restructuring of commodity production, and partly because the expanding volume of merchandise necessitated a larger to and fro flow of trade in services. Agriculture too was outside the GATT purview[7].

GATT, GATS AND TRIPS

It is essential to makea note of the overall guiding principles that would govern the flow of international trade. The two most significant principles, ostensibly highly assuring to the so-called weak partners (developing and the least developed economies) are the Most Favoured Nation (MFN) Principle and the National Treatment Clause.[8] Under the former, no discrimination is to be exercised among member countries; any trade concession offered by one member to another must be offered to all members. Under the later, imported products and domestic products are to be accorded the same treatment; moreover, besides import duty; no extra tax other than ones also levied on domestic products is to be imposed. Then, the multilateral trade system must be predictable; foreign companies, investors and governments must feel assured that trade barriers (including tariffs, non-tariff barriers and other measures) would not be raised arbitrarily by any trading partner. Lastly the new trade regime should work to a greater advantage of the less developed countries,[9] they must be given more time to adjust, greater flexibility and some special privileges. In overall terms, it would appear that for the developing economies, the incentive to join the multilateral trade system would be no less justified than for the developed world. Jumping into international trade arena would look too good to ignore.

Let us now briefly look at some of the agreements. On a broad plane, the canvas of WTO agreements is spread over three compartments; goods, services and intellectual property rights. First, Trade in goods[10] of all descriptions (agricultural, industrial or others) is to be governed under GATT re-formulations. Second. Trade in Services of all kinds (e.g. business services including professional and computer; communication; construction and engineering; distribution, educational and environmental services; financial services (banking and insurance); health services; tourism and travel services; recreational, cultural and sporting services; transport services, and consultancy) is to be regulated under General Agreement on Trade in Services (GATS). Trade in services thus encompasses practically all varieties of services in use the world over (e.g. service supplied from one country to another such as telephone calls, or consumers making use of service in another country, such as tourism, or a foreign company setting up a subsidiary or branch such as a foreign bank, or individuals working abroad on a service contract such as Indian software professionals in USA and so on). Third, Trade Related Aspects of Intellectual Property Rights (TRIPs)[11] would set out the terms and conditions for the international flow of intellectual property. While GATT and GATS are based on three-part structures (namely, general principles, associate agreements on specific sectors/issues, and commitments of individual members), the TRIPS agreement contains only general principles expected to be followed by member countries.

Under GATT, thirteen major agreements (on customs valuation, pre-shipment inspection, technical barriers to trade, sanitary and phytosanitary measures, import licensing procedures, safeguards, subsidies and countervailing measures, anti-dumping, trade-related investment measures, textiles and clothing, agriculture and rules of origin) have been signed. A few of these, viz. Agreement on Textiles and Clothing (ATC), Agreement on Agriculture (AoA), and Agreement on Antidumping Measures (ADP) attract our pointed attention given the structure of India's external trade, the employment stakes involved in ATC and AoA, and the hurt that these agreements are likely to cause to the Indian economy. Under the ATC, the restrictions hitherto maintained by the developed countries on import of textiles, clothing and ready-made garments from the developing economies, are to be progressively phased out by the end of 2005. Under the AoA, the member countries would have to drastically reduce subsidies granted to the farm sector and convert them into tariffs. The tariff rates would be reduced and appropriately bound, against subsequent increases. Finally, under the ADP, if a country exports a product at a price lower than the one it normally charges in its domestic market or if it sells it at less than the cost of production, it can be complained against for anti-dumping activities; retaliatory measures can be instituted.

The serious implications of anti-dumping activities for small producers can be easily visualized.[12]

TRIPS AND DEVELOPING COUNTRIES

The GATS Agreement requires all governments to publish laws and regulations and to establish 'inquiry points' for information, calls upon the member countries to enter into mutual or multilateral arrangements to facilitate mutual acceptance of standards, qualifications, etc., to work for the elimination of monopoly of service providers, through WTO's intervention, and so on. In particular, it requires that persons who are themselves service suppliers or employed by service suppliers shall be governed in terms of the specific commitments given by countries relating to the entry and temporary stay of such persons, and that, with the exception of cable or broadcast distribution of radio and television programming, a country must provide all service suppliers (domestic and foreign) access to any public telecommunication network; developing countries are allowed to impose reasonable conditions to strengthen their telecommunication infrastructure and so on.

The broad objective of the TRIPS[13] Agreement is to let individual countries reap the exclusive fruit of human intellect emanating in their local traditions, scientific discoveries and research, work experiences and so on. In fact, the Agreement links and clarifies, the existing international conventions on intellectual property rights with international trade, by delineating the areas where patents can be granted against those where patenting is not permissible. For the time being, the IPR Agreement covers seven areas only; patents, copyright and related rights; trademarks, industrial designs, layout designs of integrated circuits, geographical indications and undisclosed information. Detailed guidelines are prescribed as to how the international IPR agreements should be applied, how to give adequate protection to IPRs and how to settle disputes on IPRs and so on.

With the advent of science and technology, the importance of protecting intellectual property rights has got much prominence. Intellectual property is the new wealth of nations and it grows much faster than other industrial properties. Japan is the most technologically advanced country in the world, which got highest number of patents registered in the world followed by US and Europe. In Asia, two other countries, i.e. South Korea and China, which have highest number of patents registrations every year. Obviously, foremost position is occupied by Japan followed by South Korea and China. Number of patent applications in China was three lakh last year which shows tremendous increase in patent applications after modernization of its patent system.

There are seven areas of intellectual properties viz. patents, industrial designs, trade marks, geographical indications, copyrights and related rights, layout and designs (topographic) or integrated circuits and protection of undisclosed information. Among all intellectual properties mentioned above, patent is the most important issue these days not only in India but also world over. The countries, which are more technologically advanced, invest more money into R&D activities which results more inventions and thus they get patent for the protection of their intellectual properties. China, who is latecomers in protecting intellectual properties, has set up 5000 IPR training institutes. To get patent, one has to fulfill three criteria viz. novelty, non-obviousness (inventive step, which means that the invention has to involve technical advances as compared to existing knowledge or having economic significance or both and its industrial application.

TRIPS AND INDIAN AGRICULTURE

India is far behind in the area of patent compared to its. Asian giants. During 2002-03, 11466 patent applications were filed out of which 9538 applications were examined and finally 1379 patents were granted compared to 3,00,000 patents were granted in China in 2002-03[14]. Until 31 December 2004, Indian Patent system was guided by Indian Patent Act 1970, which acted as major catalyst of massive growth of India's drug and pharmaceutical industry. Term of patent was patent was seven years from the date of application or five years from the date of grant of patent for process patents for drugs & pharmaceuticals, agro-chemicals and processed food and a period of 14 years for other products.

India has signed TRIPS (Trade Related Intellectual Property Rights) of the Final Act of the Uruguay Round of multilateral trade agreement in 15 April 1904. As per India's commitment to the TRIPS Agreement, India has given product patent for drugs and pharmaceuticals. Agro-chemicals and processed food from 1 January 2005. Terms of patent would also to be 20 years from the date of filing. In order to fulfill its commitment made in the TRIPS Agreement, India was required to amend its Patent Act 1970. Accordingly, it made first amendment in 1999 providing mailbox facility to the product patent applications. Second amendment it made in 2002 extending the terms of patents for 20 years for product patents and third amendment it made in March 2005 giving effect to its product patent system to drugs and pharmaceuticals, agro-chemicals and process food. According to new act, India cannot give process patent in these three lines of industrial production, but the companies, which are already producing generic drugs of patented version they can continue to produce so after paying royalty to the patent holder in commercial terms and conditions. Another important issue is patenting traditional knowledge. India is a very rich country in biodiversity having stock of six per cent of world's total flora and fauna. First such vast biodiversity can be protected from the piracy of developed countries without paying any remuneration to the local communities, who are the main catalysts for improving and protecting traditional knowledge and maintaining rich biodiversity. There has been several occasions when Multinational Corporations (MNCs) of the developed countries got patent of our traditional knowledge like neem, turmeric and basmati rice, but finally CSIR was able to revoke them in the US and European patent offices. Issue relating to seed patenting is also equally important for India, because MNCs have been trying to introduce their new chemical and pesticide-resistant seeds which they develop with the help of recombinant DNA technology. This will gradually remove our traditional varieties of seeds which our local communities have developed and maintained over generations.

One of the most important issues in the GATT/WTO agreement has been the inclusion of agricultural trade into its provisions. This is for the first time in the history of GATT that agricultural trade has been brought into the international forum.[15] This inclusion has meant a particularly serious development for the developing countries which are highly dependent on their farm sector not only for export earning but also for people's incomes and development. It is not that the inclusion of agricultural trade into the WTO framework itself is being objected to, but the whole gamut of issues like subsidies, intellectual property rights, investments, and new trade barriers like environment, and labour standards have become controversial.

Though a lot has been written about the benefit of WTO agreement to developing countries, most of the studies on supply response in agriculture in the developing countries show that it is likely to be highly inelastic to change in terms of trade due to WTO implementation. In fact, some of the studies show a negative response. Even if there are positive benefits of trade in agriculture due to WTO provisions, they are not likely to be very large for developing countries as the markets in agricultural commodities are highly imperfect due to the fact that international commodity markets are controlled by a few Multinational Corporations practically in each commodity sector. In fact, in some of the commodity markets, 3-6 firms control as much as 85-90 per cent of the trade. Further, most of these multinational trading agencies belong to the Western Europe, the U.S. and Japan. Therefore, a rise in international prices due to agricultural trade reforms may not go over sizeably to the farmers in developing countries.[16]

So fast as the implementation of WTO provisions is concerned, there have already been quite a few manipulations by the developed world. For example, developed countries engaged themselves in dirty tarrification, that is, they used data which allowed tariffs to be bound as high as possible.

These countries went in for higher reduction in low tariff sectors than in the high tariff ones. Thus, they could reduce tariffs at an average rate of 36 per cent but average tariff levels were reduced by less than this percentage. In contrast, India has agreed to tariff bindings of 0 per cent in some commodities like milk powder which are now being renegotiated to at least 50 per cent as the domestic market is witnessing its adverse effects.

Unless recently, agriculture had remained out of the purview of international trading regime. Attempts to extend IPR's to agriculture were resisted by the developing countries. Even the US Department of Agriculture (USDA), specially the Agricultural Research Service of USDA, was opposed to IPR's in agriculture as it felt that IPR's would restrict free exchange of germ-plasm, an essential requirement for future plant breeding activities. However, the developments in the field of biotechnology, the declining levels of financial support to publicly funded research institutions and the increasing role of private sector companies in bio-tech research gave an impetus to the movement for extension of IPRs to agriculture. the debate on the desirability of IPR in agriculture has been long and acrimonious. The resolutions of Food and Agriculture Organisation (FAO), which initially considered germ-plasm as a common heritage of mankind, and the demand of the plant breeding industry for protection of plant variety, were sought to be resolved under the CBD. CBD enjoins upon the countries to promote exchange of genetic material, recognises the sovereign rights of the countries over the germ-plasm and the need for compensation for use of genetic material. The GATT agreement only addresses the issue of IPR's and is silent on compensatory payments for farmers' rights.

In view of the very clear enunciation of farmers' rights in the Indian plant variety legislation, the existing system of seed procurement which largely depends on the seeds produced by the farmers themselves is unlikely to be affected. In a study of Punjab Wheat it was found that even for a state like Punjab, over 92 per cent of total seed requirements were met by the farmers themselves. The commercial seed sources, supplied only 8 per cent of the required seeds. The seed replacement rates for wheat are also extremely low. As against a norm of seed replacement of 25 per cent per annum, the replacement rates achieved were less than 7 per cent in 2002-03. The importance of price factor in small share of commercial seeds in total seeds and low seed replacement rates is not very significant. The seed cost in total variable cost of production for major wheat growing states of Haryana, Punjab and Uttaar Pradesh was less than 10 per cent; as a proportion of total cost of production, it was less than 5 per cent. Studies on appropriability of benefits from newly developed seeds conducted outside India indicate that for self pollinating crops like wheat, farmers were passed on over 90 per cent of the incremental benefits to induce them to adopt the variety. The passage of plant variety protection bill in India, therefore, is unlikely to adversely affect the wheat production in the country. On the contrary, it might lead to higher investments by private sector companies in research, distribution and marketing networks which might ultimately lead to availability of quality seeds on time and contribute to higher production.[17]

CONCLUSIONS

The increased pace of globalisation of trade in agricultural commodities which was expected with GATT 1994 is not likely to be fully realised in view of the experience of the implementation of the accord across countries. The adverse impact on Indian agriculture which was feared by many in the country seems to be unfounded given the inherent competitiveness. Enough safeguards are available to counter the threat of cheaper imports. India is not required to reduce support to farm sector due to GATT accord. There is however a pressing need to target the subsidies more effectively to benefit small and marginal farmers for whom these subsidies were originally intended. Greater attention needs to be devoted to the provision of inputs such as seeds, fertilizers and uninterrupted power supply to the sector to boost agricultural production.

The international trading environment has not opened upto the extent predicted. The developed countries have managed to hold on to their position of the main cereal exporters by delinking support to farmers from market prices. Non-tariff barriers have been replaced by tariffs but the effective level of protection has not declined. In view of the above integration of Indian agriculture in the global trade which is a competitive trade scenario can be realized only by reducing domestic cost of production through measures which increase productivity and control procurement and distribution costs. The road to globalisation lies in productivity increases and not on the pre-supposed opening up of markets abroad.

REFERENCES

Gulati, A. and Narayan, S., (1999), Indian Agriculture in the Global Economy, Focus WTO, Indian Institute of Foreign Trade, p. 31.

Bhagwati, J. and Srinivasan, T.N., (1993), Indian Economic Reforms, Govt. of India Ministry of Finance, p. 15.

Nayyar, Deepak, (1995), "Globlisation-The Past is our Present" Presidential Address, 78th Annual Conference, I.E.A. Chandigarh.

Gordon, M., (1998), The Global Economy, Oxford University Press, p. 44.

Reddy, C.R., (2000), "WTO Stirs Again", The Hindu, May 11, 2000, p. 4.

Aggarwal, Yogi, (1994), Is GATT Really Bad for India, The Tribune, Chandigarh, Vol. 114 (51) Feb. 21, p. 15.

Gulati, A and Narayan, S., (1999), Indian Agriculture in the Global Economy, ibid. p. 35.

WTO (1995), Global Trade-WTO's Assessment of Recent Trends, Report of WTO, 1995, p. 99.

Kwa, A., (1998), WTO and Developing Countries, Economic Policy in Focus, Vol. 3, No. 37, Nov. 1998, p. 29.

Nayyar, Deepak, (1995), "Globlisation-The Past is our Present", ibid, p. 51.

Reddy, C.R., (2000), "WTO Stirs Again," The Hindu, ibid., p. 6.

FICCI (2000), Seminar on "Impact and Implications of WTO on SSI Sector", FICCI, New Delhi, March, 2000.

Gulati, A. and Narayan, S., (1999), Indian Agriculture in the Global Economy, ibid., p. 30.

Khare, V.V., (2004), TRIPS-"One Step Forward and Two Steps Backward", Times of India, 21 March, 2004, p. 14.

Gulati, Ashok, (1998), "Indian Agriculture in an Open Economy : Will it Prosper"? India's Economic Reforms and Development, Oxford University Press, New Delhi, p. 69.

Gulati, Ashok, (1998), ibid., p. 73.

Gulati, Ashok and Kelly, Tim, (1999), "Trade Liberalisation and Indian Agriculture", Oxford University Press, New Delhi, p. 24.

BIOTECHNOLOGY AND PATENT LAW

Sreenivasulu N.S & Dr. C. Basavaraju***

INTRODUCTION

Biotechnology is a study relating to microorganisms and related things. It concerns with the practical application of microorganisms or their components. Biotechnology is broadly defined as 'any technique that uses living organisms or parts of organisms to make or modify products, to improve plants or animals, or to develop microorganisms for specific uses'.[1] Biotechnology is not one single technique, but rather a collection of techniques utilized to manipulate living organisms in directed fashions. By its very nature, Biotechnology when utilized towards practical applications is multidisciplinary, requiring a team approach directed at targeted goals.[2] 'A series of advanced technologies spanning biology, chemistry, biochemistry, microbiology, protein engineering, process engineering and genetic engineering put together and collectively called as biotechnology.[3] Biotechnology is a new area of science, being notable for employing processes and products that are alive.[4] It is a technology that compounds life sciences and chemical science.

APPLICATION AND SCOPE OF BIOTECHNOLOGY

Though the concept biotechnology is new, historically speaking, biotechnology was an art in the production of wines, beers and cheers. At that time the nomenclature" biotechnology" was not there.[5] Traditionally biotechnology comprised of fermentation processes to produce beers and

* Research Scholar Department of Postgraduate Studies and Research in Law, Manasagagotri, University of Mysore, Mysore - 570 006.

** Reader & Chairman, Department of Postgraduate studies & research in Law, Manasagangothri, University of Mysore, Mysore-570006, Karnataka, India.

cheers. Presently biotechnology comprises modern techniques such as DNA technology and genetic engineering. Genetic engineering is a process of transformation or manipulation of genes to produce new living forms such as new varieties of plants, animals or microorganisms, which are hitherto not in existence. It involves technical interference into biological processes to produce novel living forms.

In modern days biotechnology is being applied in diverse fields such as agriculture, medicine, environment etc. Biotechnology is being used to produce new and developed varieties of plants and animals. It is used to produce microorganisms, which are useful in the therapeutic and surgical processes, in the production of consumable products, and also in the cleaning up of pollutants in the environment.

Though biotechnology is a modern science less than 30 years old, it is revolutionizing production in certain areas of industry and agriculture.[6] In agriculture field, biotechnology is being used to invent new plant varieties with the qualities of high yield, resistance to pests, resistance to viruses[7] and capacity to with stand drought conditions. It is estimated that 20 to 40% of the world's agricultural production is lost due to pests, weeds and diseases, and an additional 40% would suffer the same fate without pesticide application. The control of insects pests and weeds may be achieved by diverse strategies encompassing a mix of traditional and modern biotechnologies.[8] This technology may also be used to incorporate different characteristic features of two or more plants into one plant. The genes in plants providing for certain special features can be isolated and put together into one plant with the help of biotechnology. A new and improved variety of plant possessing different characteristic features can be produced through manipulation of genes or incorporation of foreign genes into the cells of existing plant. This process is called genetic engineering.[9]

Genetic engineering could be made use of to produce a plant bestowed with different features that it was not earlier. For example we can take BT cotton, BT rice and also BT soybean. These are the varieties of plants produced through genetic engineering. BT cotton is a cotton variety, which is produced by incorporating foreign genes from different cotton varieties providing for different qualities into the intended plant. This BT cotton is a new variety possessing different features. Here the characteristic features of different varieties are put together into one variety.

In plant inventions genetic engineering intends to provide for high yield (genetically engineered wheat, rice are said to yield upto 30% more under same cultivation conditions compared to regular, wheat or rice), resistance to pests, resistance to particular herbicides, raising the consumer value of foods derived from the plants.[10] (Eg: Farmer tomatoes, potatoes with a longer shelf life and higher protein fortified Soya) The new biotechnology methods will not replace traditional agriculture, forestry or horticulture approaches, but rather will provide deeper insight into productivity and quality factors, while reducing the time required to introduce improved products and services into these important economic sectors.[11] In fact new species are not created by biotechnology; rather existing species are given some new capability.[12]

Biotechnology has significant role to play in improving the capacity of plants producing consumable foods. It has revolutionized the food industry with its innovative genetically modified food. Hopefully it may solve many fold problems of the present day, especially energy and food crisis to cater the needs of growing population of the world.[13] Here plants producing consumable food such as vegetables or rice or wheat etc., can be modified and genetically manipulated to produce high yield with high protein values. Genetic engineering has clearly enhanced the techniques available for use in food production. It may increase food quality, taste, and improve storage capacity.[14]

Biotechnology is poised to change the field of agriculture in ever-so-many unprecedented ways and will, no doubt, influence the way we live.[15] Biotechnology has revolutionized the agriculture industry with its transgenic plants. As these transgenic plants are bestowed with different advantages, scientific community is encouraged to involve in the invention of new varieties of plants. As early as in 1995, fifteen transgenic plants were given market permission and thirteen were waiting for permission in U.S.[16] The European community countries were reported to have released 496 transgenic plants during 1986-1994.[17] In India the growth of biotechnology is bit slow, some field trials have been made by importing transgenic plants during 1995–96,[18] Proagro an Indian seed company has a joint venture with plant genetic systems (PGS International) of Belgium to develop hybrid oil seed rape (canola) and vegetable seeds for the Asian market. Mahyco, a large Indian seed company has proposed to undertake trials in glass houses of imported BT cotton by crossing it with Indian lines.[19]

Biotechnology is being applied on animals in different ways. Inside an animal body many proteins are produced that are useful in the manufacture of drugs and medicines. Through biotechnology, proteins produced inside the body of any animal can be identified and can be produced industrially to use in the manufacture of drugs and medicines. For instance Pig; its body is called as pharmaceuticals factory. There are many proteins produced inside the body of a pig, which are useful in the manufacture of drugs and medicines. Likewise proteins produced inside any animal body can be isolated to produce industrially to use in the medical field. Moreover biotechnologically produced animals can be used in testing new medicines and curing processes. Usually any medicine or any curing process will be tested and experimented on animals before it is used for human usage. One such example is Oncomouse, the animal invented through biotechnology to use for cancer testing.

Animals are used as bioreactors to produce human metabolic products. One of the famous cases is that of Tracy, a sheep whose germ line contains a genetic construction comprising a human gene plus 'Promoter". As a result Tracy's milk glands produce proteins identical to human ones, which can then be removed from the milk by using known processes. Examples of such protein are human insulin. Human genes and hormones are being isolated to use in the production of medicaments. One such example is relaxin hormone naturally produced in women's ovaries at the precise onset of labor, and its function is to relax the muscles used in giving birth. It is produced by a gene, which is activated at this particular time. The invention claims the isolation of the gene from the ovarian cells and its insertion into the genome of a bacterium from which relaxin can then be produced on an industrial scale. Artificial relaxin can help prevent unavoidable complications in labor.[20]

Biotechnology is being used to produce new drugs, medicines, surgical process and diagnostic methods. In the nineteen eighties many new inventions have been made in the medical field. This field has witnessed remarkable changes and has made tremendous progress during that time. In 1982, genetically engineered insulin approved for use in diabetics in U.K and U.S.A. In the mid nineteen eighties, genetically engineered growth hormone approved for treatment of dwarfism, new antibiotics have been produced by cell fusion, genetically engineered proteins used to treat heart attacks and strokes, new vaccines are invented against foot and mouth disease, monoclonal antibodies employed to boost the body's defense against cancer and other diseases were introduced. A genetically engineered yeast derived vaccine became available in 1986 for the hepatitis-B, which is a major public health problem.[21]

The process of gene therapy an innovation of biotechnology that can be used in the treatment of hereditary diseases. First gene therapy method to treat deceases has been patented in the year 1995. Biotechnology represents a powerful alternative to traditional pharmaceutical methods of drug discovery, which as practiced for most of this century involved the laborious screening of thousands of organic compounds found naturally in soil, plants, and molds.[22] Roughly $175 to $300 million to develop a new biotech medicine compared to cost of a new pharmaceutical drug run from $ 300 to $ 500 million.[23] Biotechnology firms have brought more than 50 new medicines to market, have more than 350 medicines and therapies in various stages of clinical testing and garnered in excess of $ 16 billion in sales in 1998.[24] Now a days matters concerning environment are given much importance. Nations are much concerned in the protection and preservation of environment. Abetment of pollution is a matter of high priority in the domestic policies of different Nations. Biotechnology can play a vital role in the abatement of pollution For cleaning up of pollutants in the environment, microorganisms produced through biotechnology can also be used. This has come to limelight when Dr Anandha chakraburthy, a microbiologist in America invented a microorganism, which is being capable of splitting the oil pollutants in the environment.

Biotechnology is the result of intellectual labor; it is an application of human ingenuity to biological processes. It involves human interference to a biological process. Human intervention differentiates biotechnological process from biological process. Naturally biological process takes place without human intervention. When there is human intervention to this biological process, it results in producing new things hitherto not in existence. This effort of intellectual labor deserves protection under patent law. Patent law protects any new, and useful invention by a grant of patent. These non-naturally occurred, human made and synthetically produced inventions of biotechnology shall be protected to get the desired fruits and also to encourage further research and development.

BIOTECHNOLOGY INVENTIONS AND PATENTS

Patent law intends to promote science and technology. Patents are incentives for research and developments. Universally, Patents are given to any new and useful invention having industrial application. The requirements of patentability are universally recognized. Any inventor has to satisfy that his invention is new, hitherto not existed in the public domain and also it has got industrial application. Patent gives an exclusive right to the inventor to exploit, use produce, sell, license, and assign the invention for a limited period of time. Here the term invention is defined to mean: any useful art, machine of manufacture and composition of matter. Infact, living subject matter was not included in the definition of invention.

With the advent of biotechnology, when non-naturally occurring living inventions started rocking the world, the term invention has been redefined to include living things. In the definition of the term invention, the phrase "composition of matter" now includes within its fold living things produced through biotechnology. This brings biotechnology inventions within the canopy of patent law. Now patent protection has been extended to living things produced through biotechnology such as; microorganisms, bacteria, algae, plants, animals, enzymes, viruses, cells (cells being considered as microorganisms) and also genetic elements such as DNA etc.[25] Three universally recognized patentability requirements; novelty, non-obviousness and industrial application are also applied to biotechnology inventions. Any biotechnological invention that satisfies all the above requirements is eligible for the grant of patent. Patent grant is a "monopoly right given to the inventor on his invention for a certain period of time. Once patent is granted after satisfying the above-mentioned requirements, except the patent owner no other person is entitled to use, exploit or to deal with the patented invention. The inventor will be rewarded for his intellectual labor in inventing a new thing, which is useful to the society. Intellectual property rights are universally recognized and patent protection is available on universal basis for any new, innovative and industrially applicable invention irrespective of its field of application.

PHILOSOPHY AND JUSTIFICATION FOR THE PATENTING OF BIOTECHNOLOGY INVENTIONS

The basic premise of patent law is to promote the progress of science and technology. Research and development activities leading to new inventions provide for the progress of science and technology. These research activities and inventions need some stimulation. There should be incentives to the inventors to endeavor. Patent grant provides necessary stimulation to the inventors. It is an incentive provided to encourage an inventor. The philosophy behind the patent law is to promote the progress of science and technology by providing incentives to inventions with an ultimate objective of economic development.

Since the days of first patent statute enacted by the Venetian Republic[26] till the time the philosophy behind the patent, laws remained the same. The economic development is possible through the promotion of science and technology. The innovations of science, if applied industrially, if exploited commercially could serve different purposes of the society. There is no doubt in saying that; patent law has stimulated research. One has to agree that patents promoted the progress of science and technology, as a mean for the economic development. The advent of biotechnology, the new kid of science has merited the progress of science. Biotechnology being capable of catering to the needs of the society is now at cross roads seeking patent protection.

The rationality behind giving patent protection to any invention is that; it rewards the inventor for his efforts. Lockean labor theory says that inventor's labor in the invention deserves protection. The theory states that patent is recognition for the hard work of the inventor.[27] The utilitarian theory[28] says that there shall be maximum benefit of the maximum members of the society. As per this theory a patent is justified, if it provides for the maximum benefit to the maximum members of the society. In the sense, an invention should provide for the benefit of the community. Patent is an incentive for the inventor to disclose his invention. If an invention is disclosed, then society can use it, and enjoy the fruits of it. That is how a patent serves for the maximum benefit of maximum members of the society.

PARIS CONVENTION ON INDUSTRIAL PROPERTY

The Paris convention on industrial property says that states shall endeavor to protect industrial property. Here industrial property is understood in the broadest sense and shall apply not only to industry and commerce but also to agriculture and extractive industries and to all manufactured or natural products. For example grain, tobacco, leaf, fruit, cattle, minerals, mineral water, beer, flowers, etc.,[29] Biotechnology is industrially applied in diverse fields such as agriculture, cattle, medicinal and food sector. In the sense biotechnology comes within the purview of the meaning of industrial property. So, if we want to protect industrial property, we have also got to protect biotechnology.

The rationale behind the protection of industrial property is to provide stimulation to research and development. By stimulating the growth in research and development the convention aims at the proliferation of technology and finally at economic development. Biotechnology having its application in diverse fields is playing a vital role in the economic and industrial development. Patenting biotechnology is well justified under the convention as it is extensively applied in diverse fields. So if we want to protect industrial property under the Paris convention, we should not forget biotechnology inventions, then only the real purpose behind the convention would be served.

PATENT CO-OPERATION TREATY AND INTERNATIONAL PATENT PROTECTION

The contracting states under this treaty are desirous to make a contribution to the progress of science and technology. The treaty intends to foster and accelerate the economic development of developing countries by increasing the efficiency of their legal system to protect inventions. Biotechnology is such an invention that has got its role to play in the economic development.

With its diverse applications biotechnology has got all the capabilities to mark its impact on the economy of the Nations. Inventions of biotechnology in agriculture field such as new plant varieties, animal verities with qualities of high yield, high quality, faster growth rate may foster the growth of any economy. At the same time inventions in the medical field may serve the societies health concern with drugs at affordable prices and also with innovative life saving drugs. Further the treaty aims to facilitate access to ever expanding volume of modern technology. Access to the modern technology can be provided if we give patent protection for such inventions.

Once patent is given for a particular period of time, at the expiry of such period such invention falls into the public domain, so that any one can have access to it. If patent protection is given to any biotechnological invention, at the expiry of the patent duration, such biotechnology falls into the public domain, which can be used by the public. Moreover Patent cooperation treaty provides for International patent protection. Once application is filed under the treaty and patent is granted; then there is no need for individual applications in member states. Such patent is valid and enforceable in all the member states. Such being the case, once patent protection is given to biotechnology.

However, in case of biotechnology inventions patent application shall accompany a deposit of the claimed invention. The reason is that it is not possible to give complete and clear description of biotechnology inventions in writing. So the deposit of invention serves the purpose. Budapest treaty[30] provides for international deposit of microorganisms for the purpose of patent procedure. Application for patent on biotechnology inventions has to accompany the deposit of the claimed invention in any depositary recognized by the treaty. It is possible to give patent protection to biotechnology inventions under the above conventions. The language of the conventions is broad enough to encompass biotechnological inventions. Patent protection to biotechnological inventions is very much justified under the conventions.

EVOLUTION OF THE PATENT LAW ON BIOTECHNOLOGY

The evolution of patent law relating to biotechnology dates back to nineteen sixties. In famous "Red Dove" case of 1969, which confirmed a rejection by the German patent office of a method for breeding doves with red plumage only on grounds that the method was not repeatable. In fact it was the first case to open the door to the patenting of biotechnological inventions, as these became eligible for patent protection if they met the criteria for patentability.[31] In the early seventies in Europe, issues relating to biotechnology invention have raised eyebrows. In the early 1970's German Federal Supreme Court upheld patent protection for new microorganisms, if the inventor were to demonstrate a reprodusable way for its generation.[32]

However the path breaking decision of patenting of Biotechnology inventions can be found in of Chakraburthy's case. After this decision in 1980 by the U.S Supreme Court there was spur of patent application on Biotechnology inventions. In *Diamond Vs. Anandha Chakraburthy,*[33] the claim was a synthetically produced, genetically engineered microorganism being capable of breaking down multiple components of crude oil. When USPTO and Board of Patent Appeals rejected the claim finally the issue reached the Supreme Court. Chief Justice Burger delivering the opinion of the Court held that; Chakraburthy's microorganism is not available naturally, it is human made, it is a novel invention capable of industrial application, hence is eligible for patent. The Court opined that 35 U.S.C. 101 is broad enough to cover biotechnological inventions. The invention was held as satisfying all the necessary requirements of patentability. The law relating to biotechnology inventions can be traced to the wordings of U.S constitutions Article 1; Sec: 8 Clause (8), which states that: "the congress shall have the power to promote the progress of science and useful arts, by securing for limited times to inventors the exclusive right to their respective inventions".[34] The United States patent law is justified based on Article: 1, Sec: 8, Clause (8) of the U.S Constitution.

Biotechnology is new wing of science. Science has progressed to invent new living things through biotechnology. This progress of the science deserves to be protected under Art: 1 of the U.S constitution. Biotechnology inventor shall be granted exclusive rights for a limited period of time to promote and encourage further development. Title 35 of the United States code has codified the patent Act of 1952. 35 U.S.C 101 states that "whoever invents or discovers any new and useful process, machine, manufacture or composition of matter or any new and useful improvement thereof, may obtain a patent" therefore subject to the conditions and requirement of this title.[35] Biotechnology inventions can be given patent protection by considering as composition of matter under.

U.S.C. however for many years, products of nature doctrine acted as a bar to patents from being issued on living matter. This doctrine limited composition of matter to exclude products of nature from patentable subject matter.[36] The practice of considering living matter as products of nature has broken with the decision of U.S Supreme Court in Chakraburty case. The products of nature doctrine was purportedly overturned in this land mark case[37] This remarkable decision has laid a foundation to the development of patent Law on biotechnology inventions. It has opened floodgates for the patenting of biotechnology inventions. After this decision United States Patents and Trademarks Office (USPTO) started issuing patents on biotechnology inventions. There was major upsurge in the patent applications on microorganisms and related biotechnology inventions before USPTO. Chakraburthy decision has paved the way towards the changing contours of patent Law. It has affected the patent canopy to be extended to cover biotechnology inventions.

PATENTING OF TRANSGENIC PLANTS AND RELATED INVENTIONS

The journey of patent law in patenting of biotechnology inventions has not confined just to microorganisms, but it has continued to extend patent protection to plant and related inventions. In 1986 in *Expart Hibberd,* the US patent office Board of Appeals overturned the refusal of a patent examiner to allow a patent on maize mutants. The patent examiner had argued that the invention was 'product of nature'. With this decision the USPTO began issuing patents protecting biotechnological inventions in plants, including in plant varieties.[38] There was a spur of applications for patenting of plant related inventions after this decision, as Plants, seeds, plant tissues could be patentable. Likewise BT cotton and BT rice were patented in 1992 and BT soyabean in 1994.

PATENTING OF TRANSGENIC ANIMALS

The voyage of patent law in patenting of biotechnology inventions has shifted to animals and related inventions in the second half of the 1980's. Societies ethical and moral concerns were more in case of patenting of animals. Opponents of patenting of animals took recourse to nature doctrine to prevent animals from being patented. However scientific community's pursuit of getting reward for their efforts in animal and related inventions has outweighed the oppositions. The progress of the science and technology was given much concern than that of doctrine of nature. In 1987, in Ex parte Allen[39] a claim for an animal invention had come before the court. The PTO rejected the patent on the grounds that it was naturally occurring subject matter and obvious. Allen appealed the PTO's rejection to the Board of Patent Appeals and interferences, but the board ultimately rejected his application on the grounds of obviousness.

Although Allen's patent application was denied, the board rejected the claim that the Oysters were naturally occurring subject matter and consequently left alive the issue of patenting of living organism. Consequently, this decision kept open the possibility of patenting of living organism.[40] Here the Board of appeal rejected the patent on the ground of obviousness but it rejected the stand the PTO that Oysters claimed in the patent application was naturally occurring subject matter. To put it otherwise, the Board of Appeal accepted that Oysters is a non-naturally occurring living subject matter.

Soon after this decision USPTO issued a statement where it stated: The USPTO now considers non-naturally occurring non human multicultural living organisms, including animals to be patentable subject matter within the scope of 35 U.S.C 101. On the basis of this policy the United States Patent and Trademark Office granted the first patent on an animal the Harvard Oncomouse in 1988.[41] In the Harvard Oncomouse case, the claim was a genetically modified mouse useful for cancer testing. The patent was granted, as the oncomouse was non-naturally occurring non-human, melticellular living being.

With this decision animal inventions have become patentable subject matter.

After patenting of Oncomouse, the mice race continued and at least 16 patents have been granted on inventions relating to transgenic mice. On the same lines transgenic sheep producing targeted protein milk patented, pigs that produce low cholesterol meat and animals that produce pharmaceuticals in bioreactors were patented.[42] The race continued and patents were also granted on pig, goat, and cattle expressing diverse proteins. Now it is possible to build a farm with transgenic animals[43] be a nucleus, inside that nucleus there will be chromosomes and on the chromosomes genes will be there.

PATENTING OF CELLS AND GENES

The law relating to biotechnology inventions has furthered to include within its realm cells and genes. The advent of recombinant DNA technology, gene splicing, gene manipulation have poised towards the patenting of cells and genes. Cell is considered as a microorganism, which is a part of every living being plant or animal or human being. Cell is having the capacity of self-replication and can grow into number of cells. It was estimated that in human body there are more than 3 trillion cells. Inside cell there found a nucleus. Inside nucleus, there exist genes. There are many genes inside a cell. Gene is a specific chemical pattern on chromosome (cell structure) that is received from the parents on hereditary basis and it controls the development of particular characteristics in any living matter. In 1984 in U.S a patent was granted on human cell line. The cell line was taken from the spleen of a person called John Moore. Moore cell line was producing valuable antibacterial and cancer fighting proteins. Here onwards the patenting of human cells, gene sequences and genes were started. In 1995 U.S has granted a patent on the cell line of a Hagahai man from Papua New Guinea. Recently a patent claimed on the cell line of Guayana Indian women in the U.S was forced to be given up because of worldwide protests against patenting of indigenous women. In Europe an attempt was made to file a patent claim on a women's breast, which was genetically engineered to produce pharmaceuticals in her breast milk.

Under the current practice of the European patent office cells and parts thereof are considered as microorganisms. According to the latest decision of the EPO's Enlarged Board of Appeals in the "Novarties" case decided on 20th Dec, `1999, this appears to be justified since modern biotechnology has developed from traditional microbiology and cells are comparable to unicellular organism.[44] In *Novarties* case genes were held to be patentable.[45] Much of the developed world seems to be moving towards patent protection for inventions such as genes. An element isolated from the human body or otherwise produced by means of a technical process, including the sequence or partial sequence of a gene, may constitute a patentable invention.[46] Thus human genes are unambiguously patentable in the European Union, if these can be shown to be industrially applicable. In U.S and Australia apart from human beings and the biological processes for their generation, all other inventions relating to animals or animal parts or even a part human inventions are patentable, subject to the overall exception on morality and public order. In Singapore patents Act 1994, there is no bar to the patenting of living organisms at all. Living things including human genes, gene sequences, cells are unambiguously patentable in Singapore.[47]

However USPTO believes that transgenic humans are excluded under the U.S Constitution. In Pioneer *Hibred International*[48], it was held that while human cloning is excluded, aspects such as a components for use in human cloning and methods of human cloning are patentable. In the U.S. there is a major upsurge in the patenting of genes. There is a plethora of gene patent applications. One has to believe that in the year 2001 alone USPTO awarded 20,000 gene patents and another 25,000 were pending.[49] It is anticipated that with the decoding of the entire human genome, medical science will be revolutionized and it is possible to cáre hereditary diseases. At the USPTO more than 1,00,000 provisional patent applications are pending a decision on various segments of human genome.[50] Indian patent Act of 1970 was not providing for patenting of living things. There was no scope under this patent Act for the patenting of biotechnological invention. However having signed TRIPS agreement India has brought changes in its patent law. Now under Indian patent law patents are made available for biotechnological inventions also. Living matter produced through biotechnology is now in India patentable.

TRIPS AGREEMENT AND EXTENSION OF THE CANOPY OF PATENT LAW

After having a long run of negotiations, finally TRIPS agreement came into being. TRIPS says under Art: 27 (3) (b) that patent shall be available for non biological, microbiological, processes and microorganisms provided that they are new, involve an inventive step and are capable of industrial application. In fact TRIPS article 27 (3) (b) is based on the article 53 (b) of European convention.[51] It is important to note that three universally recognized criteria of patentability now incorporated into Art: 27 of TRIPS namely novelty, non-obviousness and industrial applicability or utility which applie to all inventions including biotechnology inventions.[52] It further provides that patent rights shall be enjoyable without discrimination as to the place of invention and the field of technology. The TRIPS agreement has become a means to promote a strong and comprehensive standard of patent protection for the increasingly valuable contribution made by science and industry.[53]

When patents are made available to all types of inventions in all fields of technology, patents shall also be made available to the inventions of biotechnology. As biotechnology is a scientific innovation it is a new wing of science and as it is a new face of technological development in life sciences, it is included within the meaning of 'invention' under TRIPS. Now the term 'invention' includes inventions of biotechnology. Moreover the agreement intends to give patent protection for processes as well as products. So patent can be sought for new processes as well for products of biotechnology under the agreement.[54] There is adequate scope under the TRIPS for the biotechnology invention to be patented. By virtue of TRIPS agreement in many countries now Patents are made available to living being such as new verities of plants, animals and microorganisms[55] produced through biotechnology. Recent European directive on biotechnological invention 1998[56] provides further encouragement to biotechnological inventions. It has clarified that plants and animals as well as their separate elements are eligible for patents.[57] Moreover when an element from human body isolated by technical process including the sequence or partial sequence of a gene may constitute a patentable invention under the directive. Thus genes of living beings including human genes are unambiguously patentable under the European union directive.

CONCLUSION

However moral standards of the society say that; plant and animals being the creation of God are not patentable. The argument to support this contention is that plant and animals are products of nature, gifted by god and are not patentable. Living things such as plants, animals, and microorganisms are considered as common heritage or common property which can't be monopolised by private individuals. Private rights should not be acquired over common property. But these moral standards of the society have been altered by the Chakraburty decision. After this decision, common heritage principle has become obsolete and non-naturally produced living things have become patentable.

The position in a country like U.S is such that "anything under the sun is patentable" provided there is some human intervention. This voyage of patent law providing for patenting of living subject matter started from patenting of non-naturally occurring microorganisms which has now reached a stage where in technically isolated human genes, gene sequences, cell lines are getting patented. European unions directive on biotechnological inventions has clarified that; an element isolated from human body by technical means including human genes, gene sequences are unambiguously patentable.

Countries like Australia, Japan and the like are following almost same way. But countrys like India, where in traditions are respected, moral standards are followed, the principle such as common heritage or common property is very much relevant. In fact in India living things such as plants and animals are considered as sacred and god given. People are reluctant on acquiring ownership over such natural and living things.

Indians use to worship few plants and animals as a resemblance of God. At this juncture the patent protection given to living things produced through biotechnology is not fully acceptable to Indians. The provisions of TRIPS, provisions of EU directive providing for the patenting of biotechnological inventions and also the amended patent Act are against the principle of common heritage in allowing patenting of living beings. Still being a signatory to TRIPS agreement, India has to give patent protection to living beings such as microorganisms produced through biotechnology.

TRIPS agreement provides for the patenting of new plant, animal varieties and microorganisms produced through biotechnology. All the member countries have to bring changes in their patent laws to confirm to the provisions TRIPS. India was intransition period till January 2005 to change its laws and to adopt the provisions of TRIPS agreement. India has thrice amended its patent law to bring itself in conformity with the provisions of TRIPS agreement. (India amended patent law in 1999, 2002 and in March 2005) Now in India, there provided patent protection for biotechnological inventions; such as microorganisms since January 2005 onwards. This clearly shows that there is a diversion from the traditional principles of the country. India is getting diverged from its traditional and customary practices to give patent protection to living beings produced through biotechnology. The stage is set and the show has just begun in India.

NOTES

1. Gabrielle J., Agricultural Biotechnology: Opportunities for International Development, C.A.B International, Wallingford, U.K. 1990, Page No. 31).

2. Ibid, Pg. No. 378.
3. John E. Smith, Biotechnology, Cambridge University Press, London, Third Edition, 1996.
4. Christopher Arup, The new world trade organization agreements, Cambridge University Press, U.K, 2000. First published, Page No. 224.
5. Supra Note 3.
6. Jayashree watal, Intellectual property rights, Oxford University press, London 2002, Pg. No. 128.
7. The first virus resistant transgenic crop was given marketing permission in 1995 in the U.S., see, Gene exchange, Aug 1994, Pg. No. 9.
8. Gabrielle J. Parsley, Agricultural Biotechnology: opportunities for International development, C.A.B International, Wallingford, U.K. 1990, Page No. 123, 124.
9. Genetic engineering originally developed in bacteria; the technique was first used to move novel genes into plants in 1983. (See Hooykas and Schilperoort 1985, for review). Since then progress in crops has been dramatic, and as early as in 1986 field trials of crops engineered for insect resistance were under way in the United States, see, Gabrielle J. Parsley, Page. No. 108.
10. Swaminathan, An introduction to the principles of patent law, Bahli brothers, Delhi, first edition, 2000, Page No. 335.
11. Gabrielle J., Parsley, Agricultural Biotechnology: opportunities for International development, C.A.B International, Wallingford, U.K. 1990, Page No. 379.
12. Ibid. Pg. No. 434.
13. Ranga, Animal biotechnology, Agrobios (India), Jodhpur, 1999-2000, Pg. No. 3.
14. Christopher Arup, The new world trade organization agreements, Cambridge University Press, U.K, 2000, first published, Page No. 216.
15. Shivramiah Shantharam, Jan Montgomery, Preface, Biotechnology, Biosafety and Biodiversity, scientific and ethical issues for sustainable development, Oxford and IBH publishing company private limited, New Delhi, 1999, reprinted 2000.
16. Ibid, Pg. No. 19.

17. Gene exchange, Dec. 1994, Pg. No. 7.
18. Annual report of the Department of Biotechnology1995-96.
19. Shivramiah Shantharam, Jan Montgomery, preface to "Biotechnology, Biosafety and Biodiversity, scientific and ethical issues for sustainable development", Oxford and IBH publishing company private limited, Delhi, 1999, Reprinted, 2000, Pg. No. 2-4.
20. Swaminathan, An introduction to the principles of patent law, Bahli brothers, Delhi, first edition, 2000, Pg. No. 335-336.
21. Supra Note No. 13, Pg. No. 4-10.
22. Rochelle drayfuss, Diane L., Zimmerman, Harry first, Expanding the boundaries of intellectual property, Innovation policy for the knowledge society, Oxford University press, New York, 2004, Pg. No. 257.
23. See, Daniel, Vasella, Novartis role in 21st century drug development, 15, Nature Biotechnology, 485 (1997).
24. Pharmaceutical manufacturers Association Annual Report for 1998; Scotorrison & Glen Giovannetti, Bridging The Gap; 13th annual Biotech industry report (Ernst & Young, 1999).
25. Rajiv Jain, Rakhee Biswas, Law of patents (Procedure & Practice, Vidhi publishing (P.) Ltd., New Delhi, Second Edition, 1999, Page. No. 1.35.
26. Donald S. Chisum, Craig Allen Vard, Herbert F. Schwartz, Pauline Newman, F. Scott Kieff, Principles of patent law cases and materials, University case book series, Foundation press, New York, 1998, Pg. No. 11.
27. Ibid, Pg. No. 35-37.
28. Ibid, Pg. No. 45-47.
29. International legal instruments of Intellectual property rights law, Volume: 1, National Law School of India University, Bangalore, Paris Convention for the protection of industrial property. Article" 1 (3).
30. Budapest Treaty was made in the year 1977.
31. Jayashree watal, Intellectual property rights under the WTO and developing countries, Oxford University Press, New Delhi, 2002, Pg. No. 152, See also wegner (1976), P. 156.
32. Ibid, 152, See also Adelman etal, (1998), P. 235.
33. 447, U.S 303 (1980).

34. Manu Luv Shahalia, Perspectives in intellectual property Law, Many sided to a coin, Universal Law Publishing Co Pvt Ltd, Delhi, 2003 edition, Pg. No. 171.
35. Ibid.
36. Ibid Pg. No. 172, see also, Carrie F. Walter Beyond the Harward Mouse; current patent practice and the necessity of clear guidelines in biotechnology patent law; 73 Ind L.J, 1025)
37. Ibid.
38. Jayashree Watal, Intellectual property rights, Oxford University press, London, 2002, Pg. No. 152.
39. 1987 2 USPO 2d 1425.
40. Manu Luv Shahalia, Perspectives in intellectual property Law, Many sided to a coin, Universal Law Publishing Co Pvt Ltd, Delhi, 2003 edition, Pg. No. 173.
41. Ibid.
42. Supra Note No.38, Pg. No. 164.
43. Prabudha ganguli, Pg. No. 125, 126.
44. Supra Note No. 38, Pg. No 132, See also WWW. European-patent-office.org.
45. Ibid, Pg. No. 151, See also, www. European-patent-office.org.
46. European Union Directive on Biotechnology Inventions, Art: 5.2.
47. Supra Note No.38, Pg. No. 166, 167.
48. Pioneer Hi-bred International V. Holden Foundation seeds Inc., 35F, 3d.1226.31 USPQ, 2d.1385 (8th Cir. 1994) as cited in Morges et al (1997). P. 68.
49. Albright. M., (2002), "The end of the revolution, "Gene watch, 15.3.
50. Supra Note No. 38, Pg. No. 169, See also www. Ncbi.nlm.nih.gov/ genome/guide.
51. European convention provides that patent shall not be granted fir plant and animal verities essentially biological processes for the production of plants and animals, inventions whose exploitation would be contrary to morality or order public. But the position in the article does not apply to microbiological process.
52. Supra note No. 50, Para No. 3, Pg. No. 132.
53. Christopher Arup, The new world trade organization agreements, Cambridge University press, New York, 2000, Para No. 4, Page. No. 248.

54. In India we have already seen inventions of biotechnology such as BT cotton, BT rice.
55. Article 27of Trade Related aspects of Intellectual Property Rights. 1994. 56 European directive on biotechnology inventions came into force in 2000.
56. Jayashree Watal, Intellectual property rights, Oxford University press, London, 2002, Pg. No.155.
57. Bibek debroy, Intellectual property rights, B.R. Publishing Corporation, Delhi, 1998. Pg. No. 239.

IMPORTANCE OF INDIGENOUS HEALTH CARE PRACTICES OF MONPA TRIBE OF ARUNACHAL PRADESH UNDER IPR AND NEW REGIME

*Manish Sharma**

The significance of Indigenous Knowledge System (IKS) in health care has been an area of growing concern to the society as well as to the Government of India as alternative Medicinal System (AMS) in this new regime of World Trade Organization when every country is talking about Intellectual Property Rights (IPR).

Knowledge, practice and attitude vary from one society to another. It depends on how the societies have possessed, organized and preserved this knowledge, further it depends on various aspects of their surroundings. This paper reflects on the knowledge and nature of indigenous health practices among the Monpa tribes of Tawang district in Arunachal Pradesh. This paper explores also the ways of dealing with the IKS with the development and profound changes taking place in the Monpa society. This paper has been divided in to three parts. In part one, concept and importance of Indigenous knowledge has been dealt with special reference to IPR, and materials and methods have also been discussed in this section, in part two knowledge and practices of traditional medicine (TM) among the Tawang Monpa Tribe of Arunachal Pradesh has been discussed and in last part conclusion and suggestion have been given.

* Lecturer in Economics, Government College, Bomdila , Arunachal Pradesh.

I

India harbors a varied diversity of plants and animals and impressive variety of habitants and ecosystem. Now a days, a lot of discussions are there concluding "It is the treasure house from which future needs will be met with and where elements will be found that will form the basis of a new knowledge and technology". But the environmental problem such as climatic changes, depleted resources, pollution, and undamaged and untrammeled use of the natural resources have enhanced the problem of habitants and ecosystem. Against this scenario, now it has been felt that environmental relationship must be symbiotic for sustainable development of the human society. After further analysis it has been observed that it is at the local level that both the wealth of diversity and threats to it are more tangible. And hence importance of Indigenous Health Practices based on Indigenous Knowledge System (IKS) emerges as an important issue. Indigenous knowledge system (IKS) means institutionalized form of indigenous knowledge (IK) of any society, which is transferred from generation to generation in a systematic and informal way. This knowledge is the outcome of hundreds of years of researches, experiments, experiences and adaptation to local culture and environment. Indigenous knowledge (IK) covers a wide range of subjects such as agriculture, education, food preparation, small-scale industries, health care and many more aspects of life. Often this traditional knowledge is looked against the modern knowledge system, but in actuality both are complementary and supplementary to each other.

Importance of Indigenous Knowledge System (IKS) is ingrained in an African proverb: When an old knowledgeable person dies a whole library dies. Due to less cost and readily availability the importance of Traditional Medicine (TM) is much more, in under developed countries. Indian Government has also realized it and has taken steps to create Traditional Knowledge Digital Library (TKDL).

World Health Organization (WHO) has also felt the importance of it and recognize it by defining traditional medicine (TM) as "the sum total of all the knowledge and practice, whether explicable or not, used in diagnosis prevention and elimination of physical, mental and social imbalances and relying exclusively on practical experience and observations handed down from generation to generation whether verbally or in writing.

Major multinational pharmaceutical giants are turning to incorporate many of the traditional medicine (TM) in to their products and are making efforts to access them either directly or through the use of modern tools of breeding and cultivation (tissue culture, cell culture, and transgenic technology). All these activities reveal the importance of traditional medicine (TM) under IPR and new regime. Traditional medicine do not consist only of plants and herbs but many other things also such as animals organs, insects, flies, animal's products and spiritual activities (though spiritual activities are out of scope of the present paper due to various limitations).

Under the new economic order of the world particularly with the emergence of the WTO, a lot of discussions are there for Intellectual Property Rights (IPR) raising issues like feasibility of protection of indigenous knowledge system (IKS) with existing Intellectual Property Right (IPR) system. In this connection World Intellectual Property Organisation (WIPO) held a conference in October 1998 and under the aegis of the WIPO, an agenda for the future of Intellectual Property right (IPR) in the field of traditional medicine was prepared, which patronize activities in this area, namely development of standards for the availability, scope and use of IPRs (Intellectual Property Right) on traditional medicine in the Asian countries. The grant of patent to many known traditional medicine (TM) of the under developed countries to the developed countries is now causing a great concern to the developing countries. Now the developing countries gradually perceive that they are getting or importing the same product at dearer prices what they were producing at cheaper cost by traditional method with the help of traditional knowledge. There are several examples of it, such as the patent registered for wound-healing properties of turmeric by US which was challenged by India through CSIR to US Patent No. 54015041 in 1997 and by COICA an organization of the tribal of Amazon region against US patent No. 5751 in 1996 for B. Caapi a herbal plant.

All these examples signify the importance of indigenous knowledge system (IKS) particularly in health care, where with less cost and easy availability of the medicine, people can get better health care facilities. Tawang of Arunachal Pradesh being a remote area with a treasure of huge biodiversity keeps much relevance for this type of study.

MATERIALS AND METHOD

This study is based on field work conducted in Tawang district covering all the 05 circles (administrative blocks) during 2003-04 .The survey was under taken to study the health seeking behaviour of the Monpa through a structured questionnaire. The results discussed in this paper are based on the informations given by 350 household on the common diseases prevailed in the area and their local treatment. Botanical or scientific identification of the species is still in process.

II

Tawang is the western most district of Arunachal Pradesh with 2085 Sq. K.M. area having a population of 28,287 (1991 Census) and the population density of the district is only 13. The majority of the population belong to the Monpa tribe and the religion professed by them is the Buddhism of Mahayana sect .The Monpa of Tawang have their own age old style of traditional medicine (TM), which includes the naturopathy, herbs in various forms (Powder, leaf, oil, inhaling of vapour etc.), animal organs, birds, and of course spiritual practices by the lamas and the shamans. (Spiritual Man) They are simple and religious in nature. Due to tough hill terrain with a range varying from 4, 000 ft. altitude to 13,500 ft. altitude and cold whether (Severe cold during winter) they are subjected to cold prone diseases. They use firewood to keep their living room warm, added with poor ventilation facilities and no proper chimney for exhaustion of smoke; they are also prone to various respiratory diseases.

They practice traditional medicine (TM) for the minor diseases particularly the people living in inaccessible area with scarce means of communication. Mostly the knowledge and information was passed from generation to generation. The speciality of this tribe is that, their social organization or rural organic structure revolves around the monasteries and the Buddhist Monks (Lamas) and they have the expertise and are trained in selection, collection and processing, and the use of various parts of the herbs. During our survey we found a lot of information about the practices of traditional medicine (TM), which have been shown in Table 1 in brief. Now-a-days the impact of modernization is also seen in the villages in the health care sector. So this is the high time to discuss about it and documentise it and popularizes it among the masses.

Table 1
List of Plants/Animal Organs Used as Traditional Medicine by Tawang Monpas to Cure Various Ailments

Sl. No.	*Disease/Ailments/ Symptoms*	*Local / Vernacular Name*	*Type of Medicine*	*Parts Used*	*Mode of Appli-cation*
1.	Eye Infection	Nyulum	Herbal	Leaf, boiled in water	Wash
2.	Mild Fever, Body ache etc.	Bashakaseng	Herbal	Leaf, stems, fruits and roots	Swallow
3.	Boils	Chomcha	Herbal	Leaf, boiled in water	Drink
4.	Dysentery	Bashaka	Herbal	Flower	Chew
5.	Constipation	Lhabho and Chuto	Herbal	Flower	Chew
6.	Sleeplessness	Nyes	Herbal	Flower	Chew
7.	Weak Mind and or Weak Memory	Yeers	Herbal	Leaf	Take with water
8.	Respiratory Problem	Chalum and Namlpa	Herbal	Leaf	Take with water
9.	Fever	Chandoseng, Ohla, Chumik-tang, and Chomcha	Herbal	Stems and Roots	Chew

Contd....

Sl. No.	*Disease/Ailments/ Symptoms*	*Local / Vernacular Name*	*Type of Medicine*	*Parts Used*	*Mode of Application*
10.	Cough, Cold	Chandoseng	Herbal	Stems and Roots	Chew
11.	Wound	Chumiktang	Herbal Poisonous	Roots	Chew
12.	During Pregnancy	Chomcha	Herbal	Stems and Roots	Chew
13.	Cut/Metal Cut	Glangseng and Damerapseng	Herbal	Branches	Application in affected area after heating it
14.	Burn	Youngha (Turmeric)	Herbal	Stems and Roots	Application of Powder
15.	Constipation/ Indigestion	Samerep, Komerep, Damerep etc.	Herbal	Fruits	Chew
16.	Cough	Ginger	Herbal	Roots	Chew
17.	Skin Problem	Pine Gum	Herbal (Cosmetic)	Gum	Application
18.	Severe Pain	Changseng+ Nyulum+ Poiye leaves	Herbal	Leaves	Bath after boiling together
19.	Cancer	Jalapa	Herbal	Flower	Chew
20.	Respiratory Tract Infection	Chandusheng	Herbal	Flower and leaf	Chew
21.	Pain in Limbs	Shaaksheng	Herbal	Leaf	Chew
22.	Fracture	Chapsheng	Herbal	Leaf	Application of the leaf juice
23.	Sinus	Damrepsheng	Herbal	Leaf	Application of the leaf juice
24.	Itches	Changsheng and thulasriful	Herbal	Leaf	Application of the leaf juice
25.	Measles	Baigum	Herbal	Flower	Chew
26.	Small Pox	Chang	Food Product		Drink

Sl. No.	*Disease/Ailments/ Symptoms*	*Local / Vernacular Name*	*Type of Medicine*	*Parts Used*	*Mode of Application*
27.	Sleeplessness with headache and stomachache	Dutpa	Food Product		
28.	Fresh Bath	Changseng	Herbal Cosmetic	Leaf	Bath
29.	Weakness	Akmer, Sengmer	Animal Product	Ghee	Eat
30.	Krackage of Foot, Lips etc.	Sengmer	Animal Product	Ghee	Eat
31.	Stomach Trouble	Lever of Bear	Animal Organ		Take after boiling it
32.	Skin Problem/ Leprosy in initial stage	Jushmangsha, Vamosha etc.	Animal Organ		Take after boiling it
33.	Fever	Heart of bear	Animal Organ		Take after boiling it
34.	Viral Fever	Bile of snow bear	Animal Organ		Take after boiling it
35.	Liver Problem	Bile of snow bear	Animal Organ		Take after boiling it

Source: Field Survey held in 2003.

III

CONCLUSION

There is a paucity of published Literature providing Information regarding traditional medicine in the Tawang district considering the richness of the biodiversity of this region. This work is a small step towards the documentation of the traditional medicine (TM). Government should also take up initiative to take scientific researches to verify and testify the medicinal value of the traditional medicine (TM). Patents regime of today can be utilized favorably in terms of economics if we make Traditional Knowledge System in general and traditional medicine (TM). In particular readily available to the majority of the people after its scientific verification.

SUGGESTIONS

The following suggestions may be forwarded to tap the Indigenous Knowledge System (IKS) of the Tawang Monpas.

- Indigenous Knowledge (IK) is still in original form so priorities should be given to utilize it properly by utilizing unutilized resources.
- Intensive and extensive research practice should be adopted to give scientific base to popularize it.
- Proper documentation should be their right, from micro level disseminates Indigenous Knowledge System (IK S) for preservation.
- Recognition and encouragement should by rewarding etc to the conserver of biodiversity and medicinal practicenor for their invaluable contributions.
- Priority should be given for the integration of Indigenous Knowledge System (IK S) with science and technology.
- An organized body at micro level (at least circle level) should be established to integrate widely scattered knowledge of medicine.
- Sustained effort on the modernization of the traditional medicine should be given a priority.
- Last but not the least there is a need to set-up a people's biodiversity Register a programme of documentation to protect their Intellectual Property Right (IPR).
- Awareness programmes among the local people about the importance of traditional medicine (TM) should be implemented.

ACKNOWLEDGEMENT

I am thankful to ICSSR, New Delhi for funding a project entitled "Health Seeking behaviour among the Monpa tribe of Tawang District in Arunachal Pradesh" I wish to record my sincere thanks to Dr. B.N. Jha, my colleague for his valuable comments and suggestions. I am also grateful to my student

Miss Tenzing Chomu & Tsering Chotten for providing required assistance during survey to me.

REFERENCES

Bhattacharjee S., Tiwari, K.C., Majumdar, R.S. Mishra, A.K., "Folklore Medicine from Kamrup District (Assam), Bull of Medicos-Ethno Research. (1980).

Bhyan D.K., "Herbal Drugs Used by the Tribal People of Lohit District of Arunachal Pradesh for Abortion and Easy Delivery. A Report Advances in Plant. Sciences, (1944).

Haridasan K., Bhuyan L.R., and Deori N.L., "Wild Edible Plants of Arunachal Pradrsh, Arunachal Forest News, 8 (1 & 2), (1990).

Nath, S.C. & Bordoloi D.N., "Ethonobotanical Observation on some Medicinal Folkore of Tirap District, Arunachal Pradesh, Journal of Eco.Tex Botony. (1989).

Sharma Manish, "Cost of Health Care Among the Tribals of Jabalpur District in Madhya Pradesh", An Unpublished Ph.D. Thesis Submitted to R.D.V.V. University, Jabalpur, (1999).